E. M. FORSTER AND MUSIC

E. M. Forster and Music illustrates music's vital role in Forster's positioning of his own ideology, awakening the ideological potency in the allusive force of Forster's representations of music and revealing the political significance of his engagement with music. It shifts criticism's attention from the 'musicality' of Forster's prose to his awareness of the contentious relationship between music and politics. Examining unobtrusive, often overlooked, musical allusions in a variety of Forster's writings, this book demonstrates how music provided Forster with a means of reflecting on race and epistemology, material culture and colonialism, literary heritage and national character, hero-worship and war, and gender and professionalism. It unveils how Forster's musical representations are mediated through a matrix of ideas and debates of his time, such as those about evolution, empire, Britain's relationship with the Continent, the rise of fascism, and the emergence of musicology as an academic discipline.

TSUNG-HAN TSAI is an independent scholar specializing in music and twentieth-century literature. Since receiving his PhD from the University of St Andrews, he has co-edited, with Emma Sutton, *Twenty-First-Century Readings of E. M. Forster's* Maurice, and has published articles on E. M. Forster, Goldsworthy Lowes Dickinson, and life-writing.

E. M. FORSTER AND MUSIC

TSUNG-HAN TSAI

CAMBRIDGE
UNIVERSITY PRESS

University Printing House, Cambridge CB2 8BS, United Kingdom

One Liberty Plaza, 20th Floor, New York, NY 10006, USA

477 Williamstown Road, Port Melbourne, VIC 3207, Australia

314–321, 3rd Floor, Plot 3, Splendor Forum, Jasola District Centre, New Delhi – 110025, India

79 Anson Road, #06–04/06, Singapore 079906

Cambridge University Press is part of the University of Cambridge.

It furthers the University's mission by disseminating knowledge in the pursuit of education, learning, and research at the highest international levels of excellence.

www.cambridge.org
Information on this title: www.cambridge.org/9781108844314
DOI: 10.1017/9781108943604

© Tsung-Han Tsai 2021

This publication is in copyright. Subject to statutory exception and to the provisions of relevant collective licensing agreements, no reproduction of any part may take place without the written permission of Cambridge University Press.

First published 2021

A catalogue record for this publication is available from the British Library.

Library of Congress Cataloging-in-Publication Data
NAMES: Tsai, Tsung-Han, 1984– author.
TITLE: E. M. Forster and music / Tsung-Han Tsai.
DESCRIPTION: Cambridge, United Kingdom ; New York, NY : Cambridge University Press, 2021. | Includes bibliographical references and index.
IDENTIFIERS: LCCN 2020042852 (print) | LCCN 2020042853 (ebook) | ISBN 9781108844314 (hardback) | ISBN 9781108948029 (paperback) | ISBN 9781108943604 (epub)
SUBJECTS: LCSH: Forster, E. M. (Edward Morgan), 1879-1970–Political and social views. | Music and literature.
CLASSIFICATION: LCC PR6011.O58 Z875 2021 (print) | LCC PR6011.O58 (ebook) | DDC 823/.912–dc23
LC record available at https://lccn.loc.gov/2020042852
LC ebook record available at https://lccn.loc.gov/2020042853

ISBN 978-1-108-84431-4 Hardback

Cambridge University Press has no responsibility for the persistence or accuracy of URLs for external or third-party internet websites referred to in this publication and does not guarantee that any content on such websites is, or will remain, accurate or appropriate.

Contents

Acknowledgements		*page* vi
Abbreviations		viii
Introduction		1
1	The Rhythm of the Racial Other: Before *Aspects of the Novel*	22
2	The Queering of Musical Instruments	48
3	From Literary Heritage to National Character	75
4	The Problem of the Wagnerian Hero	103
5	Amateurism, Musicology, and Gender	132
Postlude		159
Bibliography		177
Index		194

Acknowledgements

This book started as a doctoral thesis at the University of St Andrews in 2009, and since then, I owe everything to Emma Sutton, who first saw the potential of the project and has stood by it. For many years, her insights and her own work have enriched my work, and her generosity, kindness, and encouragement have sustained me through all sorts of difficulties. This book could not have been written without Emma, and I cannot be more grateful to her.

I would like to acknowledge with many thanks The Provost and Scholars of King's College, Cambridge and The Society of Authors as the Literary Representative of the Estate of E. M. Forster for giving access to and granting permission to quote from Forster's unpublished papers. I am particularly grateful to Patricia McGuire, archivist at the Archive Centre of King's College, Cambridge, for her knowledge of Forster and useful advice. I would also like to thank Geoffrey Cox and John Corner, editors of *Soundings: Documentary Film and the Listening Experience* (Huddersfield: University of Huddersfield Press, 2018), for permission to develop my chapter 'The "Appassionata" Sonata in *A Diary for Timothy*' and weave it into the Introduction of this book.

Many thanks are due to Angela Hobart, the director of Centro Incontri Umani, Ascona, who granted me two periods of residence in the Centro in summer 2017 and in spring 2019, respectively. I was encouraged to enjoy the freedom and tranquillity there, and both times I had the most precious experience of delicious reflection and produced work that surprised me later. During my first residence in 2017, I was privileged enough to have met David Nugent, with whom I had many inspiring conversations. Also integral to my wonderful experience in Ascona is the care and understanding of Betina Hermes and Reto Mordasini. I am delighted to acknowledge them with gratitude.

I am enormously grateful to the many people who have read earlier versions and sections of the book, including Michael Herbert, Peter Dale,

Acknowledgements vii

and Brandon Chao-Chi Yen. Brandon, in particular, provided a sensible voice of calm and kindness when I was finalizing the book. Delia da Sousa Correa and Christina Alt, who examined my thesis and made extremely useful comments and suggestions then, have given me unflinching support and sagacious advice during my postdoctoral years. Important thanks as well to Janie Brooks, who helped me refine my English writing in St Andrews and continued to ask after the book. I am delighted to acknowledge the ever so kind and resourceful Gill Plain, without whom *A Diary for Timothy* would have passed me by.

Particular thanks are due to colleagues at the Schools of English and of Modern Languages at St Andrews, especially Emma Bond, Marina Cano Lopez, Ben Davies, Emily Finer, Colette Lawson, and Anna Watson for their conversations and kindness. Thanks, as well, go to Philip Ross Bullock, Charlotte de Mille, David Deutsch, Katharine Ellis, Gemma Moss, Charlotte Purkis, Sue Reid, and Fraser Riddell for their insightful questions at various conferences where ideas in this book received their first airing and discussion.

I would like to express my gratitude to the anonymous readers for their astute and invaluable suggestions. I am grateful to Ray Ryan for taking on this project, and to Edgar Mendez, Sarah Starkey, and the team at Cambridge University Press for seeing the book through production.

Friends have given me their patience and company and kept me sane in this terribly noisy world. In particular, I would like to thank Yi-wei Chang, Agnes Chen, Jenny Yi-Chien Chen, the late Jess Desanta, Lisa Griffin, Phoebe Huang, Yawen Jen, Cathy Liao, Eric Liu, Erica Mou, J. Patrick Pazdziora, Kayshinee Rye Ramchurn, Akihiko Shimizu, Verita Sriratana, Jen Swift, Gladys Tsai, Yi-chien Tsai, and Anna West.

My greatest debt, though, is to my family – my parents and my brother – for everything they have done for me and for allowing me to do whatever I want to do. To them, my deepest thanks and love.

Abbreviations

AE	E. M. Forster, *Albergo Empedocle and Other Writings*, ed. and intro. George H. Thomson (New York: Liveright, 1971)
AH	E. M. Forster, *Abinger Harvest and England's Pleasant Land*, ed. Elizabeth Heine (London: Andre Deutsch, 1996)
AL	E. M. Forster, *Alexandria: A History and a Guide and Pharos and Pharillon*, ed. Miriam Allott (London: Andre Deutsch, 2004)
AN	E. M. Forster, *Aspects of the Novel and Related Writings*, ed. Oliver Stallybrass (London: Edward Arnold, 1974)
AS	E. M. Forster, *Arctic Summer and Other Fiction*, ed. Elizabeth Heine and Oliver Stallybrass (London: Edward Arnold, 1980)
CB	E. M. Forster, *Commonplace Book,* ed. Philip Gardner (Stanford: Stanford University Press, 1985)
GLD	E. M. Forster, *Goldsworthy Lowes Dickinson and Related Writings*, ed. Oliver Stallybrass (London: Edward Arnold, 1973)
HD	E. M. Forster, *The Hill of Devi and Other Indian Writings*, ed. Elizabeth Heine (London: Edward Arnold, 1983)
HE	E. M. Forster, *Howards End*, ed. Oliver Stallybrass (London: Edward Arnold, 1973)
JD	E. M. Forster, *The Journals and Diaries of E. M. Forster*, ed. Philip Gardner, 3 vols (London: Pickering & Chatto, 2011)
LJ	E. M. Forster, *The Longest Journey*, ed. Elizabeth Heine (London: Edward Arnold, 1984)
M	E. M. Forster, *Maurice*, ed. Philip Gardner (London: Andre Deutsch, 1999)
MS	E. M. Forster, *The Machine Stops and Other Stories*, ed. Rod Mengham (London: Andre Deutsch, 1997)

List of Abbreviations

ix

MSS-PI	E. M. Forster, *The Manuscripts of* A Passage to India, ed. Oliver Stallybrass (London: Edward Arnold, 1978)
NT	E. M. Forster, *Nordic Twilight* (London: Macmillian, 1940)
PI	E. M. Forster, *A Passage to India*, ed. Oliver Stallybrass (London: Edward Arnold, 1978)
PT	E. M. Forster, *The Prince's Tale and Other Uncollected Writings*, ed. P. N. Furbank (London: Andre Deutsch, 1998)
RV	E. M. Forster, *A Room with a View*, ed. Oliver Stallybrass (London: Edward Arnold, 1977)
SL	*Selected Letters of E. M. Forster*, ed. Mary Lago and P. N. Furbank, 2 vols (London: Collins, 1983–85)
TCD	*Two Cheers for Democracy*, ed. Oliver Stallybrass (London: Edward Arnold, 1972)
UEE	E. M. Forster, *The Uncollected Egyptian Essays of E. M. Forster*, ed. Hilda D. Spear and Abdel-Moneim Aly (Dundee: Blackness Press, 1988)
WA	E. M. Forster, *Where Angels Fear to Tread*, ed. Oliver Stallybrass (London: Edward Arnold, 1975)

Introduction

The opening of the 'Appassionata' Sonata is almost inaudible in Humphrey Jennings's *A Diary for Timothy* (1945).[1] About ten minutes into the film, the camera shows a man listening to a radio report on the British forces' struggle in Arnhem, where an airborne force has been surrounded by the German army. Behind the voice of the newsreader come, almost eerily, the first few notes of Beethoven's Piano Sonata in F minor, Op. 57, or, as it is more commonly known, the 'Appassionata'. The music only becomes clearer towards the end of its first theme. When the theme moves to G-flat major with the camera cutting to a close-up of two hands gliding over a Steinway & Sons grand piano, what originally came across as background music turns out to be somebody's actual performance. The camera slowly zooms out – as the low D-flat and low C in the bass set up the second motif – and we recognize Dame Myra Hess at the piano, dressed completely in black, playing the sonata. It zooms out further and shows a stage surrounded by the audience. In bar 20, the camera zooms in and focuses on Hess's expression: frowning slightly, she follows the juxtaposition of *fortissimo* and *piano* by lifting her eyebrows every now and then. When the motif re-emerges in E-flat in bar 24, a shot of a concert poster shows that this performance is one of the National Gallery concerts during the Second World War. The billing is '5th Birthday Concert, Myra Hess'; the date is Tuesday, 10 October 1944, with Elena Gerhardt's recital to take place the next day. Before long, we are led back into the Gallery, not towards the stage but into the audience. The camera pans across the rows of listeners, male and female, old and young, military and civilian. Eventually, it stays focused on an attentive young woman just when the A-flat major second theme unfolds its warm lyricism. Yet it does not last long: as the minor key is reimposed in bar 42, the

---

[1] *A Diary for Timothy*, dir. Humphrey Jennings, in *Humphrey Jennings Collection* (UK: Crown Film Unit, 1945; DVD, Film First, 2005).

E. M. Forster and Music

camera goes back to the pianist and then her hands. No sooner does Hess start the three trills in bars 44–46 than the same newsreader's voice floats in, reiterating the endurance of the soldiers in Arnhem: 'For the last three days' – his voice has a certain mechanical clarity against the music's downward passage at its *pianissimo* – 'they have had no water, very little but small arms and ammunition, and rations were cut to one sixth. Luckily or unluckily, it rained, and they caught the water in their capes and drank that'. The end of his sentence is interrupted by the A-flat minor explosion in bar 51, with the image cut to a street corner in London: a hose, a small pool of water, a bus, a pedestrian walking by, and incessant rain. Other shots of the city follow – houses in rubble, a man on the rooftop relaying the slates, another group of men busy with more repairs. 'It's the middle of October now', a male voice suddenly emerges, 'and the war certainly won't be over by Christmas, and the weather doesn't suit us. And one third of our houses have been damaged by enemy action'. His voice is low, his pace slow. He starts to comment on the music: 'They do like the music that the lady was playing; some of us think it's the greatest music ever'. The semiquavers of the high treble and the slowly descending bass eventually end on A-flat in the *pianissimo* bar 65. 'It is German music', the commentator continues as the main theme, this time in E major, recurs, 'and we are fighting against the Germans'. His words are accompanied by a montage sequence, during which the shot of urban rubble is overlaid with Hess's hands on the piano. The commentator says: 'There is something you have to think over later on'. The end of his sentence overlaps with the silence in the latter part of bar 70. When the music shortly resumes, it cuts to a shot of heavy rain, the volume of which almost obscures the music. The commentary continues: 'Rain, too much rain, and it's even wetter under the earth'. The camera follows accordingly, showing coal mines, accompanied by the E major cadence in bars 73–75, though the sound of the piano grows dimmer. Just before it can resolve into an E major triad, the sound of drilling bursts out.

This unfolding of the 'Appassionata' Sonata does not just provide a two-and-a-half-minute vignette of wartime London; rather, the interweaving of the music with images, sounds, and human speech highlights a range of political issues – about war and patriotism, as well as about gender, class, and generational differences. While the Britain the documentary is projecting is a sanctuary of art where Myra Hess and Elena Gerhardt, Jewish and German, respectively, can continue their lustrous musical careers, the commentary's emphasis on the German identity of Beethoven's sonata poses questions about the relationship between Britain and Germany

Introduction 3

during and after the war. If the symbolic cultural status of Beethoven and his music as heroic adds volume to the BBC report's championing of the toughness of the soldiers in Arnhem, the commentary's challenge to the continuation of Anglo–German antagonism punctures the victor's glorification of the foreseeable defeat of the enemy. The concept of heroic manliness is particularly problematized by the prominence of Myra Hess in the scene. Her presence as an established woman pianist mastering the work of Beethoven, long hailed, in Romain Roland's words, as 'the most virile of musicians',[2] exudes authority and makes her an embodiment of characteristics traditionally marked as masculine. Presiding over the attentive audience with her virtuoso performance, Hess underpins the tableau of a unified Home Front. Yet the montage of her hands and the house rubble, the overlapping sounds of the music and the rain, and the sharp cut between the concert and the mining tunnel not only remind us of the conditions beyond the National Gallery, but also form a dialectic between composition and destruction, art and nature, the contained and the exposed. What underlies the documentary's interrogation of the boundary between music and politics is an alertness to the differentiation between classes and their material circumstances, and the commentary that declares that 'some of us think it's the greatest music ever' is one that is deeply aware of the lines demarcating different social groups in Britain. One of these lines is generational: the documentary itself is a dialogue between the avuncular commentator and his young addressee: 'you', the infant Timothy. Though some critics retrospectively characterize the commentary's tone as didactic and condescending,[3] one can also argue that it represents an elderly man whose primary aim is to educate upcoming generations and to invite them to 'think over' difficult issues on the horizon instead of making decisions for them. The 'Appassionata' passage thus creates a challenging conversation about the future of the nation, highlighting, in Gill Plain's words, the documentary's 'self-conscious engagement with the process of readjustment demanded by war's end'.[4]

Music is at the very centre of this passage in *A Diary for Timothy*, intersecting with and contributing to all the political debates. Rather than an apolitical artwork detached from its context, Beethoven's 'Appassionata', as presented here, is firmly embedded within and

[2] Roland Barthes, *Beethoven the Creator*, trans. Ernest Newman (New York: Harper & Brothers, 1929), p. 27.
[3] Kevin Jackson, *Humphrey Jennings* (London: Picador, 2004), p. 305.
[4] Gill Plain, *Literature of the 1940s: War, Postwar and 'Peace'* (Edinburgh: Edinburgh University Press, 2013), p. 214.

E. M. Forster and Music

evaluative of a specific historical circumstance. While some might argue that the sonata itself is a highly potent signifier, what is important is the documentary's deliberate use of the music to make interventions into topical issues such as war and patriotism. That is, music was understood and employed as politically suggestive by the passage's creators. As the opening credits show, the documentary is a collaboration between the director Humphrey Jennings (film-maker and the author of *Pandæmonium 1660–1886*), the producer Basil Wright, the composer Richard Addinsell, the actor Michael Redgrave, the pianist Myra Hess, the cutter Jenny Hutt, and the writer E. M. Forster (1879–1970).[5] Scarcely acknowledged and rarely commented upon, Forster's involvement in the *Timothy* project – which he described wryly as 'Hollywood' in a letter to Christopher Isherwood – is unknown to most literary scholars.[6] While it is now difficult to determine in what ways and to what extent Forster contributed to the final presentation of this 'Appassionata' passage, one might argue that there are explicit Forsterian resonances with the famous concert scene in his 1910 novel, *Howards End*, especially in the commentary's caution against Anglo–German antagonism and its celebration of Beethoven's music. More importantly, it is significant that Forster participated in shaping the documentary's contentious use of Beethoven's music to question national identity in wartime Britain. Here, music is unquestionably political.

Illustrating music's vital role in Forster's positioning of his own ideology, this book examines the political significance of his engagement with and representations of music. It challenges previous criticism's formalist approach to music's influence on Forster, shifting the attention from the 'musicality' of Forster's prose, especially the narratological connotations of his notion of 'rhythm' in *Aspects of the Novel* (1927), to his awareness of the contentious relationship between music and politics. It also redresses the tendency of recent assessments of Forster's legacies for later writers by gesturing towards the interpretative possibilities of close-reading Forster's texts and paying attention to their contexts.[7] Rather than enshrining the

---

[5] P. N. Furbank is the only biographer who has recorded, albeit briefly, Forster's participation in the project. P. N. Furbank, *E. M. Forster: A Life*, 2 vols (London: Secker & Warburg, 1977–78), II, p. 256.

[6] Forster's letter to Christopher Isherwood, 26 August 1945, in *Letters between Forster and Isherwood on Homosexuality and Literature*, ed. Richard E. Zeikowitz (Basingstoke: Palgrave Macmillan, 2008), p. 136.

[7] See e.g. Alberto Fernández Carbajal, *Compromise and Resistance in Postcolonial Writing: E. M. Forster's Legacy* (Basingstoke: Palgrave Macmillan, 2014), and *Only Connect: E. M. Forster's Legacies in British Fiction*, ed. Elsa Cavalié and Laurent Mellet (Bern: Peter Lang, 2017). Wendy

Introduction

posthumous influence of Forster's ideas, my study seeks to awaken the ideological potency inherent within the allusive force of Forster's musical representations. Building on Lawrence Kramer's reconfiguration of music as 'a cultural *agency*' to focus on its 'participa[tion] in ... discursive and representational practices',[8] the following chapters tease out the textual nuances of Forster's portraits of musical composition, performance, and consumption as mediated through broader political events and cultural matrices of his time. Through an examination of unobtrusive, often unnoticed, representations of music in a variety of Forster's published and unpublished writings, the book demonstrates how music provided Forster with a means of reflecting on race and epistemology, material culture and colonialism, literary heritage and national character, hero-worship and war, and gender and professionalism. This is not to neglect the literariness of Forster's prose and to identify what is written in his work as straightforward manifestations of his own views; rather, the book stays alert to Forster's ironic voice in its recovery of previously unacknowledged complexities in his musical and political concerns. It seeks to do justice to the scale and scope of Forster's writing, drawing attention to the political charge of the versatility of his musical enthusiasms and the variety of his musical-political emphases. In so doing, the book reveals how Forster's musical politics resonate across his entire oeuvre.

***

'I love music', Forster declared at the opening of his 1947 lecture at a symposium on music at Harvard University.[9] An ardent and astute musical amateur, Forster's engagement with music was diverse as well as enduring – from the first decade of his life in the 1880s to the last decade in the 1960s, when his deafness became a major hindrance to his enjoyment of music. He was a listener, a pianist, a concertgoer, an opera enthusiast, an occasional music critic, a librettist, a friend of musical

---

Moffat's work also participates in confirming Forster's legacies, especially queer ones. Her recent biography, *E. M. Forster: A New Life* (London: Bloomsbury, 2010), pays particular attention to Forster's relationships with and influence on younger gay friends. See, additionally, Wendy Moffat, 'E. M. Forster and the Unpublished "Scrapbook" of Gay History: "Lest We Forget Him!"', *English Literature in Transition*, 55.1 (2012), 19–31, and Wendy Moffat, 'The Narrative Case for Queer Biography', in *Narrative Theory Unbound: Queer and Feminist Interventions*, ed. Robyn Warhol and Susan S. Lanser (Columbus: The Ohio State University Press, 2015), pp. 210–26.

[8] Lawrence Kramer, 'Culture and Musical Hermeneutics: The Salome Complex', *Cambridge Opera Journal*, 2.3 (1990), 269–94 (p. 270).

[9] 'The *Raison d'Être* of Criticism' (1947), in *TCD*, pp. 105–18 (p. 105).

6   E. M. Forster and Music

professionals, a collaborator with musicians, and, most importantly, a writer who wrote constantly about music.[10] The longevity of his engagement with music, the diversity of his musical activities, the tenacity of music's presence in his daily routine throughout the years – all of these demonstrate that music played an important part in his life. His interest in and knowledge of music were repeatedly noted by his contemporaries; that music influenced his novels was also admitted by Forster himself and noted by many others.[11] Whilst some, like Elizabeth Bowen, felt that they possessed inadequate knowledge to comment on it, others did elaborate on the significance of music to Forster's fictional writing.[12] Peter Burra, in 1934, called Forster 'a musician who chose the novel because he had ideas to utter which needed a more distinct articulation than music could make'.[13] Wilfred Stone, in contrast, describes Forster's work as 'literature turned to music', where abstraction, unworldliness, and idea transcend the existence of human society.[14] Perhaps most famous is Benjamin Britten's tribute to Forster in 1969 as 'our most musical novelist', which can be read as a defining summary of Forster's life in music, not just because Britten recounted and indicated all the extensive musical allusions in Forster's oeuvre.[15] Also, by praising Forster for his understanding of music, Britten professionally and authoritatively endorsed all these musical efforts of a lifelong amateur. Although the tone of Britten's tribute, as Frank Kermode rightly suggests, should always be taken cautiously due to the friendship between the two,[16] Forster's engagement with music, nonetheless, garnered public and professional recognition.

[10] For a detailed biography of Forster's musical taste; piano skills; listening habits; concert, ballet, and opera attendances; and relationships with musicians and composers, see Michelle Fillion, *Difficult Rhythm: Music and the Word in E. M. Forster* (Urbana: University of Illinois Press, 2010), pp. 1–23 and pp. 145–50. Forster's major biographers – including P. N. Furbank, Nicola Beauman, and, more recently, Wendy Moffat – have documented Forster's attachment to music and provided useful records of his musical activities. See e.g. Nicola Beauman, *Morgan: A Biography of E. M. Forster* (London: Hodder & Stoughton, 1993), especially p. 162.

[11] In several of his interviews, Forster mentioned music's structural influence on his fiction. See e.g. P. N. Furbank and F. J. H. Haskell, 'E. M. Forster: The Art of Fiction No. 1', *The Paris Review*, 1 (1953), 28–41.

[12] Elizabeth Bowen, 'A Passage to E. M. Forster', in *Aspects of E. M. Forster*, ed. Oliver Stallybrass (London: Edward Arnold, 1969), pp. 1–12 (p. 12).

[13] Peter Burra, 'Introduction to the Everyman Edition', in *PI*, pp. 315–27 (p. 321). Burra's article originally appeared as 'The Novels of E. M. Forster' in *The Nineteenth Century and After* in November 1934.

[14] Wilfred Stone, *The Cave and the Mountain: A Study of E. M. Forster* (Stanford: Stanford University Press, 1966), p. 118.

[15] Benjamin Britten, 'Some Notes on Forster and Music', in *Aspects of E. M. Forster*, ed. Stallybrass, pp. 81–86 (p. 81).

[16] Frank Kermode, *Concerning E. M. Forster* (London: Weidenfeld & Nicolson, 2009), p. 29.

Introduction

7

Intriguingly, what Britten did not mention in his tribute is Forster's idea of 'rhythm', a point seminal to the majority of modern criticism of Forster and music, especially to the consideration of the 'musicality' of Forster's prose. Forster was among innumerable contemporaries employing the term 'rhythm', one of the key words that cut through multifarious disciplines in early twentieth-century culture and recurred in discourses on art, literature, science, medicine, philosophy, and many other subjects.[17] In the last section of *Aspects of the Novel*, Forster 'edge[s] rather nervously towards' rhythm for something that could lead fictional writing to another dimension.[18] In his definition, there is 'easy' rhythm and there is 'difficult' rhythm: the former can be exemplified by the opening rhythm of Beethoven's Fifth Symphony, which 'we can all hear and tap to', whilst the latter is the effect through which, 'when the orchestra stops', we hear the Symphony 'as a whole', as an 'entity' whose 'three big blocks of sound' have been linked together.[19] For Forster, if practised in the novel, 'easy' rhythm is 'repetition plus variation', exemplified by Vinteuil's *petite phrase* in *À la recherche du temps perdu*: Proust's novel, even though it appears 'ill-constructed', 'hangs together because it is stitched internally'.[20] As for 'difficult' rhythm, Forster provides no literary examples, only suggesting that Tolstoy's *War and Peace* is the work closest to producing this 'rhythmic' effect.[21] Like the end of a symphony when 'the notes and tunes composing it have been liberated', the last page of Tolstoy's novel gives one an impression that 'every item . . . lead[s] a larger existence than was possible at the time'; it is, Forster suggests, '[e]xpansion' rather than 'completion'.[22]

Critics have consistently discussed the affinity between Forster's idea of 'rhythm' and his aesthetics of narrative form, and have established that Forster's fictional writing is stylistically inspired by, and comparable to, music. E. K. Brown, David Medalie, Frank Kermode, Judith Scherer Herz, and others have analysed the ways in which Forster employs complicated verbal and thematic repetitions and variations to structure and unfold the narrative of his novels.[23] There has also been a consensus that

---

[17] For a brief discussion of the topicality of rhythm in the early twentieth century, see Faith Binckes, *Modernism, Magazines, and the British Avant-Garde* (Oxford: Oxford University Press, 2010), pp. 61–64.

[18] *AN*, p. 112.   [19] *AN*, pp. 113 and 115.   [20] *AN*, pp. 115 and 113.   [21] *AN*, p. 116.

[22] *AN*, p. 116.

[23] E. K. Brown, 'Rhythm in E. M. Forster's *A Passage to India*', in *E. M. Forster: A Passage to India, A Casebook*, ed. Malcolm Bradbury (London: Macmillan, 1970), pp. 93–113; David Medalie, *E. M. Forster's Modernism* (Basingstoke: Palgrave, 2002), pp. 124–40; Kermode, *Concerning E. M.*

8 E. M. Forster and Music

the unnamed example of Forster's 'difficult' rhythm can be found in his last novel, *A Passage to India* (1924).[24] This critical trend was partially mobilized by Forster himself when he endorsed Peter Burra's article, 'The Novels of E. M. Forster' (1934), which identifies his notion of rhythm as '*leit-motif*', as a literary device of making 'one passage [call] back to another'.[25] Making the article the introduction to the Everyman edition of *A Passage to India* in 1942 and saying in 1957 that 'Burra saw exactly what I was trying to do', Forster directed the focus of critical evaluation of his novels from ideological towards stylistic considerations.[26] As Finn Fordham suggests, Forster 'was happiest with [Burra's] formalistic, "musical" non-ideological, non-content-driven reading' perhaps because 'it attends to the presumably conscious intention of formal structures that were being made more visible by the author'; this, for Fordham, indicates Forster's intention to 'modernize' his work.[27] Such a reading aligns Forster with contemporary writers who also saw in music the potential to reconfigure the form and elements of literary narrative. As Eric Prieto has demonstrated, Aldous Huxley, James Joyce, Samuel Beckett, and many others 'incorporate[d] musical principles into the construction of the narrative text' and found in music a model for the development of storytelling different from 'the causal and sequential rules that have traditionally governed narrative form in literature'.[28] Arguably, then, the 'rhythmicity', or 'musicality', of Forster's fiction becomes an indication of his experiments in form. That is, in exploring the formal aesthetics of 'rhythm', Forster articulates a modernist dissatisfaction with the expressive capabilities of English fiction's narrative conventions.

For all its insights and coherence, this reading of music's influence on Forster has two problems. First, while the direction of the argument is certainly correct in linking Forster's attempt to 'musicalize' his fiction to an aspect of his modernism, there is an almost rushed readiness to place Forster's indebtedness to music within a modernist context of intermedial

---

Forster, pp. 39–46; and Judith Scherer Herz, 'Forster's Sentences', *English Literature in Transition*, 55.1 (2012), 4–18.

[24] This is implicit, for example, in Lionel Trilling's cursory remark that the novel has 'a cohesion and intricacy usually only found in music'. Lionel Trilling, *E. M. Forster: A Study*, 2nd ed. (London: New Directions, 1964), p. 156.

[25] Burra, 'Introduction', in *PI*, pp. 319–20.

[26] 'Forster's Prefatory Note (1957) to the Everyman Edition', in *PI*, pp. 313–14 (p. 313).

[27] Finn Fordham, *I Do I Undo I Redo: The Textual Genesis of Modernist Selves in Hopkins, Yeats, Conrad, Forster, Joyce, and Woolf* (Oxford: Oxford University Press, 2010), p. 204.

[28] Eric Prieto, *Listening In: Music, Mind, and the Modernist Narrative* (Lincoln: University of Nebraska Press, 2002), pp. ix and 57.

Introduction 9

exchange and genre crossing. Linda Hutcheon, for instance, studies how conceptions of music echo and differ in the critical writings of Forster, Roger Fry, and their mutual friend Charles Mauron. Whilst Hutcheon notes that the mystical quality Forster endows music with suggests a perception different from Fry's emphasis on music's formalist purity, her study nevertheless reinforces the understanding of Forster's attachment to music as an aesthetic and – however partially – formalist enterprise.[29] Her reading contextualizes Forster within a specific moment of cultural history during which music was perceived as the paradigm of all arts and viewed, in Daniel Albright's words, as 'the vanguard medium of the Modernist aesthetic'.[30] It depicts Forster as deeply invested in what Brad Bucknell defines as music's 'expressive potential [that] go[es] beyond the mere rationality of language' and aligns Forster with many of his contemporary writers who celebrated 'music' as 'an art which transcends referential or lexical meaning' in their representations of modern subjectivities.[31] No one would deny that music was significant for modernism's literary experimentation, yet this trend of making the unqualified term 'music' speak for Forster's modernist qualities often stems from an anxiety about Forster's status in current modernist scholarship and drives a counterargument against those who agree with evaluations such as Randall Stevenson's 'Forster was scarcely a modernist'.[32] While it may secure Forster's place in the literary pedigree of modernism, it reveals more of these critics' attempt to mark Forster as a product of modernist *Zeitgeist* than of Forster's actual engagement with contemporary musical cultures.

This tendency to use music as a springboard to reach the conclusion that Forster is a modernist writer is related to the second, and more pressing, problem. The formalist argument that music provided Forster with a means of reinventing literary form often simplifies music into a purely aesthetic and conceptual presence. Yet, as previously noted, music played a protean role in Forster's domestic and social lives. It was not merely a cultural metaphor, or an aesthetic concept, or a formalist device, but an actual practice of art to which Forster was deeply attached and in

---

[29] Linda Hutcheon, '"Sublime Noise" for Three Friends: Music in the Critical Writings of E. M. Forster, Roger Fry and Charles Mauron', in *E. M. Forster: Centenary Revaluations*, ed. Judith Scherer Herz and Robert K. Martin (London: Macmillan, 1982), pp. 84–98.

[30] *Modernism and Music: An Anthology of Sources*, ed. Daniel Albright (Chicago: University of Chicago Press, 2004), p. 1.

[31] Brad Bucknell, *Literary Modernism and Musical Aesthetics: Pater, Pound, Joyce, and Stein* (Cambridge, UK: Cambridge University Press, 2001), pp. 2–3 and 1.

[32] Randall Stevenson, 'Forster and Modernism', in *The Cambridge Companion to E. M. Forster*, ed. David Bradshaw (Cambridge, UK: Cambridge University Press, 2007), pp. 209–22 (p. 209).

which he was constantly involved as a player, a listener, and a writer. It is worth returning to Fordham's words and commenting on his use of the quotation marks around the adjective 'musical': they remind us how the formalistic properties that Forster and other early twentieth-century writers might have emphasized in music are not its sole characteristics and instead signal a particular perception of music within a specific network of aesthetics. Moreover, Forster not only engaged with music in various ways but was also aware that there were multiple kinds, types, and systems of music. Forster's writing in Egypt and in India, as the first two chapters of this study will show, register his alertness to musical cultures beyond Western art music, revealing his unease with the dominance of a monolithic 'Music' and his exploration of a world of 'musics'.[33] From this point of view, it becomes evident how simplistic, and implicitly Eurocentric, it is to read music's influence on Forster purely in terms of form. Interpreting the contexts in which Forster writes about music is thus necessary to a reappraisal of music's significance to him. Here, the recent reconceptualization of music as politicized and political within the discipline of musicology needs to be taken into account.

The changing perception of music in musicology in the past four decades has destabilized the conventional perception of music as an apolitical art form. Critics such as Joseph Kerman, Steven Paul Scher, Lawrence Kramer, and Susan McClary have questioned music's detachment from politics.[34] They draw attention to music's role in social formation and its political resonances. It is from this perception of music as attentive to and evaluative of specific historical contexts, as constructing political ideologies as well as being constructed by them, that these musicologists protest against music's purported non-referentiality and apoliticality. As Phyllis Weliver observes, this 'disciplinary shift' in musicology has given rise to new, contextual readings of nineteenth-century

---

[33] Although the exact definition of 'art music' has been intensely contested in recent years and has become increasingly difficult to obtain, the term still circulates today and is being understood as referring to musical works that are distinct from 'popular' or 'folk' music. See Denise Von Glahn and Michael Broyles, 'Art Music', *Grove Music Online*, www.oxfordmusiconline.com [accessed 30 December 2018].

[34] Joseph Kerman, *Musicology* (London: Fontana, 1985); *Music and Text: Critical Inquiries*, ed. Steven Paul Scher (Cambridge, UK: Cambridge University Press, 1992); Lawrence Kramer, *Music as Cultural Practice, 1800–1900* (Berkeley: University of California Press, 1990); Susan McClary, *Feminine Endings: Music, Gender, and Sexuality* (Minneapolis: University of Minnesota Press, 2002). See also *Queering the Pitch: The New Gay and Lesbian Musicology*, ed. Philip Brett, Elizabeth Wood, and Gary C. Thomas (New York: Routledge, 1994).

Introduction

literary works that deal with music.[35] While musical-literary studies have been burgeoning, it is in modernist studies where scholars have commented on how music was central to the aesthetic aims and political views of a diverse range of early twentieth-century writers.[36]

That there is as yet no book-length study of the musical politics of 'our most musical novelist' is thus both striking and curious. In recent years, critics such as Bret L. Keeling, Josh Epstein, and David Deutsch have analysed the queer nuances of Forster's representations of music.[37] Their focus on the link between music and Forster's homosexuality is understandable, yet it inadvertently overlooks areas in Forster's writings where there are demonstrable intersections between music and subject matters beyond gender and sexuality. Of all the studies of Forster and music, Mi Zhou's 'Sublime Noise: Reading E. M. Forster Musically' and Michelle Fillion's *Difficult Rhythm: Music & the Word in E. M. Forster* more comprehensively contextualize Forster's musical allusions within early twentieth-century musical cultures and explore the ramifications of their significance.[38] As Fillion suggests, music enables 'the dialectics of gender,

---

[35] Phyllis Weliver, 'A Score of Change: Twenty Years of Critical Musicology and Victorian Literature', *Literature Compass*, 8.10 (2011), 776–94 (p. 786). For one of the exemplary studies of music in nineteenth-century literature, see *The Idea of Music in Victorian Fiction*, ed. Sophie Fuller and Nicky Losseff (Aldershot: Ashgate, 2004).

[36] See e.g. Emma Sutton, *Virginia Woolf and Classical Music: Politics, Aesthetics, Form* (Edinburgh: Edinburgh University Press, 2013); William May, 'Modernism's Handmaid: Dexterity and the Female Pianist', *Modernist Cultures*, 8.1 (2013), 42–60; Gemma Moss, 'Music, Noise, and the First World War in Ford Madox Ford's *Parade's End*', *Modernist Cultures*, 12.1 (2017), 59–77; Susan Reid, 'In Parts: Bodies, Feelings, Music in Long Modernist Novels by D. H. Lawrence and Dorothy Richardson', *Pilgrimage: A Journal of Dorothy Richardson Studies*, 7 (2015), 7–29; *T. S. Eliot's Orchestra: Critical Essays on Poetry and Music*, ed. John Xiros Cooper (New York: Garland, 2000); Delia da Sousa Correa, 'Katherine Mansfield and Music: Nineteenth-Century Echoes', in *Celebrating Katherine Mansfield*, ed. Gerri Kimber and Janet Wilson (Basingstoke: Palgrave Macmillan, 2011), pp. 84–98; *Essays on Music and Language in Modernist Literature: Musical Modernism*, ed. Katherine O'Callaghan (New York: Routledge, 2018). See also Nathan Waddell, 'Modernism and Music: A Review of Recent Scholarship', *Modernist Cultures*, 12.2 (2017), 316–30. My discussion cannot allude more extensively to Nathan Waddell's exciting book, *Moonlighting: Beethoven and Literary Modernism* (Oxford: Oxford University Press, 2019), which was published after the current book had been finalized.

[37] Bret L. Keeling, '"No Trace of Presence": Tchaikovsky and the Sixth in Forster's *Maurice*', *Mosaic: A Journal for the Interdisciplinary Study of Literature*, 36.1 (2003), 85–101; Josh Epstein, *Sublime Noise: Musical Culture and the Modernist Writer* (Baltimore: John Hopkins University Press, 2014), pp. 235–78; David Deutsch, *British Literature and Classical Music: Cultural Contexts 1870–1945* (London: Bloomsbury, 2015), pp. 139–84.

[38] Mi Zhou, 'Sublime Noise: Reading E. M. Forster Musically' (unpublished doctoral thesis, University of Cambridge, 2009). Fillion, *Difficult Rhythm*. Another work, Erik Alder and Dietmar Hauck, *Music and Literature: Music in the Works of Anthony Burgess and E. M. Forster, An Interdisciplinary Study* (Tübingen: Francke, 2005), pp. 69–178, is useful but limited in interpretation. It also follows a work-by-work order, commenting on Forster's musical allusions

sexuality, class, politics, and nationhood that drive all [Forster's] novels' and 'sings a mysterious song of uncertainty'.[39] Zhou and Fillion indeed demonstrate the multivalent roles music plays in Forster's work, but their novel-by-novel analyses confine the interpretation of Forster's musical allusions to the local contexts of individual works.[40] Their privileging of longer published novels over Forster's other shorter texts also omits a large proportion – and the majority – of Forster's oeuvre, missing the opportunity to uncover themes which Forster consistently tackles through drawing music into his writing.

To draw attention to the political – political in its broadest sense, be it sexual, racial, national, or social – significance of Forster's engagement with and representations of music, this book uses Forster's own idea of 'not listening' as a methodology. In the opening of his essay, 'Not Listening to Music' (1939), Forster admits his inattention 'during the greater part of every performance':

> I wool-gather most of the time, and am surprised that others don't. . . . I fly off every minute: after a bar or two I think how musical I am, or of something smart I might have said in conversation; or I wonder what the composer – dead a couple of centuries – can be feeling as the flames on the altar still flicker up; or how soon an H.E. bomb would extinguish them. Not to mention more obvious distractions: the tilt of the soprano's chin or chins; the antics of the conductor, that impassioned beetle, especially when it is night time and he waves his shards; the affectation of the pianist when he takes a top note with difficulty, as if he too were a soprano; the backs of the chairs; the bumps on the ceiling; the extreme physical ugliness of the audience.[41]

One could ask whether Forster would give precedence to these distractions or to his other much more orthodox ways of listening to music; what he describes as the 'muddle' of putting a musically affected consciousness into words is demonstrated by this seemingly disjointed and rhapsodic reflection.[42] Even though this reflection is only a brief one, and even though the rest of the essay – in which Forster discusses how he distinguishes music that reminds him of something from music itself – is more commonly quoted and analysed by critics, it is his tendency to 'not listen' to music

---

in two of his short stories, 'The Celestial Omnibus' and 'Co-ordination', and all the novels except *The Longest Journey* and *Maurice*.

[39] Fillion, *Difficult Rhythm*, p. xviii.

[40] Zhou discusses three of Forster's novels: *Howards End, A Room with a View*, and *A Passage to India*. Fillion studies all of the novels, but her analysis of *A Passage in India* is only a brief one

[41] 'Not Listening to Music' (1939), in *TCD*, pp. 122–25 (p. 122).   [42] *TCD*, p. 122.

Introduction   13

that becomes the title of the essay. Forster's choice to highlight 'not listening' as his primary occupation during a concert can be read as a musical amateur's disclaimer, but it also signifies his awareness that musical sounds do not take place in a vacuum. His inattention here, whether viewed contemptuously or humorously, reflects how the listener seeking to pay exclusive attention to music is instead invaded by random thoughts about war, class, and performativity.

Postmodern theorization of music listening celebrates such inattentiveness. In *Classical Music and Postmodern Knowledge*, Lawrence Kramer argues that 'not listening' should not be regarded as a failure to appreciate music. Asking whether he himself is 'failing to experience the music when I vary my attention level or simply let it fluctuate', Kramer suggests that 'not listening' is, in fact, a 'more flexible, more plural, more contingent logic of postmodern musical experience'.[43] If we apply Kramer's words to the consideration of musical references in a literary work, such distraction can be understood as attention deliberately set adrift; that is, the consciousness is allowed to wander into details before, after, or around an extensive description of music, thus bringing together multifarious textual details in a single musical scene, and giving focus to the relation between music and its surroundings. 'Not listening', then, revises the musical-literary methodology proposed by Werner Wolf in 1999. In *The Musicalization of Fiction: A Study in the Theory and History of Intermediality*, Wolf defines allusions to music in a written text as 'covert' musical-literary intermediality and separates them into two groups: 'thematization' and 'imitation'.[44] For him, 'thematization' can be in forms textual (e.g. direct references to musical works in a text), paratextual (e.g. titles associated with music), and contextual (e.g. an author's biographical engagement with music), while 'imitation' refers to the imaginary verbalization of music and musical aesthetics through written words. To study the 'musicalization' of fiction, Wolf uses 'thematization' as 'flags', which signal the site where an author might be modelling his or her text on a certain musical work.[45] Wolf suggests that 'the mentioning of music or musical terms' in a text merely plays an 'indicative' role and, for him, a 'really musicalized' text contains more than just that.[46] Effective as it may be, Wolf's methodology reveals a limited understanding of what he calls

---

[43] Lawrence Kramer, *Classical Music and Postmodern Knowledge* (Berkeley: University of California Press, 1995), p. 65.
[44] Werner Wolf, *The Musicalization of Fiction: A Study in the Theory and History of Intermediality* (Amsterdam: Rodopi, 1999), pp. 41–45.
[45] Wolf, *Musicalization*, pp. 51–67.   [46] Wolf, *Musicalization*, pp. 51–52.

14   E. M. Forster and Music

'thematization'. In the case of Forster, rather than musical works cited or mentioned only spontaneously by him, these 'flags' are, as I shall demonstrate throughout this book, informed by and responsive to various topical issues. However minute or unobtrusive they are, these references to music are more than names and titles Forster randomly selected from his repertoire of personal favourites and then dropped. They are crucial to analyses of Forster's engagement with music in political terms, and it is through 'not listening' that their protean implications for Forster's politics can be uncovered.

To test the interpretative possibilities of 'not listening', we may revisit Forster's 'musical *locus classicus*', the Beethoven concert in chapter 5 of *Howards End*.[47] Many critics have offered persuasive readings of the scene, either by close-reading it or analysing it in relation to numerous references to Beethoven and his works scattered in Forster's other novels and non-fictional writing, thereby shedding light on the scene's layers of meanings and suggesting the writer's deep attachment to the composer's music.[48] However, if we consciously distract ourselves from Forster's description of the concert – if we engage in 'not listening' to what is happening during the concert, including all the social encounters (or blunders), and 'not listening' to Helen Schlegel's inner thoughts about the hero and the goblins, the elephants and the shipwreck, or her repeated evocation of the sense of 'panic and emptiness' and its variations in later chapters – we may then discover what has been bypassed by readers and critics alike since the novel's publication. At the end of the chapter, when the Schlegels are back in their house after the concert, Helen jokes that Tibby, her younger brother, 'only cares for cultured females singing Brahms'.[49] This is not only a mocking comment on the artistic, pedantic young man but also a suggestive example of the richness of Forster's reference to music. In some

---

[47] Britten, 'Some Notes', p. 81.
[48] See e.g. Barry R. Westburg, 'Forster's Fifth Symphony: Another Aspect of *Howards End*', *Modern Fiction Studies*, 10.4 (1964), 359–65; Andrea K. Weatherhead, '*Howards End*: Beethoven's *Fifth*', *Twentieth-Century Literature*, 31.2–3 (1985), 247–64; Anne Foata, 'The Knocking at the Door: A Fantasy on Fate, Forster and Beethoven's Fifth', *Cahiers Victoriens et Édouardiens*, 44 (1996), 135–45; Cecilia Björkén-Nyberg, '"Listening, Listening": Music and Gender in *Howards End, Sinister Street* and *Pilgrimage*', in *Literature and Music*, ed. Michael J. Meyer (Amsterdam: Rodopi, 2002), pp. 89–115; Phyllis Weliver, *The Musical Crowd in English Fiction, 1840–1910: Class, Culture and Nation* (Basingstoke: Palgrave Macmillan, 2006), pp. 182–84; David Deutsch, 'Reconnecting Music to *Howards End*: Forster's Aesthetics of Inclusion', *LIT*, 21.3 (2010), 163–86; Zhou, 'Sublime Noise', pp. 22–76; Fillion, *Difficult Rhythm*, pp. 79–92; Gemma Moss, 'Music in E. M. Forster's *A Room with a View* and *Howards End*: The Conflicting Presentation of Nineteenth-Century Aesthetics', *English Literature in Transition*, 59.4 (2016), 493–509.
[49] *HE*, p. 40.

Introduction 15

respect, Brahms's vocal music seems an adequately erudite set of works that caters to Tibby's musical taste, aligning, as it does, Tibby – who has just listened to Beethoven's Fifth with a full score on his knees – with the serious and cerebral character of the German musical canon. At the same time, however, it invites us to imagine whether or not Helen, even though she has missed the second half of the concert as she left abruptly after Beethoven's symphony, is referring to the Brahms on the programme – his 'Four Serious Songs' (*Vier ernste Gesänge*, Op. 121) – when mocking her brother. This raises further questions, for these songs were written for bass voice and piano rather than for female singers. Did Forster mistake 'Four Serious Songs' for another vocal work by Brahms for women's choir, 'Four Songs' (*Vier Gesänge,* Op. 17)? Or is it simply Helen's parody to have this bass song cycle, which Margaret has previously described as Brahms's 'grumbling and grizzling', sung by 'cultured females'?[50] Why the adjective 'cultured'? Does it make a commentary on the public appearance of contemporary female performers on stage? Or is it an allusion to upper-middle-class amateur musical groups in early twentieth-century London? Or, as Helen advocates women's suffrage, can the adjective be read as her ironic critique of the conventional association of 'cultured' women with domestic musical activities? Most importantly, what is the implication of the tableau of Tibby, a young man anything but manly, listening to a group of singing females? All these questions – about gender, class, the boundary between public and private, the reception of Brahms's work in Britain and his cultural status – illustrate the ambivalence that can be produced by a single reference to music.

Focusing on unobtrusive textual details like those just mentioned, this book picks up what would have been readily labelled by Wolf as 'thematization' in Forster's novels, short stories, essays, letters, diaries, lectures, and broadcast talks. This is not to say that the book will bypass Forster's better-known descriptions of musical performance and consumption; rather, the strategy is to 'not listen' to the obvious but to 'wool-gather' and contemplate the meanings of what is often briefly mentioned and overlooked. In so doing, I suggest that Forster's engagement with music is mediated through a matrix of ideas and debates about evolution, empire, Britain's relationship with the Continent, the rise of fascism, and the emergence of musicology as an academic discipline. My discussion's thematic structure provides the necessary liberation from strict chronology to allow disparate examples to be brought together and unacknowledged

---

[50] *HE*, p. 33.

links to shine, thus foregrounding the width and connections of Forster's political concerns. By analysing Forster's representations of music as his responses to differing, sometimes conflicting, perceptions of music, my study seeks to illustrate how the wide-ranging associations of music serve as a conduit for Forster's contemplation of issues he felt ambivalent about, such as racial and national differences, imperialism, hero-worship, individualism, and patriarchy. Music's intersections with discourses on gender and sexuality, racial identity, colonial rule, national character, and anti-Semitism, I shall suggest, provided Forster with a means of reflecting and commenting, sometimes contradictorily, on the repercussions of ideological conflicts of his time.

This is therefore not a formalistic study of the 'musicality' of Forster's text, of how his narratives are modelled on certain musical works, or of the ways in which a text can be 'rhythmically' dissected and charted out. Instead, this book is interested in Forster's engagement with and representations of music as contingent on external historical and social situations, as modulated according to different audiences so as to meet discrete purposes, and as politically nuanced even when they appear apolitical. For example, his aesthetics of 'rhythm', as the first chapter will argue, is not purely concerned with the narrative styles of the novel but informed by the topicality of the term 'rhythm' in contemporary delineations of the racial other. While my study is an interdisciplinary project, its primary focus is literary analysis rather than musicology. I shall discuss a variety of musical works and performances, but only in so far as they shed light on Forster's representations of, and commentaries on, his musical material. It is, then, from Forster's perspective that I approach these musical works, without intending to provide evaluation of any of them. Even when Forster's text does subjectively assess the quality of a musical work, a composer, or a performance, this book is not concerned with critiquing the validity of his judgement, but with exploring the implications of his assessment. At the same time, the book is mindful that Forster's writings are not merely documents that record social reality from an authorial view. Rather, as we will see in the following chapters, a discussion of Forster's musical representations is often inseparable from an interpretation of the irony of the narrative voice, and an emphasis on ideology frequently prompts us to contemplate Forster's aesthetic choices.

The first chapter contextualizes Forster's idea of 'rhythm' in *Aspects of the Novel* within the contemporary currency of the term in evolutionary discourses on non-Western cultures, arguing that his conception of 'rhythm' as an aesthetics of fiction is preceded by his use of the term to

Introduction

reflect on the conditioning of epistemology in cross-cultural encounters. Analysing two little-discussed newspaper articles on music Forster wrote in Egypt, a 1912 essay by his friend Goldsworthy Lowes Dickinson about Anglo-India as well as *A Passage to India*, the chapter proposes that Forster was alert to the many problems of subjectivity, perspective, and language in delineating the racial other. It examines how Forster's references to actual rhythm in *A Passage to India* suggest a significant, and so far undiscussed, negotiation of the plurality of musical cultures. The chapter thus challenges the critical notion of rhythm as reflective purely of modernist fascination with form and intermediality. Complicating the long-held dichotomy of aesthetics and politics in modernist scholarship, it recovers the racial connotations of Forster's employment of 'rhythm' in his writing, shedding new light on his recognition that his questioning of imperialism had profound implications for his own conception of epistemology and representation.

Following the discussion of 'rhythm', the second chapter continues to focus specifically on *A Passage to India*, examining the ways in which Forster's representations of Western musical instruments in the novel destabilize and subvert – or queer – colonial norms. It continues the previous chapter's investigation into the conventional dissociation of modernist aesthetics from politics by going against Forster's aforementioned preference for a formalist, 'abstract' reading of the work and against his consistent dilution of the novel's political resonance with contemporary nationalist movements in India.[51] This is not to vandalize authorial intention, but to suggest that, whether Forster intended politics as the novel's theme or not, his alertness to the colonial reality is worked into the novel. Documenting Forster's awareness of the dissemination of Western musical instruments as an embodiment of the Empire's material invasion of the colony, the chapter explores this rarely discussed attention to the material existence of Western music as part of Forster's criticism of colonialism. Informed by postcolonial theories, material culture studies, and queer musicology, the chapter suggests that Forster's descriptions of Ronny Heaslop's viola, the Maharajah's harmonium, and a piano in a European Guest House delineate the individual subjection to and negotiation of external forces in a colonial environment.

---

[51] In 'Three Countries' (1959), a lecture read in Milan and in Rome, Forster said that '[f]or the book is not really about politics, though it is the political aspect of it that caught the general public and made it sell. It's about something wider than politics'. *HD*, pp. 289–99 (p. 298).

18   E. M. Forster and Music

The materiality of music is exemplified not only by musical instruments but also by the abundance of textual forms in the musical industry, such as music scores, teaching materials, and a vast literature about music. The third chapter focuses on Forster's transformation of the opera-box literary trope of seduction into a comical, almost riotous, opera scene in his first novel, *Where Angels Fear to Tread* (1905).[52] The scene is liberally scattered with allusions to nineteenth-century musical and literary texts and to national stereotypes about musical idiosyncrasies. Arguing that Forster's parodic use of these allusions reflects both his negotiation of the weightiness of literary heritage and his participation in topical debates about national character, the chapter considers his stylistic and ideological ambitions for his debut novel. The chapter thus brings together considerations of the novel's literary history and its national politics. Unearthing what lies beneath the beguiling social comedy of the novel, the chapter puts its emphasis on the intertextual and contextual resonances of the opera scene, analysing them as evidence of Forster's strategy of writing against existing material to distinguish his debut work from others.

Forster's Wagnerism is the focus of the fourth chapter. Although he never called himself a Wagnerite or a Wagnerian,[53] Forster was one of numerous contemporaries under the cultural impact of Wagner in the first few decades of the twentieth century, his many allusions to Wagner and Wagner's work informed by and responsive to the controversies surrounding Wagnerism at the time. According to Michelle Fillion, Forster first heard Wagner's *Tristan und Isolde* in Covent Garden in 1898; his first *Ring* cycle was in Dresden in 1905.[54] While his interest in and knowledge of Wagner's music and ideas have been documented as well as contextualized within the broader cultural movements of British and European Wagnerism,[55] past commentaries on Wagner's influence on Forster's work

---

[52] On opera-box literature conventions, see Ruth A. Solie, *Music in Other Words: Victorian Conversations* (Berkeley: University of California Press, 2004), pp. 187–218.

[53] Oliver Stallybrass and Frank Kermode have called Forster a 'Wagnerite' or a 'Wagnerian'. As Emma Sutton suggests, 'labelling oneself a Wagnerite was an act replete with political (in its broadest sense) resonance' in the 1890s, as it 'place[d] oneself ... in relation to a range of contemporary and antecedent Wagnerians, and in relation to contemporaries uninterested in or hostile to Wagner'. Considered in this context, that Forster never called himself a Wagnerite or a Wagnerian suggests his alertness to the complexity of contemporary Wagnerism. Emma Sutton, *Aubrey Beardsley and British Wagnerism in the 1890s* (Oxford: Oxford University Press, 2002), p. 2. For Oliver Stallybrass's comment, see *RV*, p. 233. For Kermode's discussion, see Kermode, *Concerning E. M. Forster*, p. 46.

[54] Fillion, *Difficult Rhythm*, pp. 5–6.

[55] Fillion, *Difficult Rhythm*, pp. 40–43. For British Wagnerism in the late nineteenth and early twentieth centuries, see Sutton, *Aubrey Beardsley*, passim. For European contexts, see *Wagnerism*

Introduction

have been scattered and uneven, with the majority of them straining to identify the Wagnerian model behind a particular text.[56] Instead of trying to map out the narrative parallels between Wagner's music and Forster's fiction, the chapter turns to the way in which Forster confronts the monumentality of Wagner's cultural status through tackling and questioning the heroism of Siegfried. Examining a variety of texts – ranging from his 1907 novel, *The Longest Journey*, to his political essays in the 1930s and a wartime pamphlet, *Nordic Twilight* (1940), and to a postwar radio broadcast, 'Revolution at Bayreuth' (1954) – the chapter considers how Forster was attentive to a complex web of discourses on Wagner's anti-Semitism, posthumous reception in Britain, and links to the Nazis in the first half of the twentieth century. Forster's consistent critique of Wagnerian heroism for its apocalyptical vision suggests his opposition to the political extremism and masculine exceptionalism celebrated and advocated by many contemporaries. Analysing Forster's criticism of the Wagnerian hero, the chapter discusses his reflection on fascism, war, violence, and hero-worship.

In the fifth chapter, I turn to Forster's ironic representations of musical scholarship in its institutional form, contextualizing his own self-proclaimed status as a musical amateur within the increasingly professionalized and institutionalized discipline of musicological research in the early twentieth century. The chapter examines his portrayals of two rarely discussed women characters – Vashti in the 1909 short story, 'The Machine Stops', and Dorothea in his unfinished novel, *Arctic Summer*, first drafted between 1911 and 1912 – as his championing of musical amateurism and his criticism of the professionalization of musicology. In particular, the chapter analyses Forster's satirizing of early twentieth-

---

in European Culture and Politics, ed. David C. Large and William Weber (Ithaca: Cornell University Press, 1984).

[56] Tony Brown, 'E. M. Forster's *Parsifal*: A Reading of *The Longest Journey*', *Journal of European Studies*, 12.1 (1982), 30–54; W. J. Lucas, 'Wagner and Forster: *Parsifal* and *A Room with a View*', in *Romantic Mythologies*, ed. Ian Fletcher (London: Routledge & Kegan Paul, 1967), pp. 271–97; Judith Scherer Herz, '"This is the End of Parsival": The Orphic and the Operatic in *The Longest Journey*', in *Queer Forster*, ed. Robert K. Martin and George Piggford (Chicago: University of Chicago Press, 1997), pp. 137–50; and Peter E. Firchow, 'Germany and Germanic Mythology in *Howards End*', *Comparative Literature*, 33.1 (1981), 50–68. Compared to these works, John Louis DiGaetani's book, *Richard Wagner and the Modern British Novel* (Cranbury: Associated University Presses, 1978), is an incomplete study of the relationship between literary modernism and Wagner. His chapter on Forster (pp. 90–109) neglects some of Forster's important Wagnerian allusions and oversimplifies Forster's Wagnerism as an application of musical leitmotifs to prose writing. Alexander H. Shapiro's article, 'McEwan and Forster, the Perfect Wagnerites', *The Wagner Journal*, 5.2 (2011), 20–45, is equally unconvincing in its unsuccessful attempt to read characters in *Howards Ends* as modelled on those in *Die Walküre*.

century academia's antiquarian interest in folk revival. What problematizes his satire, the chapter argues, is Forster's conception of gender: on the one hand, Forster exposes that professionalism is often constructed by gendered discourses that depend on the conventional mind–body dualism of patriarchal culture; but on the other, he casts professional women in roles against which his narratives rebel. Asking whether the portrayals of the two women hide his misogyny, the chapter suggests that Forster's advocacy of musical amateurism is at the same time an attempt to negotiate women's place in his often homoerotically charged envisioning of companionship.

***

'I was going to a Busch Quartet and much looking forward to it', Forster once wrote, 'but just before starting I heard a decent and straightforward story of misfortune – quite unprintable, even in these advanced columns. ... I got to the Wigmore Hall so occupied and worried over it, that I could not listen to the music at all, and yet I heard the whole of the music'.[57] This might have been a one-off experience, but if it demonstrates Forster's perception of music as a form of art vulnerable to external disturbances, it also suggests that he is aware of the difference between listening and hearing, and of the extramusical ramifications of not listening. By demonstrating how Forster explores musical politics of various kinds to reflect on epistemology, material culture, national identity, fascism, and institutional intellectualism, this book highlights music's vital role in Forster's ideology and recovers a previously underappreciated eclecticism in his writing. Although there is no doubt about Forster's preoccupation with homosexuality and empire, his creative and critical antennae – as we shall see in the chapters that follow – stretch to explore a wide variety of fields and areas of study, many of which intersect with early twentieth-century musical cultures. In focusing exclusively on Forster's musical representations and their historical contexts, the following chapters exemplify how a retrieval of textual nuances and their contextual links brings out new ways to read and understand Forster's writing. As the Postlude will suggest, through a brief discussion of Forster's listening to Hugo Wolf's lieder in 1935 and a reflection on the limits of past 'gay' interpretations of Forster's contribution to the opera *Billy Budd*, a renewed close investigation into the relation between text and its historical context will enable us to uncover the complexity in Forster's ideology and generate

---

[57] 'A Note on the Way' (1934), in *AH*, pp. 69–72 (p. 70).

fresh readings of Forster's work. Contrary to the recent critical interest in Forster's legacies for subsequent generations of writers and artists, *E. M. Forster and Music* places the spotlight back on Forster himself and studies his work on his own terms. In so doing, my study simultaneously seeks to lend a new lens to the widely noted ambiguity in Forster's prose, reassesses the width and depth of his writing, and invites a reorientation of critical perspectives and approaches within Forster scholarship. This is therefore a study deeply wary of the need to give Forster a critical 'label' or enter him into an existing narrative. By paying attention to his musical enthusiasms and emphases, the book recovers a more complicated Forster. What shall emerge is not merely his attachment to music. Rather, we will see a writer whose engagement with and representations of music, like the 'Appassionata' passage in *A Diary for Timothy*, produce ideological interventions into political contingencies.

CHAPTER I

The Rhythm of the Racial Other
Before Aspects of the Novel

> I remember that on one occasion the player of the *tawak* [a large gong] becoming tired, he passed on the instrument to another Malay who proceeded to beat it just as a European would do, keeping strict time with the orchestra. He was laughed at by his audience and very soon retired covered with ridicule.
>
> C. S. Myers, 'A Study of Rhythm in Primitive Music'[1]

In his final Clark Lecture in 1927, Forster addressed the subject of 'rhythm' in the novel. His discussion of 'rhythm' has since then provoked diverse, sometimes contradictory, critical inquiries. While acknowledging Forster's deliberate vagueness, critics, as we have seen, have frequently used his notion of 'rhythm' as an important point of reference to consider his conception of narrative form and the 'musicality' of his prose; they have read Forster's notion of 'rhythm' as his attempt to renew the aesthetics of fictional form. What has not been done – and what should come before such readings – is a contextualization of Forster's discussion of 'rhythm'. Forster's use of the term is one of many examples of contemporary explorations of the properties and associations of rhythm, and his discussion of 'rhythm' as an aspect of the novel needs to be situated in this context of, not influence per se, but cross-disciplinary parallels and echoes. Specifically, it is this chapter's intention to demonstrate that Forster was aware of the contribution of contemporary racialized, universalizing discourses about evolution to the term's topicality.

The chapter explores what preceded the section of 'rhythm' in *Aspects of the Novel*, unearthing many new contexts to consider what might have informed Forster's concept and employment of the term. It retrieves a forgotten link to a 1912 essay by Goldsworthy Lowes Dickinson and draws attention to Forster's writings in Egypt during the First World War, a part

---

[1] C. S. Myers, 'A Study of Rhythm in Primitive Music', *The British Journal of Psychology*, 1.4 (1905), 397–406 (p. 398).

The Rhythm of the Racial Other: Before Aspects of the Novel

of his oeuvre rarely touched upon by critics.[2] What emerges from this examination of previously underdiscussed texts, as the chapter shall illustrate, is Forster's familiarity with the application of the term 'rhythm' to portrayals of the racial other. This prompts us to reconsider key moments in *A Passage to India*, particularly the trial scene and Gokul Ashtami, where references to actual rhythm generate profound racial implications for our understanding of Forster's reflection on his own writing. In so doing, the chapter questions the critical notion that characterizes Forster's 'rhythm' in *Aspects of the Novel* as his modernist aesthetics of novel writing, offering instead a new understanding of it as ideologically, especially cross-culturally, significant. By complicating Forster's 'rhythm' through highlighting his rumination on issues surrounding race and evolution, the chapter illustrates that Forster perceived 'rhythm' not simply as a metaphorical or aesthetic concept but as a term highly suggestive of Western value judgement. The broader concern of the chapter is therefore with Forster's view on Western epistemology in cross-cultural encounters. The chapter explores how Forster's writing, while negotiating rhythm's association with Western stereotypes about 'the East', reflects on the challenges in representing the racial other.

As mentioned in the Introduction, the chapter suspends critics' immediate alignment of 'rhythm' in *Aspects*, often via a discussion of *A Passage to India* as a 'rhythmic' novel, with modernist aesthetics of narrative form. For example, E. K. Brown analyses the images of 'wasps' and 'echoes' in the novel, observing how Forster 'combin[es] phrases, characters, and incidents, rhythmically arranged, with a profusion of expanding symbols, and with a complex evolution of themes'.[3] The novel thus explores and represents both 'an order and a mystery', creating 'a rhythmic form that enables us to respond to it as prophecy and song'.[4] David Medalie expands this interpretation, using 'rhythm' and *A Passage to India* to present Forster 'as a sceptical formalist [who] neither liberates nor completes'.[5] Forster's 'easy' rhythm is a 'contrived repetition of words and phrases' that 'accrue[s] meaning through [its] changing contexts', thus signalling a modernist conception of 'language as encoding memory and yet indicating that memory will not suffice', while 'difficult' rhythm is 'a formal device transporting itself to an evocation of that which lies

---

[2] One exception is Claire Buck, *Conceiving Strangeness in British First World War Writing* (Basingstoke: Palgrave Macmillan, 2015). One of Buck's chapters focuses on Forster's Alexandrian output.

[3] Brown, E. K., 'Rhythm', p. 93.   [4] Brown, E. K., 'Rhythm', p. 113.

[5] Medalie, *Forster's Modernism*, p. 157.

beyond form'.[6] For Medalie, the verbal repetitions in *A Passage to India*, plus the novel's tripartite structure, represent Forster's 'rhythm', which creates a 'cyclical movement' and 'grants solace in that it may bring back what has been lost', but 'it may also bring back what has been repressed or wished away'.[7] *Passage* is therefore Forster's 'most modernist novel'; his 'technical experiments', Medalie suggests, 'have much to do with the avoidance of "aesthetic absolutes"' in the novel's exploration of *'formalistic alternatives'*.[8] For all their insights, both readings rely on Forster's terminology as well as on the assumption that music's influence on modernist writers was purely aesthetic and formalist. For Forster and his contemporaries, however, rhythm never simply appeared in discussions of literary aesthetics and form. As Thaddeus L. Bolton claimed in his influential essay 'Rhythm' in 1894, 'Rhythm is so universal a phenomenon in nature and in physiological activity'.[9] Overlooking these contexts in which rhythm was constantly referred to and debated means that studies like Brown's and Medalie's unveil only a fraction of the meaning of Forster's 'rhythm'.

Recent modernist scholarship has demonstrated that the topicality of rhythm in the late nineteenth and early twentieth centuries was manifest in the ways in which the word cut through a wide range of areas of study. In her essay 'The Rhythm of the Rails: Sound and Locomotion', Laura Marcus explores the prominence of rhythm in various contemporary discourses, such as those on the human body, the cycle of the natural world, gender and sexuality, human labour and mechanical production, and – her focus – locomotion and avant-garde aesthetics.[10] By highlighting rhythm's highly effective pertinence to the many areas of study, Marcus's essay, I suggest, carries an implicit but important lesson. The cross-disciplinary overlap and historical connotations of rhythm remind us of how loaded the term was, and perhaps remains, yet too often in existing criticism it percolates down into critical vocabulary without being clarified. Often, rhythm is employed by critics interchangeably with either musical beats (but what kind of music and what kind of beat?), a certain repetition (in what form?), or bodily pulsation. Frequently, it is not clear whether

---

[6] Medalie, *Forster's Modernism*, pp. 124–25 and 128.   [7] Medalie, *Forster's Modernism*, p. 143.

[8] Medalie, *Forster's Modernism*, pp. 157–58, and 101. This interpretation of the novel's formal inventions was already present in earlier readings of the novel: see e.g. Richard S. Cammarota, 'Musical Analogy and Internal Design in *A Passage to India*', *English Literature in Transition*, 18.1 (1975), 38–46.

[9] Thaddeus L. Bolton, 'Rhythm', *The American Journal of Psychology*, 6.2 (1894), 145–238 (p. 146).

[10] Laura Marcus, 'The Rhythm of the Rails: Sound and Locomotion', in *Sounding Modernism: Rhythm and Sonic Mediation in Modern Literature and Film*, ed. Julian Murphet, Helen Groth, and Penelope Hone (Edinburgh: Edinburgh University Press, 2017), pp. 193–210.

The Rhythm of the Racial Other: Before Aspects of the Novel   25

rhythm is used literally or metaphorically (but for what?). Furthermore, references to rhythm in art are in need of further specification themselves. For instance, what is meant by 'prose rhythm'? Is it an auditory effect of up and down or a special arrangement of words and phrases? For twenty-first-century critics, rather than resorting to the evocativeness of the term, it is necessary to attend to the connotations of rhythm and interrogate its wide-ranging referentiality.

One of the contexts noted by Marcus is rhythm's contribution to explorations of the physiological and psychological functioning of the human body and its involvement in late nineteenth- and early twentieth-century debates about race and evolution. Herbert Spencer's controversial 'The Origin and Function of Music' (1857) popularized the view that the variety and complexity of modern European music were the fruition of evolution.[11] Despite being much contested by his contemporaries, numerous descriptions, factual or imaginative, of non-Western music supported and augmented this line of thinking, presenting the strong 'rhythm' in 'savage' music as a feature of the primitiveness of non-Western civilization. For example, Thaddeus L. Bolton claimed that '[s]avages are well aware of the exciting effects of certain rhythms, and are accustomed to use them to bring about the state of frenzy in which their priests give their prophecies and in which religious dances are danced'.[12] On the contrary, in his early work on non-Western music, the psychologist C. S. Myers proposed a less linear logic than that of Spencerian evolution. As the epigraph to this chapter shows, Myers, who went to Sarawak to study its indigenous music, was aware that the musical culture he encountered celebrated a rhythm distinct from that of Western art music. As Bennett Zon observes, Myers's description, though still rooted in a Western perspective, 'decries European inadequacy in comprehending primitive rhythm', 'attempting to equalize ... the value of European and primitive musical cultures, by making them appear related yet independent'.[13] Myers's reflection, I suggest, can find resonance in Forster's writing. Forster's negotiation of the intersection between rhythm and race was simultaneously a reflection

---

[11] For a discussion of the impact of Spencer's work, see Bennett Zon, 'The "Non-Darwinian" Revolution and the Great Chain of Musical Being', in *Evolution and Victorian Culture*, ed. Bernard Lightman and Bennett Zon (Cambridge, UK: Cambridge University Press, 2014), pp. 196–226.

[12] Bolton, 'Rhythm', p. 163.

[13] Bennett Zon, *Representing Non-Western Music in Nineteenth-Century Britain* (Rochester: University of Rochester Press, 2007), p. 236.

on the plurality of musics and a recognition of the Eurocentrism inherent in Western delineations of cross-cultural encounters.

There is growing critical interest in reading the influence of the racialized science of rhythm on modernist writers.[14] Michael Golston's *Rhythm and Race in Modernist Poetry*, for example, comments on the impact of the scientific (or pseudoscientific) rhythmicization of the human body as racially specific in the early twentieth century:

> By the late 1930s ... experimental work on rhythm had coalesced into a series of theoretical equations comprising a budding scientific field that linked the human pulse, genetic difference, racial metabolisms, the unconscious, machine-age work, and the geophysical environment: human bodies and minds, it appeared, were genetically precoded to respond to certain rhythms that manifested themselves in cultural productions as distinct as national fingerprints. Nazi exploitation of Rhythmics was of course an extreme use of this "science," many of the tenets of which were part of the more general Modernist zeitgeist. It is therefore not surprising that these equations appear in various configurations in the aesthetics articulating themselves at the time – particularly in poetics, where age-old controversies over the issue of rhythm were given a special spin.[15]

Arguing that the many cultural and political meanings of the term enabled multifarious loose allusions to race in formulations of poetic rhythm, Golston focuses on the writing of W. B. Yeats and Ezra Pound, observing the ways in which they engaged with the plethora of 'rhythmical' profiling of racial and national identities. His work attends to what Edward W. Said noted in the late 1980s as the tendency in intellectual and critical debates about art and philosophy to 'elevate' European ideas and inquiries 'to the level of the essential and the universal':

> To say that questions that ask 'What is music?' or 'What is the literary, or literariness?' are impressively evident in recent discussions of art and politics is to say the obvious. What has needed saying, however, is that these same fascinated discussions, whose presence is so striking in Adorno, de Man, Wagner, etc., actually occur in a much wider framework than is usually allowed: namely, the tremendous imperial expansion of the West.[16]

---

[14] William Martin, *Joyce and the Science of Rhythm* (New York: Palgrave Macmillan, 2012); Emma Sutton, '"Putting Words on the Backs of Rhythm": Woolf, "Street Music", and *The Voyage Out*', in *Rhythm in Literature after the Crisis in Verse*, Special Issue of *Paragraph*, ed. Peter Dayan and David Evans, 33.2 (2010), 176–96.

[15] Michael Golston, *Rhythm and Race in Modernist Poetry and Science* (New York: Columbia University Press, 2008), p. 47.

[16] Edward W. Said, *Musical Elaborations: The Wellek Library Lectures at the University of California, Irvine* (New York: Columbia University Press, 1991), p. 52.

The Rhythm of the Racial Other: Before Aspects of the Novel   27

What Golston unveils, then, is that Eurocentrism underlies the topicality of 'rhythm'. While his focus on poetic rhythm is different from my focus on Forster's 'rhythm' in the novel, Golston usefully debunks the universality of the term. If his is an examination of the centrifugal Foucauldian desire in early twentieth-century Europe to exert influence on and identify the other, mine is concerned with how 'others', centripetally, forced a subjectivity rooted in Western values and norms to look at the inadequacy of tools available for cross-cultural understanding and representation.

In *Play and the Politics of Reading: The Social Uses of Modernist Form*, Paul B. Armstrong states that 'Forster suggests that we can get beyond prejudice, but only by going through it – that is, by employing interpretive frameworks ironically, through a constructive act of negation that deploys epistemological categories and simultaneously suspects them'.[17] Dramatizing such a scenario of cross-cultural encounters, Forster's use of rhythm as a means of reflecting on issues of language, perspective, and epistemology suggests that he engages not just with the term's aesthetic associations but with its political, particularly racial, signification.

Goldsworthy Lowes Dickinson's 'Anglo-India'

When Forster first visited India in October 1912, he did not travel alone; with him were two of his Cambridge friends, Goldsworthy Lowes Dickinson and R. C. Trevelyan. Unlike Forster, who travelled to India on personal grounds for a visit to his long-term friend, Syed Ross Masood, Dickinson was touring India, and later China and Japan, as a recipient of an Alfred Khan Travelling Fellowship.[18] During the trip, he regularly wrote for the *Manchester Guardian*. Most of these writings, signed 'Don' when first published, were later collected in *Appearances* (1914). Forster was familiar with these writings as he kept the original clippings and later used them, with Dickinson's autobiographical writings, to recount his friend's impressions of India of the 1910s in his 1934 biography of Dickinson. In it, Forster focuses on Dickinson's attitude towards the British in India, or 'the Anglo-Indians': Dickinson 'felt either strong

---

[17] Paul B. Armstrong, *Play and the Politics of Reading: The Social Uses of Modernist Form* (Ithaca: Cornell University Press, 2005), p. 134.

[18] After his trip, Dickinson completed an official report for the Kahn Trustees in 1913, which was reprinted as *An Essay on the Civilisations of India, China and Japan* in 1914. For more background information of their trip to the East during 1912 and 1913, see *GLD*, pp. 112–13 and Furbank, *Forster*, I, pp. 215–19.

28   E. M. Forster and Music

sympathy or strong aversion, and in either case he pitied them for having such an uncongenial job'.[19]

For Dickinson, this 'job' went beyond office work and encompassed an Anglo-Indian routine of life in which Western music played a significant part, as evidenced by 'Anglo-India', one of the essays in *Appearances*, originally published on 21 January 1913.[20] Written in a satiric tone, the essay centres on an afternoon of leisure in an unspecified English Club: 'The scene is commonplace enough; twaddle and tea, after tennis; "frivolling" – it is their word; women too empty-headed and men too tired to do anything else'.[21] Accompanying this Anglo-Indian ennui is 'a band':

> The music suits the occasion. It is soft, melodious, sentimental. It provokes a vague sensibility, and makes no appeal to the imagination. At least it should not, from its quality. But the power of music is incalculable. It has an essence independent of its forms. And by virtue of that essence its poorest manifestations can sink a shaft into the springs of life.[22]

The passage indicates how the music, unspecified here, gives the Club afternoon a familiar and necessary European atmosphere, sedating the audience into a homogenously 'bored' musical crowd.[23] The selection of the repertoire and the way it is performed suggest a cautious attitude towards the affectivity of musical sounds, yet the mediocrity of the performance, Dickinson claims, does not hinder the music from becoming a catalyst for imagination. While he listens, the familiar Club life around him 'detaches itself from actuality and floats away on the stream of art' and 'symbols arise and begin to move'.[24] Here, rather than enthusing over his own enchantment with the music, Dickinson is mimicking an Anglo-Indian sense of entitlement, allowing himself to take flight with the music to indulge in the fantasy of the Empire.

Under the effect of the music, Dickinson writes rhapsodically how 'the East' becomes 'an infinite procession':

> all the generations of Asia pass and pass on, seen like a frieze against a rock background, blazing with colour, rhythmical and fluent, marching menacingly down out of infinite space on to this little oasis of Englishmen. Then, suddenly, they are an ocean; and the Anglo-Indian world floats upon it like an Atlantic liner. ... It has its first and second class and steerage well

---

[19] *GLD*, p. 114.
[20] Goldsworthy Lowes Dickinson, 'Anglo-India', in *Appearances* (Garden City: Doubleday, Page & Company, 1914), pp. 15–17.
[21] Dickinson, 'Anglo-India', p. 15.   [22] Dickinson, 'Anglo-India', p. 15.
[23] Dickinson, 'Anglo-India', p. 15.   [24] Dickinson, 'Anglo-India', pp. 15–16.

The Rhythm of the Racial Other: Before Aspects of the Novel 29

marked off. It dresses for dinner every night; it has an Anglican service on Sunday; it flirts mildly; it is bored; but above all it is safe. It has water-tight compartments. It is 'unsinkable.' The band is playing; and when the crash comes it will not stop. . . . Is it Gounod's 'Faust' or an Anglican hymn? No matter! It is the same thing, sentimental, and not imaginative.[25]

The repeated description of the music as 'sentimental' and 'not imaginative' makes a satiric commentary on the Anglo-Indians' self-characterization as a besieged few. The revelation that Gounod's *Faust*, extremely popular for its melodious sentimentalism in Europe and the United States since its premiere in 1859 and numerous lavish productions in the 1860s,[26] might have been one of the works being played demonstrates how important it is to the Club to select something non-inflammatory yet at the same time distinctively Western. As such, the music contributes to continuing the symbolization of 'the East' and 'the West' as an 'ocean' and a 'liner':

The East has swept over this colony of the West. And still its generations pass on, rhythmically swinging; slaves of Nature, not, as in the West, rebels against her; cyclical as her seasons and her stars; infinite as her storms of dust; identical as the leaves of her trees; purposeless as her cyclones and her earthquakes.[27]

Writing ironically, Dickinson observes how the Club people, beneath 'tea and twaddle', have more 'tragic' depth, as '[t]hey stand for the West, for the energy of the world, for all, in this vast Nature, that is determinate and purposive, not passively repetitionary'.[28] Concluding the essay by saying that he 'almost vow[s] never again to abuse Gounod's music', Dickinson makes a jibe at the reverence reserved for elements that uphold the imperial system.[29] Dickinson's essay thus satirizes the employment of music by Anglo-Indians to construct their national solidarity and cultural 'superiority', unveiling the cultural and aesthetic superficiality in their delusional self-indulgence.

---

[25] Dickinson, 'Anglo-India', p. 16.

[26] Intriguingly, in *Howards End*, Margaret Schlegel 'disliked' 'Faust' after Leonard Bast uses it to show that he is musically cultured. *HE*, p. 35. For an introductory discussion of the opera, see Steven Huebner, 'Faust (ii)', *Grove Music Online*, www.oxfordmusiconline.com [accessed 10 May 2018]. Individual pieces from the opera, such as the 'Jewel Song', were, and still are, frequently played as encores in concerts. The opera plays an important part in Edith Wharton's *Age of Innocence* (1920): see Cormac Newark, '*Faust*, Nested Reception and La Castafiore', *Cambridge Opera Journal*, 25.2 (2013), 165–84.

[27] Dickinson, 'Anglo-India', p. 17.   [28] Dickinson, 'Anglo-India', p. 17.

[29] Dickinson, 'Anglo-India', p. 17.

30 E. M. Forster and Music

As such, Dickinson's essay critiques a reductive understanding of 'the East'. The Anglo-Indians generalize 'the East' and use Western music to justify their rhapsodic generalization. In this respect, Western music, especially an evocation of the Western idea of rhythm, affords the Anglo-Indians the imaginative space necessary to make the contrast between 'the West' and 'the East' effective. As a 'rhythmical' 'procession' 'rhythmically swinging' and 'menacingly' moving forward, the use of rhythm enables 'the West' to evoke stereotypes about 'the East' as passive and primitive, as living in servitude to seasonal cycle ('slaves of Nature'), as unchanging, unthinking, and incapable of evolving or progressing ('infinite', 'identical', 'purposeless') in opposition to the evolution of Western civilization but at the same time potentially violent and threatening. For Anglo-Indians, rhythm brings forth the associations with these characteristics. Here, we have a glimpse into the logic and strategy behind the construction of the racial other. 'The East', unfamiliar or strange to Anglo-Indians, needs to be made accessible to their understanding. That is, its perceived 'difference' needs to be highlighted but at the same time conveyed in a familiar term. It is necessary here to sound the obvious: 'rhythm' is an English word, and its equivalents in most European languages are etymologically similar. With Gounod's music playing the role as the catalyst for the flow of symbolism, the characterization of 'the East' as 'rhythmical' is an attempt not just to simplify and associate 'the East' with the basest constituent in the Western conception of music but also to Westernize non-Western idiosyncrasies, to taxonomize a 'different' way of life into a Western knowledge system. It is therefore not enough to construe rhythm here simply as a musical repetition; rather, it is an essentially Western signifier, signifying a specifically Western concept of rhythmicity which is thought of by Anglo-Indians as able to capture the 'passively repetitionary' quality of India. Rhythm is thus part of the stereotypical reduction of 'the East' Dickinson is satirizing, suggesting his awareness of how rhythm helped the imperial and Eurocentric subjectivity define, and thus confine, the other.

Forster shared Dickinson's concern with the limit of imperial subjectivity in terms of its ability to perceive and represent a cross-cultural encounter. Most obviously, there is striking intertextuality between Dickinson's essay and *A Passage to India*. Two of the novel's most significant images, 'frieze' and 'dust', seem to have their roots in Dickinson's essay. In the novel, the frieze first appears literally on the mosque in which Aziz and Mrs Moore meet, before being mentioned in a figure of speech by Adela, who realizes that once she marries Ronny she 'would see India

The Rhythm of the Racial Other: Before Aspects of the Novel   31

always as a frieze, never as a spirit'.[30] Adela's reference to 'frieze', in particular, echoes Dickinson's description of 'frieze' in the essay, both of them laying bare the superficiality of the imperial gaze. As for the image of 'dust', the novel's protean representations of 'dust' create a kaleidoscopic display of Dickinson's phrase 'storms of dust', mutating itself into diverse significations for crumbling personal relationships as the plot unfolds.[31] That these two images were not lost during the long years when Forster was working on *A Passage to India* suggests that Forster regarded Dickinson's essay as important source material for his consideration of the inadequacy and problems of the rootedness of a Western perspective.

Forster in Alexandria

Yet Forster not only shared Dickinson's images but also Dickinson's strategy of using Western music to reflect on the epistemological rootedness in cross-cultural encounters, most evidently in his largely neglected Egyptian journalism. As a Red Cross officer in Alexandria between 1915 and 1919, Forster, unable to continue his unfinished Indian novel at the time, shifted his attention to journalism, publishing twenty-five newspaper articles for *The Egyptian Mail*, including two series – 'Our Diversions' and 'Alexandria Vignettes' – and several individual pieces.[32] His Egyptian output was by no means his first attempt at non-fiction; Forster started writing and publishing non-fiction long before his stay in Alexandria: his historical writing dated back to his Cambridge years, his travel writing developed along with his trips to Italy and to India, and his book reviews started before the First World War.[33] However, in Alexandria, Forster engaged conscientiously with various non-fictional genres within a short period of time, not excluding those which he had previously tried but including an even wider range of others, such as

---

[30] *PI*, pp. 13 and 41.

[31] Benita Parry, for instance, insightfully observes that Forster's 'text constructs an ontological scale situating the species in a universe indifferent to human purpose and intent, contiguous to an unconcerned inarticulate world, planted on a neutral earth and beneath an impartial sky. It is a position which seems to reduce existence to a respite between two epochs of dust, inducing a view of people as moving mud and contesting the centrality of human aspiration and endeavour'. Benita Parry, '*A Passage to India*: Epitaph or Manifesto?', in *E. M. Forster: A Human Exploration: Centenary Essays*, ed. G. K. Das and John Beer (London: Macmillan, 1979), pp. 129–41 (p. 135).

[32] Nine of them were later included in his 1923 pamphlet, *Pharos and Pharillon*, published by the Woolfs' Hogarth Press. See Miriam Allott, 'Editor's Introduction to *Pharos and Pharillon*', in *AL*, pp. 180–81.

[33] The three genres became, in *Abinger Harvest* (1935), three distinct sections: 'The Past', 'The East', and 'Books'.

32   E. M. Forster and Music

biographical writing and music criticism.[34] 'A Musician in Egypt' and 'Handel in Egypt', two of its kind in the latter category, echo Dickinson's 'Anglo-India' in their examination of the relation of a Western subjectivity with its non-Western surroundings.

Published on 21 October 1917, 'A Musician in Egypt' comments on Enrico Terni, a local composer in Alexandria whom Forster knew personally, and his orchestral music.[35] It appears to be a tribute to Terni, yet a closer scrutiny reveals an ambivalence produced by a series of qualifications. The article first introduces 'Egypt of the Levant – the coastal strip on which since the days of Herodotus European influences have rained'.[36] Always hatching 'a civilization of eclecticism and of exiles', coastal Egypt, not 'an eagle or a swan', is like 'a certain little bird' which accompanies a 'rhinoceros', 'perch[ing] lively and alert upon the hide of that huge pachyderm Africa'.[37] 'Though born and bred here', Terni, 'by blood an Italian', 'finds no inspiration locally, and turns for everything to Europe': from Greek mythology, he acquired the material for his symphonic poems and from César Franck and Wagner, his musical style.[38] Thus, '[h]is compositions no more smack of our soil than did the Idylls of Theocritus or the Elements of Euclid or the Enneads of Plotinus'; his music, though having 'individuality' and 'quietness', is '[n]ever noisy, never queer, avoiding excessive modernity'.[39] He is therefore 'emphatically a musician in Egypt', but 'not an Egyptian musician'.[40] The repeated negations imply a narrator cautious and reserved about its descriptions of Terni's musical merits.

Yet an interpretation of the article as a slight by an internationally renowned writer from London on someone on the Empire's periphery would be simplistic. Similar to the narrators in Forster's novels, frequently noted by critics for their ambivalence, the narrative voice in this article is uncomfortably slippery, resistant to having its belief and judgement pinpointed by readers. At times, the narrative voice is apologetic for its lack of musical expertise: 'being no musician, I can neither describe that phrase nor hum it nor even wave my finger to it in the air'.[41] At another moment,

---

[34] I suggest that Forster's three essays on Eliza Fay's letters from Egypt mark his first attempt at biographical writing. Written also during his stay in Alexandria, these three 'impressions' quote Eliza Fay's own words in length, but here and there, one can find Forster's shrewd comments in between these extensive passages, interpreting and evaluating Eliza Fay's actions, characteristics, emotions, and biases. See 'Eliza in Egypt', in *AL*, pp. 225–33.
[35] On Forster's acquaintance with Terni, Furbank, *Forster*, II, pp. 44–45.
[36] 'A Musician in Egypt', in *UEE*, pp. 37–40 (p. 37).   [37] *UEE*, p. 37.   [38] *UEE*, p. 38.
[39] *UEE*, p. 38.   [40] *UEE*, p. 38.   [41] *UEE*, p. 38.

The Rhythm of the Racial Other: Before Aspects of the Novel 33

it is only partially apologetic, laying the blame instead on the subject itself: 'The above remarks, empty as they are of musical criticism, may perhaps indicate the general quality of [Terni's] talent'.[42] Yet this seems less the composer's fault but a symptom of the time: if Terni's 'is not a heroic talent', it is because 'we do not live on heroic soil, nor, with all respect to the great war, in a heroic age' and 'out of a population of exiled little jobbers it is impossible that a heroic art should be raised'.[43] 'We', the narrative voice and the target audience alike, are thus the target of the article's criticism. The article is for 'the English here' who, unlike 'the Italian or French speaking community', 'hold so severely aloof from the arts that they may be surprised to learn that ... Egypt after all produces more than cotton, onions and eggs'.[44] By taking note of this not quite 'indigenous' composer, the narrative voice satirizes English provincialism and British colonization while aligning itself with the sophisticated Continentals.[45] In fact, it takes pride in its European identity, declaring at the very beginning of the article: 'A European personally, I feel kindly toward this coastal strip. It raises my interest and even a sense of romance'.[46] In the midst of the uncertainty of the article, the loudness of the unabashed identification of the 'I' becomes conspicuous. Its indulgence in the Levant as a displaced European 'elsewhere' illustrates how a quest for something exotic is also a search for familiarity because, for the exotic to exude its allure, its aura of exoticism is felt, construed, and delineated by the onlooker. Like Dickinson's strategy in 'Anglo-India', Forster's narrative can be interpreted as a result from his mimicking the voice of an English (and European) expatriate. Instead of celebrating the self-proclaimed European identity, this suggests Forster's critique of the overconfidence of Western values. If the article is reserved about Terni's quintessentially Levantine music, it also ironically highlights its own reliance on European cultural orientations to make value judgements.

It becomes evident that, by exposing a Western sense of entitlement in a colonial context, the article is both an example and an examination of the bias of cross-cultural evaluation. Through commenting on Terni's music, it reflexively critiques its own European rootedness. This prompts the readers to consider the Eurocentrism in the article's criteria and perspective, as revealed by the characterization of Terni as a product of its Alexandrian milieu, as

---

[42] *UEE*, p. 39.   [43] *UEE*, p. 39.   [44] *UEE*, pp. 37–38.   [45] *UEE*, p. 38.   [46] *UEE*, p. 37.

34 E. M. Forster and Music

> typical of the other artists who have preceded him on this coastal strip. Like them, he writes as an eclectic and an exile. Their hearts are in Europe, their hearts are not here. Africa, that huge and forgotten rhinoceros, never comes in at all. Indeed how could it come in? One touch of its horn would send the whole of art as we understand art, tom-tomming up to the moon.[47]

The article's repetition of 'eclectic' and 'exile' becomes ironic because the cosmopolitan culture of Alexandria and the cosmopolitanism of Terni's music are less culturally diverse than they appear. What underlies the article is an elegiac penchant for European culture only, a 'straining of the eyes beyond the sea', a European form of eclecticism worshipped by European exiles.[48] While Europe is thus identified by the Levant and the narrator as the homeland, Africa is the present habitat 'forgotten' by these 'exiles'. The rhinoceros analogy projects an image of Africa as stagnant, harmful, and inexplicable. The reference to the tom-tom conjures up the stereotype about Africa as a place of haunting drumbeats, using it to reiterate the Western fear of a tribal, primeval, and aggressive backwardness. It is also an oblique reference to an exotic type of rhythm, viscerally alarming and harmfully affective to the Western body. More importantly, the phrase 'the whole of art as we understand art' suggests an awareness that language conditions epistemology; the word 'art' defines the English, and more broadly European, understanding of 'art' shared by the narrative voice, the targeted reader, Terni, Alexandrian Egypt, and, if we read the article autobiographically, perhaps Forster as well. The phrase makes visible the linguistic confinement of subjectivity, suggesting Forster's wariness of the epistemological conundrum encapsulated in using one's language to interpret 'the other'.

There is a striking similarity between this characterization of Africa as beyond Western understanding and detrimental to Western artistic values, and Fielding's perception of India on his trip back to Europe in *A Passage to India*. Fielding's craving for 'form' when approaching Venice is in the same vein of thoughts as the narrator's compliment on Terni as a composer who 'knows how to build'.[49] 'Form' is something Fielding finds India short of and something he has lost the ability to appreciate when there; for the narrator in 'A Musician in Egypt', it is the merit of Terni's otherwise unmerited music against 'the vast, the formless, the helpless [*sic*] and unhelpful' continent.[50] For both, 'form' is, then, a European kind of architectural unity, valuable but vulnerable; as an epitome of Western civilization, it is worth being disseminated around the world but, once

---

[47] *UEE*, p. 38. [48] *UEE*, p. 39. [49] *PI*, p. 270. *UEE*, p. 38. [50] *UEE*, p. 39.

The Rhythm of the Racial Other: Before Aspects of the Novel   35

displaced from its root, becomes besieged and contaminated by the threat of the racial other. In their enchantment with 'form', and in lamenting that Western civilization is put at risk and potentially annulled as a result of being brought into contact with non-Western cultures, Fielding and the narrator in 'A Musician in Egypt' share a sense of cultural superiority. Such a perception of Westerners abroad as participants in an anxiety-ridden mission is similar to what Dickinson notes as 'tragic depth' in his depiction of the English Club. 'A Musician in Egypt' thus registers the same cultural awareness as Dickinson's 'Anglo-India' and rehearses the examination of cross-cultural relations in *A Passage to India*. By gauging the 'value' of Terni's music from a European point of view and situating music within a broader colonial economy of production and consumption, the article problematizes the relationship between 'indigenous' and 'foreign', suggesting Forster's awareness of the limits of an European subjectivity.

'Handel in Egypt' touches on many of the same issues as 'A Musician in Egypt'.[51] Drawing attention to the conflict between different national and racial identities at a performance of Handel's *Messiah* in Alexandria on New Year's Eve, 1917, the article, in a similarly ironic tone, satirizes the undue attachment of the English abroad to a composer not even English by birth, even though Handel's centrality to English music was, and has been, widely noted. The article opens with a statement that 'Few Englishmen can listen to Handel's music unmoved'.[52] As the narrator notes, 'we' the English share a childhood memory, 'tender and absurd', of listening, with 'Uncle James and Aunt Margaret', to '"Handel done really properly" at the Albert Hall'.[53] Recalling those 'expeditions' always titillates the English 'middle class sentimentality':

> How the leaves rustled as Aunt Margaret and thousands of other visitors turned over their scores [at] the same moment! As the festival proceeded the Albert Hall became a globe of fog through which the monster chorus boomed and barked, and the Soloist was diminished into a lucifer match.[54]

In comparison, while 'the effect that Handel had upon one in an Egyptian atmosphere' is almost the same, 'the emotions he awoke' are 'so curious and so poignant' as to defamiliarize the event.[55] There is 'a dense block of khaki' at the performance in Alexandria, thus sending out a more explicitly military sense of aggression than the uniformity of listeners' actions or the sonority of the chorus in the Albert Hall.[56] The facts that 'we all st[and]

---

[51] 'Handel in Egypt', in *UEE*, pp. 47–50.   [52] *UEE*, p. 47.   [53] *UEE*, p. 47.
[54] *UEE*, p. 47.   [55] *UEE*, p. 48.   [56] *UEE*, p. 48.

36   E. M. Forster and Music

up' to salute 'the celebrated Hallelujah Chorus ... because Englishmen always have stood' and that we find in the vision of *Messiah* 'a balm for the incurable wound of the world', suggest that the Egyptian performance is a site of collective zeal, rousing both nationalistic and religious fantasies.[57] For the narrator, the 'beautiful' music becomes rather 'overwhelming when heard in Egypt and at the close of another year of war'.[58] The article's disdain of the English's worship of Handel is underpinned by an aversion to war.

The article's characterization of the English audience as a susceptible musical crowd was informed by evolutionary discourses on music. As the narrator says ironically, when all stand to the Hallelujah Chorus, Herbert Spencer 'sat the better to observe the effect of great music upon his compa-triots' mentality'.[59] While this alludes to Spencer's use of music as an indicator of the level of human civilization in his evolutionary theory as well as, more broadly, to the discipline of crowd theory,[60] the satire lies in its displacement of the English from observing others to being observed. The English audi-ence's behaviour under the effect of Handel's music becomes the sample in focus; its almost irrational response to *Messiah*, from a Spencerian perspective, becomes pathological evidence of backwardness. In contrast, there are some 'intelligent and musical Levantines' whose 'clever dark heads and the big hats of their women folk showed up here and there in the acquiescent audience like notes of interrogation'.[61] Their sophisticated and measured listening indicates that the article was informed, too, by circulating stereotypes about different national musical sensibilities:

> [The music] must have seemed to them so formless and provincial. Our middle-classes, being afraid of opera because it is wicked and of church music because it is popish, have evolved this amorphous compromise, the Oratorio, which alternately coquets with the altar and the stage. To a Southerner and a Catholic this must seem very absurd.[62]

Forster's use of the verb 'evolved' to comment on the close affinity between the oratorio and English musical tradition is significant. Though not English in origin, the oratorio has had a long tradition in England: the genre was decisively revolutionized and popularized by Handel in the eighteenth century, anglicized symbolically by Mendelssohn's premiere of *Elijah* in Birmingham in 1846 and rejuvenated by Elgar, whose work in the early twentieth century, such as *The Dream of Gerontius* (1900), shows his conscious and conscientious engagement with the choral

---

[57] *UEE*, pp. 48–50.   [58] *UEE*, p. 50.   [59] *UEE*, p. 49.
[60] See Zon, 'The "Non-Darwinian" Revolution'.   [61] *UEE*, p. 48.   [62] *UEE*, p. 48.

The Rhythm of the Racial Other: Before Aspects of the Novel   37

form.[63] By saying that the English 'middle-classes' 'evolved' the genre, the article undermines the discipline of evolution, stripping it of its scientific status and unveiling the factor of human engineering.

However, though the article mocks Spencerian evolution, it appears to adhere to racial stereotypes about the musical knowledge and sensibility of non-Westerners:

> And there was some one else in the church who struck a note even more critical than the Levantines. I refer to the organ-blower. ... This organ blower – no doubt through no wish of his own – was an Arab. He blew not far from my Presbyterian window-sill, and he had dined on garlic. Being merry by nature he kept grinning in the hope that one of us would lighten his labours by grinning back, which we were too respectable to do. What would this man have thought of our performance, supposing him to think? Of course he didn't think. He was just a humble servitor. But in his person Egypt and the East were represented in that church – the East that generated Handel's religion and now receives it back in an inexplosive form. ... There is nothing mystic here – only a promise of permanent comfort such as no Oriental thinker would tolerate. As the Oriental grows thoughtful he grows sad – that organ-blower would stop smiling if his brain developed.[64]

The logic of this passage is that the organ-blower, perceived by the narrator as akin to 'Oriental' mysticism, levels the charge of superficiality at the English audience, but the essentialization and generalization of the Arab is ostensible, almost excessively so. On a biographical level, Forster was dismissive about Arabic civilization in Alexandria. In his *Alexandria: A History and a Guide*, he offers accounts of the city's Greek and Christian pasts but states that the 'Arab Period' 'is of no importance though it lasts over 1,000 years'.[65] The emphasis on the organ-blower's inability to 'think' is itself a racist characterization of non-Westerners as undeveloped. The description of him as ignorantly 'grinning' and 'smiling' while pumping the organ recalls the trick of using monkeys as organ-grinders in street performances in the nineteenth century, thus giving the character a less-than-human status.[66] One might read it as Forster's racism:

---

[63] Howard E. Smither, 'Oratorio', *Grove Music Online*, www.oxfordmusiconline.com [accessed 10 May 2018]. The article's title can be read as an allusion to another oratorio by Handel, *Israel in Egypt* (1739), often paired with *Messiah*.

[64] *UEE*, p. 49.   [65] *AL*, p. 7.

[66] Cf. Henry Mayhew's 'Italian with Monkey': 'An Italian ... had a peculiar boorish, and yet good-tempered expression, especially when he laughed, which he did continually'. 'He wore the Savoy and broad-brimmed felt hat, and with it on his head had a very picturesque appearance, and the shadow of the brim falling on the upper part of his brown face gave him almost a Murillo-like look.

to borrow Chinua Achebe's criticism of Conrad's *Heart of Darkness*, Forster, too, 'chose the role of purveyor of comforting myths', criticizing the English abroad through perpetuating the racial stereotypes about non-Westerners.[67] However, despite being an outsider who sits on a 'window-sill', the narrator's national and racial belonging to the people he is satirizing suggests, if not self-caricature, at least some degrees of awareness of the limit of his own perspective. Like Dickinson's 'Anglo-India', Forster's 'Handel in Egypt' explores how an epistemology rooted in European orientations operates in a cross-cultural encounter. The narrator's description assumes a hierarchy of racial norms; Forster's positioning of the narrator, while not exactly subverting the hierarchy, invites the readers to examine the conditioning force behind such racial assumptions. Forster's image of the Arab organ-blower certainly alludes to stereotypes about the non-Western 'other', but it becomes ambivalent when we see through the crudely delineated national and racial contrasts and consider the self-reflexivity of the narrative voice.

It is imperative, then, to notice the Eurocentrism of the narrator's perspective before we can extend a reading of the significance of the organ-blower. Martin Quinn and Safaa Hejazi, two of the very few scholars who have studied Forster's Egyptian writings, have insightfully read the organ-blower as 'a prototype' for the punkah-wallah in the trial scene in *A Passage to India*. They indicate the similarities between the two scenes, in which it is 'the lone, humble, aloof, inscrutable, undiscerning Eastern functionary – with an oddly central, crucial role of circulating air – who casts the mixed audience of English occupiers and sophisticated Orientals into high relief'.[68] However, they have overlooked that the 'undiscerning' non-Westerners in both cases are looked at and portrayed by Westerners; the portrayals become not simply Forster's reproduction of racial stereotypes but his reflection on the limit of Western subjectivity. More importantly, what Quinn and Hejazi also overlook is the parallel of the 'rhythmicization' of the body of the two. Though 'rhythm' is not

---

There was, however, an odour about him, – half monkey, half dirt, – that was far from agreeable, and which pervaded the apartment in which he sat'. Henry Mayhew, *London Labour and the London Poor*, 4 vols (London: Frank Cass, 1967), III, pp. 179–80. For nineteenth-century anti-street music movement, see John M. Picker, *Victorian Soundscapes* (Oxford: Oxford University Press, 2003), chapter 2, 'The Soundproof Study'. Cf. also Virginia Woolf's depictions of the barrel organ player in 'Street Music' (1905) and in *The Years* (1937).

[67] Chinua Achebe, 'An Image of Africa: Racism in Conrad's *Heart of Darkness*', in *Hopes and Impediments: Selected Essays* (New York: Doubleday, 1989), pp. 1–20 (p. 5).

[68] Martin Quinn and Safaa Hejazi, 'E. M. Forster and *The Egyptian Mail*: Wartime Journalism and a Subtext for *A Passage to India*', *English Literature in Transition*, 25.3 (1982), 131–45 (p. 138).

The Rhythm of the Racial Other: Before Aspects of the Novel   39

referred to in the portrayal of the organ-blower, it is written into the character as he works the bellows of the organ, thus essentially maintaining the tempo and sustaining the rhythm of the oratorio. As such, the movement of the organ-blower can be read as looking forward to the punkah-wallah, who pulls the rope that controls the punkah 'rhythmically', to which we will now turn.

Rhythm in *A Passage to India*

Recollecting her friendship with Forster, Santha Rama Rau, who adapted *A Passage to India* for the stage, wrote that 'On that distant afternoon of our first meeting, Forster and I had agreed that the beautiful, almost naked Punkah-wallah ... was a crucial figure symbolic of an eternal India impervious to the small and transitory disturbances of Britons or Indians'.[69] Many critical readings have elaborated on the functions of the character as a representation of 'divine', discussing it as a site of colonial and sexual tension.[70] In the novel, the punkah-wallah is first observed by Adela:

> Almost naked, and splendidly formed, he sat on a raised platform near the back, in the middle of the central gangway, and he caught her attention as she came in, and he seemed to control the proceedings. He had the strength and beauty that sometimes come to flower in Indians of low birth. When that strange race nears the dust and is condemned as untouchable, then nature remembers the physical perfection that she accomplished elsewhere, and throws out a god – not many, but one here and there, to prove to society how little its categories impress her. This man would have been notable anywhere; among the thin-hammed, flat-chested mediocrities of Chandrapore he stood out as divine, yet he was of the city, its garbage had nourished him, he would end on its rubbish-heaps. Pulling the rope towards him, relaxing it rhythmically, sending swirls of air over others, receiving none himself, he seemed apart from human destinies, a male Fate,

---

[69] Quoted in *E. M. Forster: Interviews and Recollections*, ed. J. H. Stape (Basingstoke: Macmillan, 1993), p. 137.

[70] The punkah-wallah is, for Allen Mendenhall, 'a representation of divine', which combines both 'the natural rejection of clear-cut categories and the synthesis of competing dualities'. Allen Mendenhall, 'Mass of Madness: Jurisprudence in E. M. Forster's *A Passage to India*', *Modernist Cultures*, 6.2 (2011), 315–37 (p. 334). For Sara Suleri, 'the untouchable no longer refers to caste alone, but is extended to include an embodiment of homosexual desire'. Sara Suleri, *The Rhetoric of English India* (Chicago: University of Chicago Press, 1992), p. 135. Charu Malik combines the two readings: 'In his aloof servility and humbleness muted by striking physical beauty, he presents a contradictory figure who simultaneously reinforces colonial authority and disturbs it'. Charu Malik, 'To Express the Subject of Friendship: Masculine Desire and Colonialism in *A Passage to India*', in *Queer Forster*, ed. Martin and Piggford, pp. 221–35 (p. 222).

40 E. M. Forster and Music

a winnower of souls. ... The punkah-wallah ... scarcely knew that he existed and did not understand why the court was fuller than usual, indeed he did not know that it was fuller than usual, didn't even know he worked a fan, though he thought he pulled a rope.[71]

At the end of the chapter, the narrator observes: 'Unaware that anything unusual had occurred, [the punkah-wallah] continued to pull the cord of his punkah, to gaze at the empty dais and the overturned special chairs, and rhythmically to agitate the clouds of descending dust'.[72] Drawn to this basest form of the exotic (the association of the punkah-wallah with 'dust'), Adela mythologizes the punkah-wallah, in free indirect speech, detaching the Hindu servant from the present and the mundane; the narrator's description echoes her perception of the punkah-wallah as outside the progression of human civilization and outside 'time'.[73] Employing the adverb 'rhythmically' to describe the movement of the Indian body as purely kinetic and beyond the constraints of time, both Adela and the narrator, although not exactly romanticizing the punkah-wallah as noble savage, recall Dickinson's ironized sentimentalization of 'the East' as a timeless 'procession'. In presenting the punkah-wallah as devoid of thoughts and ignorant of the trial, both Adela and the novel's narrator are also similar to the narrator in 'Handel in Egypt', expressing curiosity only about the non-Western body (the narrator in 'Handel in Egypt' repelled by the fact that the organ-blower 'had dined on garlic') and centralizing it as an essential force that underpins the scene. That the punkah-wallah and the organ-blower maintain the 'rhythm' of the court-room and the concert, respectively, playing, as Quinn and Hejazi remind us, the 'crucial' role of supplying air, suggests that Forster was consciously engaging with the topical discourses about rhythm in contemporary, especially Bergsonian, debates about vitalism.[74] The perceived cyclicity of 'the East' is thus regarded as vital: if it is still cyclical and repetitive, it is perceived as a repetition that drives the mechanism of human society.

Like our discussion of Dickinson's 'Anglo-India' and Forster's Egyptian journalism, it is necessary to emphasize that the perspectives from which the punkah-wallah is described are ostensibly Western and Eurocentric.

---

[71] *PI*, p. 207.   [72] *PI*, p. 219.

[73] Sarah Cole focuses on the significance of the perspectival slippage when 'Europeans looking into a scene of oriental male beauty' here: 'Indeed the perspectival slippage in this scene calls attention to the way the text more broadly goes about universalizing a very specific form of desire. The lovely, godlike figure is appreciated by one and all'. Sarah Cole, *Modernism, Male Friendship, and the First World War* (Cambridge, UK: Cambridge University Press, 2003), p. 83.

[74] Marcus, 'The Rhythm of the Rails', p. 194.

The Rhythm of the Racial Other: Before Aspects of the Novel 41

Through Adela's and the narrator's use of 'rhythm', Forster exposes an epistemology conditioned by European culture that has the privilege to know and to define. As Paul B. Armstrong has convincingly illustrated, the novel demonstrates how 'knowledge ... cannot be completely nonrepressive and nonmanipulative precisely because its very partiality is necessarily objectifying and exclusionary'.[75] Both Adela's and the novel's narrator's reliance on 'rhythm' to describe the punkah-wallah needs to be read within Forster's reflection on the 'interpretive frameworks' of cross-cultural encounters through which 'epistemological categories' are simultaneously constructed and de-neutralized.[76] If rhythm provides Adela and the narrator with the term and the concept to portray the punkah-wallah, it is equally an attempt to classify the other within their knowledge system as well as to distance themselves from the racially specific rhythm of the foreign body. Expressing something akin to the narrator's 'sense of romance' when finding familiar traces in the exotic in 'A Musician in Egypt', both descriptions of the punkah-wallah remind us of Foucault's power-knowledge. Rhythm is a means of capturing and labelling the unfamiliar, a colonial signifier to represent – and to understand and regulate – the body of the colonized. In this respect, rhythm perpetuates Western stereotypes about 'the East'. In describing how rhythm reassures a Western perception of the racial other, Forster exposes the problems of representation.

If to describe the punkah as pulled 'rhythmically' is to reveal the irremovable Western perspective, other references to rhythm in the novel suggest Forster's alertness to the existence of non-Western musical systems. The first reference to rhythm in the novel is not to a Western one: in chapter 2, Aziz hears drums and identifies the sound as Hindu because its rhythm is 'uncongenial' to him.[77] Whether the rhythm congenial to Aziz is Western or Islamic remains an interesting point to speculate on; at least the Hindu drumming produces a rhythm of its own and suggests Forster's awareness of India's diverse cultures. The fact that the novel depicts multiple forms of rhythm can also be seen at the end of Fielding's tea party. When the confused narrator attempts to grasp Godbole's song, he can only wonder that '[a]t times there seemed rhythm'.[78] The narrator's attempt indicates that rhythm is one of the important elements in a listener's processing of music. That the 'rhythm' of Godbole's song does not fit in with what the narrator understands as European musical beats

---

[75] Armstrong, *Play and the Politics of Reading*, p. 132.
[76] Armstrong, *Play and the Politics of Reading*, p. 134.   [77] *PI*, p. 13.   [78] *PI*, p. 71.

42   E. M. Forster and Music

demonstrates that the song stems from a different musical culture that consists of different requirements and understandings of rhythm.

The novel's final two references to rhythm appear in the description of Gokul Ashtami, an annual celebration of the birth of Krishna, in chapter 33. As several critics have noted, the scene has its genesis in Forster's personal experiences in India in 1921, which he detailed in his letters home.[79] Yet the fact that rhythm is not referred to in these letters suggests that the term is one of Forster's additions to the literary reworking of the scene. Like his counterparts in 'A Musician in Egypt' and 'Handel in Egypt', the narrative voice in the novel is ostensibly foreign to the local, as manifested in Forster's use of parentheses:

> They sang not even to the God who confronted them, but to a saint; they did not one thing which the non-Hindu would feel dramatically correct; this approaching triumph of India was a muddle (as we call it), a frustration of reason and form. Where was the God Himself, in whose honour the congregation had gathered? Indistinguishable in the jumble of His own altar, huddled out of sight amid images of inferior descent, smothered under rose-leaves, overhung by oleographs, outblazed by golden tablets representing the Rajah's ancestors, and entirely obscured, when the wind blew, by the tattered foliage of a banana. Hundreds of electric lights had been lit in His honour (worked by an engine whose thumps destroyed the rhythm of the hymn). Yet His face could not be seen.[80]

As Carey J. Snyder comments, the narrator's description of the celebration offers no useful guidance; failing to sympathize or to explain, it 'dramatizes the breakdown of ethnographic understanding'.[81] As casual as it sounds, the narrator's added phrase 'as we call it' acts not only as a parenthetical afterthought but also as a reminder that it is in 'our' terms that this scene is described. For 'us', the 'engine whose thumps destroyed the rhythm of the hymn', though a side note, is one that sneeringly augments the chaos, and thus the absurdity, of the scene. While it might point to the incompatibility between Western technology and Hindu music and symbolize the invasion of European civilization, the perception of the hymn's 'rhythm' as being 'destroyed' suggests two possible interpretations. It can be read as a discovery that the hymn (perhaps at moments) has a beat similar to the

---

[79] Forster acknowledged that *The Hill of Devi* 'contains some of the material utilized in the final section of the novel'. 'Forster's Prefatory Notes (1957) to the Everyman Edition', *PI*, p. 314. See also Elizabeth Heine's introduction to *HD*.

[80] *PI*, pp. 275–76.

[81] Carey J. Snyder, *British Fiction and Cross-Cultural Encounters: Ethnographic Modernism from Wells to Woolf* (New York: Palgrave Macmillan, 2008), pp. 153 and 146.

The Rhythm of the Racial Other: Before Aspects of the Novel   43

Western understanding of rhythm before this 'rhythm' is being disrupted by the engine; or it can be read as a Western misunderstanding of the hymn's 'rhythm', which has nothing to do with the engine but seems irregular or fractured to the Western ear.

Finally, the narrator's attempt at understanding, and satirizing, the ceremony turns to the figure of Professor Godbole, who scrambles to adjust his pince-nez while singing. 'Godbole consulted the music-book, said a word to the drummer, who broke rhythm, made a thick little blur of sound, and produced a new rhythm. This was more exciting, the inner images it evoked more definite, and the singers' expressions became fatuous and languid'.[82] While the narrator may have discerned a change of pace of the singing, whether there is certainly a different 'rhythm' from the singers' point of view, whether the Hindus understand a change of pace as an introduction of 'a new rhythm', and whether the change of their expression is the result of this become unclear given the limitations of the narrator. What we have is not only the narrator blending reportage with satire; also, we see the inevitability of falling back on one's own terminology and taxonomy to depict others. Rhythm is thus part of the narrator's vocabulary to identify, gauge, and present musical idiosyncrasies and imply cultural differences.

As Ambreen Hai argues, *A Passage to India* 'is fundamentally interested in language, particularly in Anglo-Indian colonial language: in the ways language deploys power by naming, labeling, or categorizing'.[83] Forster's references to rhythm highlight that the 'naming, labeling, or categorizing' of music is also conducted through language and suggestive of power. Whether it is the rhythmicization of the punkah-wallah or the narrator's attempt to identify rhythm in Professor Godbole's singing, the central issue is epistemological, and it is the perspectival specificity that Forster invites the readers to scrutinize. If, as Paul B. Armstrong observes, *A Passage to India* demonstrates Forster's alertness to 'the irreducibility of different perspectives and the obstacle they present to univocal notions of justice and consensus',[84] our discussion of the novel has taken the observation one step further by noting Forster's awareness that a universal understanding of music does not exist. This is already implicit in the previously quoted phrase from 'A Musician in Egypt': 'the whole of art

---

[82] *PI*, p. 276.
[83] Ambreen Hai, *Making Words Matter: The Agency of Colonial and Postcolonial Literature* (Athens: Ohio University Press, 2009), p. 154.
[84] Armstrong, *Play and the Politics of Reading*, p. 140.

44   E. M. Forster and Music

as we understand art'. Underpinning the multiple references to rhythm in *A Passage to India*, this awareness of the non-universality of Western culture has its most explicit manifestation in one of Forster's personal descriptions of Gokul Ashtami to his mother: 'It is the noise, the noise, the noise, the noise which sucks one into a whirlpool, from which there is no re-emerging. The whole of what one understands by music seems lost for ever, or rather seems never to have existed'.[85] If there is confusion and disorientation, Forster's words also acknowledge limitations and resist universalizing. They call attention to the boundary of *his* understanding of 'music', beyond which other 'musics' pose terminological and epistemological difficulties.

Forster's references to rhythm in *A Passage to India* thus highlight the challenge in representing cultural plurality and remind us of Benita Parry's comment that 'the novel approaches Indian forms of knowledge with uncertainty, without asserting the authority of its representations, and unaccented by a will to enforce an ontological schism'.[86] This sense of self-conscious inadequacy to represent 'other' is also evident in another of Forster's personal accounts. Describing another musical celebration in Dewas in 1921, he reflected on the inevitability of deploying terms that were common in his familiar classification system but were alien to other cultures. The occasion was a celebration of the birth of a baby of the Maharajah, where multiple types of music – Western, Indian, orchestral, instrumental, vocal – were being played incessantly. Forster noted:

> at 3.0 a.m. something unusual aroused me – the music became beautiful [.] ... I am as far as ever from understanding Indian singing, but have no doubt that I was listening to great art, it was so complicated and yet so passionate. The singer (man) and the drummer were of almost equal importance and wove round the chord of C Major elaborate patterns that came to an end at the same moment – at least that's as near as I can explain it: it was like Western music reflected in trembling water, and it continued in a single burst for half an hour.[87]

It is the indeterminacy of tonality that becomes the music's appeal. The flexible intonation of the singing is admired by Forster for its spontaneity, complexity, and expressivity; it is, overall, a 'beautiful' experience. But it is the description 'Western music reflected in trembling water' that invites more discussion. The word 'reflected' signals secondariness and

[85] *HD*, p. 65.
[86] Benita Parry, *Postcolonial Studies: A Materialist Critique* (London: Routledge, 2004), p. 169.
[87] *HD*, pp. 45–46.

The Rhythm of the Racial Other: Before Aspects of the Novel   45

derivativeness, and indicates once again that Forster's listening experience is rooted in the Western understanding of what 'music' is. Inevitably, it is through a comparison with Western music that he can describe what 'Indian' music is, yet his description is less concerned with evaluation and more with perception. The account delineates his perception of the difference between 'Indian' and Western music not as an absolute dualism but as a pair close to each other, with shared, or comparable, characteristics. If the word 'trembling' conveys his confusion about the tonal indefiniteness of the music, the adjective also evokes the bodily sensation of getting in touch with the 'foreign': it outlines a body susceptible to an external stimulus. The imagery of 'trembling water' evokes ripples and suggests constantly changing impressions. If the 'strange' music can only be understood and described as an undulation of his familiar Western musical norms, the listening experience is a process that creates an unstable, but also almost titillating, effect on the self. In his determination to record the sensations the music brought him, Forster's account reveals that writing about a cross-musical experience means an epistemological recognition through which the boundaries between 'musics' are undrawn and redrawn.

'Rhythm' in *Aspects of the Novel*

The many contexts of Forster's engagement with rhythm provide us with a new angle to approach his discussion of 'rhythm' in *Aspects of the Novel*. Read alongside Dickinson's 'Anglo-India', and his own articles in Egypt and *A Passage to India*, the section on 'rhythm' in *Aspects* seems purely – and oddly – aesthetic, as if Forster had wiped out the term's complex associations with perceptions of racial otherness. Yet, first, it is noteworthy that Forster suggests in *Aspects* that 'rhythm' 'lessens our need of an external form'.[88] If Forster, as we have seen, represents 'form' as a specifically Western concept of unity through Fielding's attitude towards Venice, his envisioning of 'rhythm' as an alternative might suggest his search for inspiration from non-Western cultures. At the same time, it seems unlikely that Forster did not have the 'rhythmically' moving punkah-wallah in mind when discussing 'rhythm' in *Aspects*, given the character's importance and the novel's chronological proximity as well as aesthetic relevance to his lectures. In this respect, one might be able to claim that Forster's discussion of 'rhythm' does attend to the racialized

[88] *AN*, p. 115.

46 E. M. Forster and Music

conception of rhythm, but appropriates the non-Western body to serve for his own aesthetic purpose. That is, from the punkah-wallah pulling the cord of the punkah 'rhythmically' to 'rhythm' in fiction, Forster abstracts a universalizing sense of beauty from its colonial contexts. The punkah-wallah's 'aloofness', the continuousness of his movement, the recurrence of the rise and the fall of the 'dust', and his elemental and vitalistic presence in the trial scene seem to be transformed conceptually by Forster into a universally applicable aesthetics of 'rhythm' in *Aspects of the Novel*. Forster's renewal of the form of fiction seems to have thus resulted from a Eurocentric aestheticization of the racial other.

However, to accuse Forster of perpetuating racial and colonial hierarchy is to assume that Forster formulates his idea of 'rhythm' through confining the racial other within a status of permanent backwardness. Rather, it is specifically rhythm's ability to 'develop' that he emphasizes in *Aspects of the Novel*.[89] His definition of 'easy' rhythm as 'repetition plus variation', as capable of 'waxing and waning' which 'fill[s] us with surprise and freshness and hope', puts the emphasis on its evolving quality.[90] His discussion of 'difficult' rhythm similarly looks forward to a sense of evolution. Inspired by his feeling after the end of a symphony that 'the notes and tunes composing it have been liberated', his vision of 'expansion' as an alternative to 'completion' delineates a reading experience during which 'great chords begin to sound behind us' when we read onward and, once we close the book, 'every item . . . lead[s] a larger existence than was possible at the time'.[91] Forster's 'difficult' rhythm thus celebrates not only the work as an 'entity' but also a sense of progression and transformation, a potential to have an allegorical layer that generates fresh resonances and new significance. While critics tend to use this to point to Forster's interest in ambiguity,[92] these qualities of 'rhythm' also suggest that, if Forster's discussion of 'rhythm' is a result of cultural appropriation, it is one that reaches beyond racial caricatures. By conceptualizing 'rhythm' in fiction as able to evolve, Forster disconnects the term's association with European stereotypes about an 'Eastern' form of repetition and unchanging cyclicity. Then, although still from a Western point of view, Forster's discussion of 'rhythm' in *Aspects of the Novel* seems to postulate parallel evolutions between the East and the West; at least for the English novel, the use of 'rhythm' in fiction, an aesthetics inspired by the perception of 'the East' as ever evolving, holds the future for the genre. In this way,

[89] *AN*, p. 115.   [90] *AN*, p. 115.   [91] *AN*, p. 116.
[92] Brown, E. K., 'Rhythm', p. 113. Fillion, *Difficult Rhythm*, p. xviii.

The Rhythm of the Racial Other: Before Aspects of the Novel 47

while Forster's formulation of 'rhythm' might have been symptomatic of modernist primitivism, the qualities he bestows on 'rhythm' suggests a divergence from stereotypical portrayals of the 'primitive' as unchanging and repetitive.

From Dickinson satirizing the Anglo-Indian indulgence in their destiny against the 'rhythmically swinging' 'East' in 'Anglo-India' to Forster reconceptualizing 'rhythm' as evolving in *Aspects of the Novel*, Forster's writing, both fictional and non-fictional, suggests his endeavour to challenge the association of rhythm with Western stereotypes about the unchangeability of non-Western cultures, as well as to reimagine that association. Although the portrayals of the Arab organ-blower and the punkah-wallah continue to align the non-Western body with the repetitive quality of rhythm, they also suggest something against, as well as aloof from, Western civilization, thus generating a new (new for Westerners) level of significance and creating a proliferation of meanings: '[n]ot rounding off but opening out'.[93] Of course, this reimagining still essentializes the racial other, pushes it into another stereotype, and, as we have seen, aestheticizes the non-Western. One might simply conclude that Forster was not able to think ahead of his time. Yet it is also evident that he was wary of the limits of his own perspective. In the often-ironic admiration for Terni's music, the self-inclusive jibe at the colonial significance of Handel's *Messiah* in Alexandria, and the unease about describing music he heard in India, Forster reflects on epistemological limitations, exploring the non-ubiquity of musical terminology, criteria, concepts, and definitions. His reimagining of rhythm's association with racial otherness is thus part of his concern with the inadequacy of tools available to represent and understand cross-culturally. His perspective is Eurocentric, but inevitably – and self-reflexively – so. As Benita Parry suggests, Forster's description and questioning of colonialism reflects on the limit of 'a western script', disorienting both 'the textual India of British writing and the empire of British self-representation'.[94] If his writing registers an awareness that to write about 'other' is to encode 'distancing, objectifying prejudgments' in one's language,[95] his numerous allusions to rhythm suggest that he lays the emphasis, not on censoring stereotyping otherness, but on exposing the correlation between subjectivity, perception, and representation.

---

[93] *AN*, p. 116.   [94] Parry, *Postcolonial Studies*, pp. 173 and 175.
[95] Armstrong, *Play and the Politics of Reading*, p. 128.

CHAPTER 2

The Queering of Musical Instruments

After my experiences in the Darien I would never think of going into a 'wild' Indian territory without a phonograph. Time and again we were to encounter surly, unfriendly and even menacing Indians. We would appear to ignore them entirely. We would bring out and start a record while proceeding with our regular task of camp pitching or what-not. The attention of the Indians would soon be diverted from us to the 'music-box'. Their hostility would cease and be replaced by curiosity. Gradually they would draw closer to the instrument, discussing it among themselves and finally would end up by crowding around it as closely as possible, touching and feeling it. From then on they would often keep us playing it until midnight, and were no longer our enemies though perhaps not yet our friends.

Richard O. Marsh, *White Indians of Darien*[1]

Writing in 1921 to his friend G. H. Ludolf from Lingsugur, in the Nizam-ruled Hyderabad State, Forster commented on the legacy of the British rule in the region:

Once it was a British Cantonment, but we cleared out in 1860, and our relics have a curious effect on me. A civilization, however silly, is touching as soon as it passes away, and I sit on the stucco curve of what was once a bandstand, or wander through ruined halls of bungalows that once smelt of whiskey and echoed to giggles, or read on the tombs in the cemetery that the 'dearly beloved sweet gentle wife of Captain Pedley' has 'gone before'. No English now, no English spoken, no soldiers, no music, railway station sixty miles away. Only an exquisite lake where the British once bathed and rowed, and where a few black Canarese now squat fishing.[2]

Semi-satirically romanticizing, Forster's description emphasizes the absence of music, which is likely to be the absence of Western musical

---

[1] Richard O. Marsh, *White Indians of Darien* (New York: G. P. Putnam's Sons, 1934), p. 81.
[2] *HD*, p. 335.

The Queering of Musical Instruments   49

activities, in this decolonized place. As we have seen in the previous chapter in Dickinson's 'Anglo-India' and Forster's 'Handel in Egypt', this passage also demonstrates the importance of Western music in the construction of the authority and national identity of British colonizers. The disappearance of Western music seems to dial back the time, resetting the place to its indigenous way of life. Yet the debris of the 'bandstand' suggests that, while the sounds of Western music might have been as evanescent as whiskey's smell and human giggling, it has a material reality that does not fade away when British civilization has retreated. Like the tombstone of the wife of the 'Captain', the bandstand, presumably for a brass band, is a concrete reminder that Western music once contributed to the Empire's self-assertion as well as military coercion. The ruin of the bandstand is a tangible conduit of the colonial past that scars the present tranquillity.

Critics have so far overlooked Forster's attention to the material existence of music, and it is his representation of Western musical instruments in *A Passage to India* on which this chapter focuses. By discussing his descriptions of Ronny Heaslop's viola, the Maharajah's harmonium, and a piano in a European Guest House – not just as symbols of Western musical culture but as objects through which human relations are mediated and by which the boundary between public and private is negotiated – the chapter examines the ways these three instruments provide a means through which the novel interrogates the subjection and resistance of the individual to external forces in a colonial environment.

By addressing the human–object relationship in Forster's portrayals of the three musical instruments, this chapter attends to the current development of material culture studies in both modernist scholarship and musicology. On the one hand, the chapter complements and broadens existing criticism of modernism's engagement with the world of objects.[3] Since previous studies of material culture in Forster's work tend to focus on representations of money, houses, furniture, and goods in *Howards End*,[4] my focus on musical instruments in *A Passage to India* in the context

---

[3] Representatively, Douglas Mao, *Solid Objects: Modernism and the Test of Production* (Princeton: Princeton University Press, 1998), and Bill Brown, 'The Secret Life of Things (Virginia Woolf and the Matter of Modernism)', *Modernism/modernity*, 6.2 (1999), 1–28. I also find Elaine Freedgood, *The Ideas in Things: Fugitive Meaning in the Victorian Novel* (Chicago: University of Chicago Press, 2006) particularly stimulating.

[4] See e.g. Paul Delany, '"Islands of Money": Rentier Culture in E. M. Forster's *Howards End*', *English Literature in Transition*, 31.3 (1988), 285–96; Henry S. Turner, 'Empire of Objects: Accumulation and Entropy in E. M. Forster's *Howards End*', *Twentieth-Century Literature*, 46.3 (2000), 328–45;

of imperial economy provides a new dimension. Additionally, although critics have examined a variety of soundscapes represented by modernist writers, few have looked at their depictions of the objects that produce the sounds.[5] Even a reference to a silent instrument speaks volumes, as such deviation from its sounding role invites inquiries into the causes of its silence. On the other hand, the chapter emulates the social turn within organology. The recent shift of focus of many organologists, especially those who work in the field of ethnomusicology – from the design, construction details, and use of an instrument to the appearance or performance of an instrument in a specific time and location and its social functions – is significant. By adopting a more historicist and contextual alertness to cultural differences, recent organologists question previous organology's efforts in museum-based collection and classification, exposing the Eurocentrism inherent in the application of one cultural frame to instruments all around the world.[6] Such a disciplinary shift is in the same critical vein as Forster's reflection on epistemology and perspectives, as the last chapter has discussed. That readers only see Western musical instruments instead of 'exotic' Indian ones in *A Passage to India* can also be read as another example of Forster's deliberate construction of an English-oriented narrative.

The spread of Western musical instruments beyond Europe has been well documented. Since the early modern period, Western musical paraphernalia – including scores, books, treatises, and instruments – had accompanied Europeans abroad, travelling to new, sometimes even 'hostile', environments and being disseminated for religious, commercial,

---

and Elizabeth Outka, *Consuming Traditions: Modernity, Modernism, and the Commodified Authentic* (Oxford: Oxford University Press, 2008), pp. 68–95.

[5] On modern(ist) soundscapes, see e.g. Steven Connor, 'The Modern Auditory I', in *Rewriting the Self: Histories from the Renaissance to the Present*, ed. Roy Porter (London: Routledge, 1997), pp. 203–23; Alex Ross, *The Rest Is Noise: Listening to the Twentieth Century* (New York: Picador, 2007); Sam Halliday, *Sonic Modernity: Representing Sound in Literature, Culture and the Arts* (Edinburgh: Edinburgh University Press, 2013). An instrument that has captured the critical attention is the pianola: see David Deutsch, 'The Pianola in Early Twentieth-Century British Literature: "Really it is a wonderful machine"', *English Literature in Transition*, 58.1 (2015), 73–90, and Cecilia Björkén-Nyberg, *The Player Piano and the Edwardian Novel* (Edinburgh: Edinburgh University Press, 2015).

[6] Henry M. Johnson, 'An Ethnomusicology of Musical Instruments: Form, Function, and Meaning', *JASO*, 26.3 (1995), 257–69; Jann Pasler, 'The Utility of Musical Instruments in the Racial and Colonial Agendas of Late Nineteenth-Century France', *Journal of the Royal Musical Association*, 129.1 (2004), 24–76; Eliot Bates, 'The Social Life of Musical Instruments', *Ethnomusicology*, 56.3 (2012), 363–95; and John Tresch and Emily I. Dolan, 'Toward a New Organology: Instruments of Music and Science', *Osiris*, 28.1 (2013), 278–98.

The Queering of Musical Instruments   51

educational, or diplomatic purposes.[7] What needs to be emphasized, however, is that these 'purposes' were set by Western travellers and explorers who knowingly cultivated the material existence of an object which was, for themselves, simply common and mundane but, for those in the place to where it was brought, became a wonder. For instance, as the epigraph to this chapter by the American engineer Richard O. Marsh demonstrates, the phonograph was used by 'the civilized' as a mediator for cross-cultural communication only after its very being served as a buffer between them and those they referred to as the Chocó Indians. That it is both the material existence of the phonograph, as well as its modern technology of sound making and recording, that Marsh and his expedition first relied on to rouse the curiosity of the others suggests that the racial other, to borrow Scott Herring's concept of 'material deviance', was expected to 'disappoint' 'normative object conduct'.[8] That is, Marsh's description reveals an assumption that those without 'our' shared under-standing of the meanings and functions of the phonograph could only form 'culturally inappropriate material relations' with the instrument.[9] Racial and cultural differentiation were thus predetermined and reinforced by the 'queer objecthood' of the phonograph. Marsh and his members queered the usage of the instrument and, through the indigenous people's queer material relation with the phonograph, obtained, literally and psy-chologically, self-anchoring.

Forster's representations of the three Western musical instruments in *A Passage to India* are, this chapter argues, similarly queer: not only are they not involved in music-making, or at least not music as traditionally understood by Westerners; they also find themselves in bizarre scenarios: Ronny's viola is silenced by Ronny himself, the Maharajah's harmonium stolen, and the piano in the European Guest House broken. In this respect, they are distinct from Marsh's phonograph, as they are not intentionally placed in roles or situations other than producing sounds; rather, they become confusingly entangled in extramusical activities in the colonial environment, where every character – British and Indian alike – contributes to augmenting their queerness. Their appearance in the novel,

---

[7] See e.g. David R. M. Irving's two articles: 'The Dissemination and Use of European Music Books in Early Modern Asia', *Early Music History*, 28 (2009), 39–59, and 'Comparative Organography in Early Modern Empires', *Music & Letters*, 90.3 (2009), 372–98.
[8] Scott Herring, 'Material Deviance: Theorizing Queer Objecthood', *Postmodern Culture*, 21.2 (2011), www.pomoculture.org/2013/09/03/material-deviance-theorizing-queer-objecthood [accessed 30 May 2018].
[9] Herring, 'Material Deviance'.

52   E. M. Forster and Music

then, goes beyond simply sustaining the national identity of the British abroad. In representing the musical instruments as things around which human interactions revolve, Forster examines their embeddedness within webs of complex relations between colonizer and colonized. In representing them as queer things, Forster exposes the normativity of colonial norms.

By attending to the representations of the viola, the harmonium, and the piano, this chapter redresses the critical neglect of the role of Western music in *A Passage to India*. As discussed in the previous chapter, the novel is consistently used as an example to discuss Forster's idea of 'rhythm'; when Forster's depiction of actual music is the subject, critics frequently turn their focus to Professor Godbole's singing at the end of chapter 7. Godbole's song is about the refusal of Krishna to come to a milkmaiden's prayer. Taking place when Ronny, Adela, and Mrs Moore are about to leave the tea party at Fielding's, it baffles its Western listeners but draws the attention of Hindu servants, before ending abruptly in the middle of a bar upon the subdominant.[10] Numerous critics have examined Forster's depiction and its significance.[11] Recently, Mi Zhou observes the ways in which the contemporary ethnomusicological work of Maud Mann informed Forster's description of Godbole's song and, more broadly, contributed to the novel's representation of India as a 'cacophony'. The novel's interest in India's aural 'presence', as Zhou argues, reflects Forster's attempt to problematize the usual epistemological confidence of imperial sovereignty.[12]

Yet, as demonstrated by examples we have seen in the previous and the present chapters, Forster also wrote about Western music in India,

---

[10] *PI*, p. 72.

[11] To name but a few of the interpretations of the singing, Mary Lago reads it as an example of Forster's understanding of Hinduism, in *E. M. Forster: A Literary Life* (Basingstoke: Macmillan, 1995), pp. 81–83, while Sara Suleri regards it as 'synecdochical of the tautological desire that vexes imperial narrative'. Suleri, *Rhetoric*, p. 141. Judith Scherer Herz calls Godbole's song 'a maze of noises' and observes how the silence after the song produces division between characters and provides no comfort. Judith Scherer Herz, 'Listening to Language', in *A Passage to India: Essays in Interpretation*, ed. John Beer (Basingstoke: Macmillan, 1985), pp. 59–70 (p. 65).

[12] Zhou, 'Sublime Noise', pp. 151–78 and pp. 168–88. In *Representing Non-Western Music in Nineteenth-Century Britain*, especially parts 3 and 4, Bennett Zon provides a useful historical context for Maud Mann's work. Zon notes that early twentieth-century scholars, Mann included, became increasingly alert to the inadequacy of using Western understanding to evaluate Indian music, as well as consistently resisted the practice of fitting Indian musical culture into an evolutionary hierarchy. The ideas and concerns of scholars such as C. S. Myers and A. H. Fox Strangways are strikingly modern, anticipating late twentieth-century ethnomusicological inquiries. See also *Music and Orientalism in the British Empire, 1780s–1940s: Portrayal of the East*, ed. Martin Clayton and Bennett Zon (Aldershot: Ashgate, 2007).

The Queering of Musical Instruments

especially about the defamiliarization of Western music and how Western music was formative to, and emblematic of, the national identity of the colonizer. In the novel, the latter is best exemplified by the performance of the national anthem by 'the amateur orchestra' in the English Club in chapter 3: 'It was the Anthem of the Army of Occupation. It reminded every member of the Club that he or she was British and in exile'.[13] Like Dickinson's 'Anglo-India', Forster's description satirizes the indulgence of the British in glorifying their suffering through Western music. The use of the word 'exile' recalls the word in Forster's own 'A Musician in Egypt', jibing at an oddly aggrandized sense of displacement among the British abroad. That the national anthem sends out 'a prayer unknown in England' implies that, like Handel's *Messiah* in Alexandria, Western music accrued augmented national and religious significance when it was played in a colony.[14] However, Forster was also aware that not all genres of Western music were employed in this way. Music that manifested a political overtone was selected precisely because of its political overtone, either to mitigate the nostalgia for 'Old England' or to assert the ownership of the subcontinent. In contrast, art music and those who engaged assiduously with it were often ostracized. In a 1913 letter to his mother, Forster recounted an incident about 'an artistic "Chelsea" sort of couple' who had just arrived in Lahore, being 'blackballed by the English Club' there. He reported that his friends Malcolm and Josie Darling were the only people who were friends with the outcasts:

> Not many Anglo Indians would encourage a guest to do queer unusual things, still less join in such themselves. Everyone is in such a terror of being out of the ordinary. Classical music, literature, intellectual tastes generally – as a rule all is dropped in a couple of years, and husbands and wives, when their day's work is done, meet other husbands and wives in a dense mass at the Club. One is told that all this has to be, and of course the outsider can't know, but it is refreshing to find people who stand up against it.[15]

Forster's description reveals an anomalous musical culture in British India which approved of mediocrity and cautioned against sophistication. His compliment on the Darlings displays a preference for individual taste over communal value judgement, which is consistent with his belief in personal relationships. The fact that this was written in a letter, moreover, suggests that Forster intended his addressee – or addressees, as he knew well that his

---

[13] *PI*, pp. 20–21. For a brief discussion of the national anthem scene, see Zhou, 'Sublime Noise', pp. 168–69.
[14] *PI*, p. 21. [15] Letter to his mother (26 February 1913). *SL*, I, pp. 193–94.

letters were usually circulated among family and friends – to envision the bias and repression within British communities in India.[16] If his description seems simplistic, it could be intentionally so because he aimed not only to satiate the curiosity of those back home but also to influence their political opinions. For Forster, this biased selection of musical repertoire was representative of colonial norms, which he challenged alongside the Darlings, the 'Chelsea' couple, and hopefully those who would read this letter in England.

The phrase 'queer little things' alludes to Forster's alertness to the perception of Western music as subversive in the English Club. As critics have demonstrated, music was often marked as 'deviant' and associated with sexuality, especially homosexuality, in the last decade of the nineteenth century, not only in literary texts and musical commentaries but in religious and scientific – evolutionary, psychiatric, and sexologist – discourses as well.[17] Susan McClary, Philip Brett, and many other musicologists have also explored the ways in which musical engagement circumvents, destabilizes, and challenges the often but not solely sexual norms of the social structures of power.[18] The queerness of musical representations in Forster's other texts has been considered elsewhere.[19] Here, my discussion is to extend the widely held critical notion that Forster's criticism of the Empire is inseparable from his resistance to contemporary British policing of sexual deviances, highlighting how music energizes his combined examination of colonialism and sexuality. In his account of a welcoming party at the mess hosted by Kenneth Searight – a young officer with whom Forster, Dickinson, and Trevelyan became acquainted on board the ship to India in 1912 – on the first night when the trio arrived in Peshawar, Forster writes:

> Band – which had waited for me to play 'Roast Beef of Old England' – performed during evening, and they danced – [Searight] far the best and inspiring them. ... Bob danced and scrummed, I felt not to know them well enough, tho' they would have drawn me in. Once 'in' with the military

---

[16] My argument here echoes Ambreen Hai's contention that Forster's Indian letters to his relatives are more political than his Indian journals because they were meant to challenge and revise what the addressees thought about India. Hai, *Making Words Matter*, p. 120.

[17] See, representatively, Sutton, *Aubrey Beardsley*, pp. 24–56; Joe Law, 'The "perniciously homosexual art": Music and Homoerotic Desire in *The Picture of Dorian Gray* and Other *Fin-de-Siècle* Fiction', in *The Idea of Music in Victorian Fiction*, ed. Fuller and Losseff, pp. 173–96, especially pp. 182–83; Emma Sutton, '"The Music Spoke For Us": Music and Sexuality in *Fin-de-siècle* Poetry', in *The Figure of Music in Nineteenth-Century British Poetry*, ed. Phyllis Weliver (Aldershot: Ashgate, 2005), pp. 213–29.

[18] McClary, *Feminine Endings*. Philip Brett, 'Musicality, Essentialism, and the Closet', in *Queering the Pitch: The New Gay and Lesbian Musicology*, ed. Brett, Wood, and Thomas, pp. 9–26.

[19] Deutsch, *British Literature and Classical Music*, pp. 162–70. Tsung-Han Tsai, 'Music as Queering in E. M. Forster's *Goldsworthy Lowes Dickinson*', *Music & Letters*, 99.1 (2018), 1–15.

The Queering of Musical Instruments 55

they take one to their bosom. No gradations between hauteur and intimacy, as is natural with unreflecting men. I imagine these are good specimens – all young and merry and some able.[20]

Underlying the hegemony of imperial patriotism, evoked by the playing of 'Roast Beef of Old England', there are moments of individual bonding. In this account, Western music accompanies, and perhaps also facilitates, such moments, augmenting the exuberance of hospitality that goes beyond class differences. Forster's relishing, almost homoerotic, gaze at those around him becomes apparent towards the end of the passage: for him, the group comprised nothing but individual men searching for friendship and intimacy.[21] This homosocial cordiality is a sharp contrast to the heterosexual compactness of the Club in Lahore, where 'husbands and wives' congregated and dominated.[22] Forster's account suggests that Western music set in motion different, presumably queer, human relationships that were alternative to those sanctioned by the official, hierarchical world of British imperialism.

Attentive to the mutability and malleability of the signification of Western music in India, Forster's representations of the viola, the harmonium, and the piano in *A Passage to India* convey more than anything the power dynamics of colonial regulation and individual resistance. The hegemony of the official collapses into an amalgamation of queer fragments of subject–object relations; the queering of the instruments, both their objecthood and their music, enables Forster to destabilize and complicate the relationship between colonizer and colonized.

Ronny's Viola

Frequently, Ronny Heaslop is read as a typical British imperial officer in India. His English public-school background leads to his propriety, but also to his insensitiveness and complacency. The characterization of Ronny and the social system he represents, as critics often tell us, signal Forster's

---

[20] Diary entry (8 November 1912). *HD*, pp. 140–41.

[21] Forster was conscious of the homoeroticism in his enjoyment of this evening in Peshawar: the letter to his mother, in which he recounted this evening, only mentioned that the party became 'friskier and friskier'. *SL*, I, p. 155. Another account of this evening is in his biography of Goldsworthy Lowes Dickinson, in which Forster draws the attention less to his homoerotic sentiments but to Dickinson's almost avuncular popularity among the soldiers. *GLD*, pp. 114–15.

[22] As Janice Ho observes in her discussion of *The Longest Journey* and *Howards End*, the homoerotic dimensions of Forster's conception of friendship should be understood not simply as a psychological or libidinal expression but as a highly political delineation of alternative ways of life in response to circulating, acceptable social relationships. Janice Ho, *Nation and Citizenship in the Twentieth-Century British Novel* (Cambridge, UK: Cambridge University Press, 2015), pp. 25–58.

condemnation of British imperialism. While Forster's depiction of the colonizers was perceived by some contemporary readers as unfair, it also propelled the novel to become topical after its publication.[23] More recently, Mohammad Shaheen alludes to *Aspects of the Novel* in his comment on Forster's British characters in *A Passage to India* as 'flat' because Forster found imperialism 'flat enough to invite no exploration into its existential order'.[24] As Shaheen argues, imperialism, for Forster, was 'not a subject for any aesthetic contemplation to warrant fictive rendering'.[25] This tendency to read Forster's British characters, especially those who hold office in the fictional Chandrapore, as negative and one-dimensional is a strategy for critics to interpret Forster's depiction of Indians as sympathetic and with depth. One contemporary reviewer, for example, described the novel's characterization of the British as 'bitten with disdain' whereas that of Aziz is 'touched with sympathy'.[26] Consequently, this dichotomized understanding of the characters in the novel often resorts to a comparison between Ronny and Fielding. Benita Parry, for instance, writes that '[t]he obtuse, coarse, arrogant and bellicose deportment of Anglo-Indians, as realised in the novel, is the very negation of those decencies defined through Fielding':

> 'When Fielding, after his courageous stand against his countrymen and women, aligns himself with the rulers of India, he is submitting to the fact of imperialism, deferring to a mode of behaviour and feeling made and needed by an aggressive political system and conceding that his liberal principles and hopes of doing good in India exist only by favour of a Ronny Heaslop'.[27]

This perceived dualism of Ronny and Fielding, of the former's 'white man's burden' and the latter's humanistic bearing, and of the official world of the Empire and the unofficial interaction between individuals, is reductive. It is simplistic to use Forster's anti-imperialism to assume that his characterization of the British lacks nuance.

---

[23] Furbank, *Forster*, II, pp. 125–30.

[24] Mohammad Shaheen, *E. M. Forster and the Politics of Imperialism* (Basingstoke: Palgrave Macmillan, 2004), pp. 16 and 89.

[25] Shaheen, *Forster and the Politics of Imperialism*, p. 86.

[26] H. W. Massingham, 'The price of India's friendship', *New Leader*, 27 June 1924, rpn in *E. M. Forster: The Critical Heritage*, ed. Philip Gardner (London: Routledge & Kegan Paul, 1973), pp. 207–10 (p. 208).

[27] Benita Parry, 'The Politics of Representation in *A Passage to India*', in *A Passage to India: Essays in Interpretation*, ed. Beer, pp. 27–43 (p. 34).

The Queering of Musical Instruments

A couple of unobtrusive references to Ronny's viola in chapter 5, the bridge party at the English Club – in which colonial and racial impressions, stereotypes, and conventions overflow – give us access to an undiscovered side of his character. During the party, the Anglo-Indians ignore their Indian guests, occupying themselves with conversation about their own recent production of *Cousin Kate*. Their manner is observed by the narrator:

> They had tried to reproduce their own attitude to life upon the stage, and to dress up as the middle-class English people they actually were. . . . Save for this annual incursion, they left literature alone. The men had no time for it, the women did nothing that they could not share with the men. Their ignorance of the arts was notable, and they lost no opportunity of proclaiming it to one another; it was the public-school attitude, flourishing more vigorously than it can yet hope to do in England. If Indians were shop, the arts were bad form, and Ronny had repressed his mother when she inquired after his viola; a viola was almost a demerit, and certainly not the sort of instrument one mentioned in public.[28]

The English Club in Chandrapore is similar to the one we have seen in Lahore, which had banished the 'Chelsea' couple; it entertains itself with artistic mediocrity while accommodating only those who join in the consensus. Read alongside Forster's satire in his depiction of the Club's warm reception of *Cousin Kate*, the references to Ronny's unspeakable viola seem nothing but another example of the British's opposition to art and culture in the colony.[29]

However, the fact that Ronny silences his mother's question about the instrument invites discussion. A preliminary interpretation might suggest that Ronny's repression of his viola stems from his subscription to the ideal of imperial masculinity. For Ronny, his viola may all too easily conjure up an aura of auditory fineness, artistic delicacy, domestic leisure, and emotive susceptibility, and thus endows him with characteristics that are detrimental to his public image. He does not mention – and does not want others to mention – his viola in the Club perhaps because 'India isn't a drawing-room'; because he does not want to be perceived as 'a vague sentimental sympathetic literary man' but only as 'a servant of the Government'; and because he fears that the disclosure of his private instrument playing would

---

[28] *PI*, p. 34.

[29] As Elaine Showalter suggests, the ignorance of the Anglo-Indian women of the anti-feminist content of *Cousin Kate* indicates their subscription to traditional notions of marriage and motherhood when they live in India. Elaine Showalter, 'A *Passage to India* as "Marriage Fiction": Forster's Sexual Politics', *Women & Literature*, 5.2 (1977), 3–16 (p. 6).

undercut 'such power as [he has] for doing good in this country'.[30] The viola, alongside 'Grasmere, serious talks and walks', might therefore belong to 'the callow academic period of his life', which Ronny believes he has 'outgrown' when he reflects on his service in India at the end of the second part of the novel.[31] As Jonathan Rutherford suggests, '[t]he strenuous exertions of the imperial hero, his refusal to contemplate, to think or to pause, suggest that his adventures involved a compulsion to escape the idleness and comfort of domesticity'.[32] Ronny may not necessarily believe that he can obtain a heroic status in India, but he certainly subscribes to this idea, and ideal, of imperial manliness by distancing himself from the qualities associated with and crystallized within the viola. As Jenny Sharpe suggests, compared to contemporary England, the imported domestic lifestyle in the novel's English Club is underpinned by a stringent, anachronistic conception of gender roles.[33] Such domesticity evokes the leisure and familiarity of 'home', but it also augments the alertness to, and anxiety with, the clarity of normative gender boundaries in the British community. Since the disclosure of the instrument, and Western art music in general, has the potential to align Ronny with what is traditionally regarded as 'feminine' and thus undercuts his masculinity, it needs to be forcefully silenced.[34]

Yet the phrase, 'the sort of instrument', is an explicit invitation for readers to reflect on the characteristics and connotations of the viola, especially when the novel's manuscripts indicate that, rather than a viola, it was originally a violin which Ronny would have.[35] What prompted Forster to make such a revision? What are the differences between a viola and a violin? Why is a viola 'almost a demerit'? Does it mean that a violin would be 'the sort of instrument' that one can mention in public? Histories of the viola are inseparable from, and often appendant to, those of the violin; nowadays viola jokes – stereotypes about violas and viola players – are still prevalent within musical groups: the viola is derided for

---

[30] *PI*, pp. 43–44.   [31] *PI*, p. 246.

[32] Jonathan Rutherford, *Forever England: Reflections on Race, Masculinity and Empire* (London: Lawrence & Wishart, 1997), p. 12.

[33] Jenny Sharpe, *Allegories of Empire: The Figure of Woman in the Colonial Text* (Minneapolis: University of Minnesota Press, 1993), p. 121.

[34] As Ambreen Hai notes, silence, or the inability to explain something, characterizes the novel's representation of Anglo-Indian rhetoric: throughout the novel, this 'unspeakability of Anglo-Indian codes' results in numerous abrupt changes of topics or fruitless discussions. It underpins the imperial structure of political domination, but it also aggravates the problem of communication. Hai, *Making Words Matter*, p. 165.

[35] *MSS-PI*, p. 49.

its bigger size, less value, and more limited range than the violin; violists are often thought of as having poorer skills than violinists. Although nineteenth-century composers became increasingly interested in the instrument's darker timbre and grander sonority, the viola was less used than the violin as a solo instrument. Used in orchestral music, the viola was either assigned to completing a chord or to accompanying the subject performed by others; more concertos were written for the violin than for the viola. More widely employed in chamber music, the viola had an important place in the string quartet and quintet, but even then the prominent role still went to the violin. When it came to works where fewer instruments were involved, like sonatas or trios, the viola was, once again, bypassed.[36]

Given the different ways the two string instruments were, and perhaps still are, perceived, Forster's revision suggests an attempt to use the instrument to symbolize Ronny's subordinate but necessary role in the imperial system. From a violin to a viola, Ronny plays his part as a cog in the gigantic imperial machine, as if Forster had intended him not to play the first theme. The viola's subsidiary role echoes Ronny's position as the City Magistrate in Chandrapore, one of the officers under the command of Mr Turton, the District Collector. The fact that Ronny appropriates his superiors' 'phrases and arguments' can be compared to a viola reiterating or harmonizing a melodic line.[37] The way he behaves – 'He always showed deference to his superiors' – sounds similar to the viola's gentle alto or tenor.[38] Or, if unsympathetically caricatured, the viola's 'characterless' tone is reflected, in this respect, by Ronny's mediocre colonial performance and his unremarkable appearance.[39] That said, Ronny is to Chandrapore what the viola is to chamber music; his role is collaborative in nature and his duty, though nondescript, is what constitutes the Empire. Alongside the Superintendent of Police, Ronny maintains the operation of a legal system imported from and imposed by the centre of the Empire. If the Turtons are 'little gods' in Chandrapore, Ronny is the one who makes this godly presence palpable, since his work is 'to dispense justice fearlessly' while being 'surrounded by lies and flattery'.[40] Secondary but loyal,

---

[36] David D. Boyden and Ann M. Woodward, 'Viola', *Grove Music Online*, www.oxfordmusiconline .com [accessed 10 May 2018].

[37] *PI*, p 28.   [38] *PI*, p. 178.

[39] In Turton's conversation with Mrs Moore, we learn that Ronny, though a 'dignified' 'sahib', has not had any specific merits. As for his appearance, he is, according to Aziz, without 'physical charm'. *PI*, p. 20 and p. 144.

[40] *PI*, p. 23 and p. 44.

60   E. M. Forster and Music

undistinguished but necessary, Ronny is thus aligned with an instrument that is compatible with his job performance and emblematic of his status in the imperial system.

This collaborativeness of Ronny's viola needs to be considered not only metaphorically but also in actual music-making. Does Ronny have his viola in India? This seems affirmative, or his mother would not have made the inquiry. Does he still play it? Forster leaves this unspecified in the novel, but it is likely that, if Ronny does play, he does so in an ensemble. If such is the case, Ronny's viola is only unmentionable in public but known – perhaps secretly – by several others among the British. This detail is made explicit in the manuscripts – 'only a few people knew he had one' – but deleted in the final published version.[41] A shared knowledge amongst a few compatriots, Ronny's viola suggests that there is perhaps private engagement with Western art music beneath the total ignorance of the arts on the surface. It also suggests the existence of heterogeneous personal interactions underlying the hierarchical officialdom of the English Club. If those who know of Ronny's viola and knowingly participate in these exclusive moments of domestic musical practice are men, the surreptitious musical enjoyment should never intersect with their imperial roles; in public, the British officials still show their unalloyed loyalty when the national anthem is played by the Club's band. They may also be more than conscious of the way their music-making transgresses the strict gender demarcations in their community. Ronny's reaction to his mother's question is thus possibly motivated by a broader concern, not just with his own unmentionable instrument, but over a secret that affects more than one individual. What we see here is how the viola, though being silenced, has an unspeakable existence among the knowing few. Its parallel with contemporary coding of homosexual desire suggests the queerness of Ronny's viola. Kept hidden, it expresses a desire for the intimacy of synchronicity, for accompanying another instrument, thus for the company of another human being.

Brought into public, however, the viola becomes a troubling object, against which Ronny shows symptoms of paranoia when he decides to adopt an official tone as if giving orders to his mother. Just as he 'commissioned her to bring' Adela to India,[42] he 'repressed [her] when she inquired after his viola'. Tellingly, the novel's manuscripts demonstrate that Forster originally described Ronny as having 'been \quite/ vexed with' his mother.[43] By replacing the phrase with the single verb 'repressed',

[41] MSS-PI, p. 49.   [42] PI, p. 19.   [43] MSS-PI, p. 49.

The Queering of Musical Instruments

Forster transforms Ronny from a passive listener to an active doer, indicating his acquisition of colonial idioms and the encroachment of the public on the private. There is a note of complacency in his interaction with his mother, an assertiveness and a willingness to flash the authority he has obtained. It can also be read as an invocation of sexual normality and patriarchal dominance: the viola is silenced by Ronny through his exertion of power over the maternal solicitude of Mrs Moore, who is here in India to facilitate the heterosexual pact that will lay the foundation for Ronny's imperial masculinity. Yet his insistence on the instrument's staying beyond public knowledge says as much about his wariness of the subversiveness of his private music-making as his subscription to imperial norms. If the viola symbolizes Ronny's position as a supporting colonial officer, his role as a secret viola player in the colony undermines the assumption that his characteristics are fully compatible with those of his official persona.

The Maharajah's Harmonium

Unlike Ronny's viola, which is forcibly pushed back to the private sphere, the harmonium in chapter 8 is ostensibly public as it undergoes several transitions of ownership:

> 'If I didn't snatch like the devil, I should be nowhere. He doesn't want the car, silly fool! Surely it's to the credit of his State I should be seen about in it at Chandrapore during my leave. He ought to look at it that way. Anyhow he's got to look at it that way. My Maharani's different – my Maharani's a dear. That's her fox-terrier, poor little devil. I fished them both out with the driver. Imagine taking dogs to a Chiefs' Conference! . . . The harmonium – the harmonium's my little mistake, I own. They rather had me over the harmonium. I meant it to stop on the train. Oh lor'!'[44]

The speaker is Miss Derek, who has stolen a car from her employer, the 'Mudkul State' Maharajah; her addressees are mainly Ronny and Adela, but the Nawab Bahadur, an eminent Muslim, is also onboard the car. The latter three are given a lift by Miss Derek; they were picked up by her from a car accident, a confusing event in which those involved could not determine whether or not it was a hyena into which their car had crashed. As one of the minor characters in the novel, Miss Derek works in a Native State as a companion to the Maharani, neither an Empire's servant nor a tourist but 'a freelance', thus neither formally affiliated to nor detached

---

[44] *PI*, p. 83.

62 E. M. Forster and Music

from the imperial system.[45] While Forster might have drawn upon his personal experiences in Dewas for the characterization of this anomalous British existence in India, Miss Derek's ambiguous role allows, and perhaps also spurs, her to take liberties with her employers' possessions. At first, the harmonium seems also one of the spoils, but her explanation quoted before reveals that the instrument is rather unwanted by her. In the manuscripts, the harmonium as mistakenly taken by her is more clearly shown as it is 'popped ... on board without [her] noticing'.[46] Yet the instrument's appearance in the car is no coincidence. The conspicuousness of the harmonium in this scene and throughout the chapter is Forster's strategy of bringing several subplots together to examine the conflict between Western material civilization and Indian indigenous culture.

The harmonium in the car reveals Forster's attention to colonialism not only as political domination or racial segregation but also as an invasion of objects. After its introduction into India in the middle of the nineteenth century, the harmonium was widely disseminated. Portable, foldable, and easy to play, the harmonium provided 'heterophonic contrapuntal texture for vocal music' and became popular in indigenous musical performances, although the instrument's inability to convey authentically the intonation of Indian music had drawn strong criticism from Indian nationalists by the early twentieth century.[47] In his personal record of Gokul Ashtami, Forster noted how a band playing 'Night of Gladness' found its music mixed with incessant noise produced by cymbals, harmoniums, and drums.[48] The harmonium is also referred to in the novel's depiction of Gokul Ashtami: Godbole 'and the six colleagues who supported him clashed their cymbals, hit small drums, droned upon a portable harmonium, and sang'.[49] The verb 'droned' can be read as Forster's awareness of the harmonium as tonally incompatible with Indian singing.

Different from these references to the harmonium which reveal the cultural insensitivity of the British, the depiction of the harmonium in the car says more about the Indians. What the Maharajah's harmonium articulates is an enchantment with 'the Western', a subscription to a value system that celebrates modern technology and abides by the concept of

---

[45] *PI*, p. 83.   [46] *MSS-PI*, p. 120.

[47] Barbara Owen and Alastair Dick, 'Harmonium', *Grove Music Online*, www.oxfordmusiconline.com [accessed 10 May 2018].

[48] All of these details were worked into the opening chapter of the third part of the novel. See the similarities between Forster's letter to his mother on 28 August 1921 (*HD*, p. 66) and the corresponding passage in the novel (*PI*, p. 276).

[49] *PI*, p. 275.

The Queering of Musical Instruments 63

capitalist ownership. The harmonium, according to Miss Derek, is one of the things – alongside the car and the fox terrier – that the Maharajah brings along to a Chiefs' Conference; the untold but telling story here is the Maharajah's eagerness to appear more Westernized and more 'advanced' than other rajahs and princes. The harmonium therefore becomes not just a token of wealth but also an indicator of Westernization. Its appearance in the car reminds us how Western material culture not only brought actual, tangible changes to the colony but also imposed a new set of cultural parameters on Indian people. Additionally, the desire of the colonialized for the concrete modernity imported from 'the West' creates the economic energy that further drives colonial expansion, evidenced by the fact that India became both the factory and the market when the harmonium, like the piano, was later mass-produced there. Contrary to the repeated accusations of overlooking the hard facts of British colonialism, the representation of the Maharajah's harmonium signals that Forster's novel explores the percolation of Western material goods into India's indigenous culture.[50]

The depiction of the harmonium can thus be paralleled with Forster's numerous observations during and after his visits to India in 1912 and in 1921 on the ways in which contemporary Indians tackled the concept of 'the West'. Forster repeatedly wrote about how – for all Indians, Hindus and Muslims alike – Western culture – including material imports, living habits, religious outlooks, social norms, political structures, and many other subjects – posed a significant and inevitable problem. Several of these articles, many of which in the form of book reviews, were reprinted in the essay collection, *Abinger Harvest* (1935), under the heading, 'The East'.[51] Among them, the short essay, 'Advance, India!' (1914), describes a local wedding in Simla, in which a 'rationalistic' family defied Islamic doctrines by not veiling the bride.[52] The genesis of the essay was a request from the bridegroom's brother, who hoped that Forster's report of this Westernized ceremony would show that Muslims in India had made 'a great step forward against superstition'.[53] The end result Forster produced, however, presents an occasion full of confusion, negotiation, and compromise: 'It was depressing, almost heartrending, and opened the problem of

---

[50] My reading therefore counters previous suggestions that the novel fails to address the economic aspect of British imperialism. See e.g. Hunt Hawkins, 'Forster's Critique of Imperialism in *A Passage to India*', *South Atlantic Review*, 48.1 (1983), 54–65 (pp. 59–60).

[51] The rest of Forster's 1913 and 1914 Indian articles are reprinted in a collection published posthumously. See *AE*.

[52] 'Advance, India!' (1914), in *AH*, pp. 298–301 (p. 298).   [53] *AH*, p. 301.

India's future'.[54] For Forster, only when the usual evening prayer took place regardless of an ongoing Western popular song on a gramophone did he find 'beauty' in 'a memorable act' in this oddly Westernized ceremony:

> They gathered on the terrace behind, to the number of twenty, and prostrated themselves towards Mecca. . . . Crash into the devotions of the orthodox birred the gramophone –
>
> I'd sooner be busy with my little Lizzie
>
> and by a diabolic chance reached the end of its song as they ended the prayer. They rejoined us without self-consciousness, but the sun and the snows were theirs, not ours; they had obeyed; we had entered the unlovely chaos that lies between obedience and freedom – and that seems, alas! the immediate future of India.[55]

If this description reveals Forster's exoticization of the indigenous culture,[56] it also expresses his scepticism about Indians' conscious, and conscientious, Westernization. Notably, it is in relation to the gramophone that Forster delineates the diverse and localized responses of Indians to Western civilization. Like the harmonium, the gramophone was powerfully influential on Indian musical cultures and, as a recording and playing device, played an important role in contemporary anthropological studies.[57] That Forster pivots the conflict between Westernization and tradition around the instrument suggests his perception of the importation and dissemination of Western musical instruments in India as illustrative of the divisive power of Western material culture.

In the novel, the Maharajah's harmonium similarly brings such a division among Indians to the fore. On the one side is the Maharajah, who, as aforementioned, relies on imported goods to define his modernization. On the other side is the Nawab Bahadur. Following Miss Derek's explanation about why the harmonium is in the car, the Nawab Bahadur gives an 'oration' on how to modernize India.[58] A prominent, educated

---

[54] *AH*, p. 299.   [55] *AH*, pp. 299–300.

[56] Ian Baucom reads Forster's preference for the traditional as a response to contemporary tourism and the memory of the Mutiny. He regards this account as a touristic tendency to search for the 'authentic': 'Forster transforms the bodies of the orthodox into souvenirs . . . that he can collect and preserve in the materiality of text'. Ian Baucom, *Out of Place: Englishness, Empire, and the Locations of Identity* (Princeton: Princeton University Press, 1999), p. 120.

[57] See e.g. Gerry Farrell, *Indian Music and the West* (Oxford: Oxford University Press, 2004), especially chapter 4: 'The Gramophone Comes to India', pp. 111–43.

[58] *PI*, p. 85.

The Queering of Musical Instruments 65

Muslim, he laments over Hindu superstition while eulogizing the 'reason and orderliness' of British India.[59] Although he speaks to show deference to the British in the car (the narrative's satiric tone is also explicit in the description of this unstoppable outburst as 'geysers'),[60] the speech of Nawab Bahadur nevertheless offers an alternative approach to Western culture: it is education and rationality, instead of Western material culture, that should be promoted. Even though the Nawab Bahadur is not explicitly commenting on the harmonium, the instrument can be read as an agent that invites two different Indian approaches to Western civilization to make their cases. Around the harmonium, we see the diffraction of Indians into the Hindu and the Muslim, the traditional and the anglicized, the materialistic and the ideological. The fact that Forster uses a Hindu ruler and an Islamic elite to exemplify the conflicts within India suggests, too, his concern with the ways in which religious differences produced inner contradictions in the colony. Like the gramophone, the harmonium represents and augments the topicality of social 'advance'; the instrument materializes and manifests the gap between the two opposite attitudes towards 'the West'.

The harmonium bears witness, then, to incompatibilities. When he is talking, the Nawab Bahadur is aware that he is boring the British trio – Miss Derek, Ronny, and Adela – in the back seat: 'he suspected that his audience felt no interest, and that the City Magistrate fondled either maiden behind the cover of the harmonium'.[61] Casting the instrument as a medium through which a male-centred 'courtship' takes place, the Nawab Bahadur ironizes his own previous emphasis on enlightened thinking, revealing a subscription to patriarchal clichés about heterosexual interaction. He is only half correct: Ronny is behaving properly when the Nawab Bahadur entertains his suspicion, but the older man's suspicion does resonate with details a few pages earlier and foreshadows what subsequently occurs. What happened in the past is before the car accident: 'owing to a jolt', Adela's hand touched Ronny's, 'and one of the thrills so frequent in the animal kingdom passed between them'.[62] As a result, the awkwardness that had lasted since the break-up of their prospective marriage disappeared. Later, the two British characters again touch each other's hand when the Nawab Bahadur gets out of the car: '[Ronny's] hand, which he had removed to say good-bye, touched Adela's again; she caressed it definitely, he responded, and their firm and mutual pressure surely meant something'.[63] These exchanges of touch seem to chart the

---

[59] *PI*, p. 84.   [60] *PI*, p. 85.   [61] *PI*, p. 85.   [62] *PI*, pp. 79–80.   [63] *PI*, p. 85.

66   E. M. Forster and Music

reconciliation of Ronny and Adela, first filling up the silence where conversations failed and later precipitating the closeness of the couple. The nascent desire contained within these exchanges, the reciprocity of physical demonstrations of passion and understanding, and the surreptitious nature of these moments all underline the importance of the body to the restoration of the relationship between the two characters.[64] Yet these moments of physical intimacy are simply a foil to the real gap between the two: no sooner does their conversation resume than the connection produced by their touch seems lost, but to Adela's and Ronny's surprise, they find themselves unexpectedly engaged again. It becomes evident, then, that, if this journey in the car creates a series of misunderstandings, misperceptions, and miscommunications, central to these faltering personal relationships is the harmonium. In fact, it was made central by Forster's revision: in the manuscripts, it was originally a 'shawl' to which the Nawab Bahadur refers in his suspicion of Ronny's impropriety.[65] Whether the revision was due to Forster's sudden recognition of the harmonium's useful availability in the car, or it was an intended detail to endow the instrument with added significance, the harmonium, instead of bringing a sense of heterosexual harmony, becomes a parody of its own etymology.[66]

If the normal relation with the harmonium is to use it to produce music, we have seen it repeatedly queered in this scene: none of the characters mean to use the harmonium conventionally for its primary function of music-making, and no one fully understands the purposes of the others' engagement with the instrument. Although the harmonium does not trouble either British or Indian understanding, its unwanted presence in the car – and, more broadly, in India, given its incompatibility with India's indigenous musical cultures – promotes non-standard, but also improvisatory, material relations and enables its meanings to proliferate. Literally intrusive and bulky, the harmonium in the car becomes, then, not simply a musical instrument, but it is instrumental in highlighting contradiction, difference, and irreconciliation. It exposes imperial misjudgement (Miss Derek taking it by mistake), casts doubts on self-Westernizing (its disappearance from the Maharajah's entourage), creates division (the Maharajah's materialism versus the Nawab Bahadur's elitism), foils colonial submission (the Nawab Bahadur's performed obsequiousness), and

[64] Hai, *Making Words Matter*, p. 186.   [65] *MSS-PI*, p. 123.
[66] One of the derivatives of Latin *harmonia*, the etymology of 'harmonium' is the same as that of 'harmony'. *OED*.

confuses heterosexual desire (Ronny and Adela's false engagement). The complex racial, cultural, and sexual fault lines of British colonialism are made explicit by Forster's centralization of the harmonium in the car as a queer object.

The Broken Piano

When he arrived in Dewas Senior in 1921, Forster wrote to his mother:

> Life here will be queer beyond description. The New Palace ... is still building, and the parts of it that were built ten years ago are already falling down. You would weep at the destruction, expense, and hideousness, and I do almost. ... I can't start now on the inside of the palace – two pianos (one a grand), a harmonium, and a dulciphone, all new and all unplayable, their notes sticking and their frames cracked by the dryness. I look into a room – dozens of warped towel-horses are stabled there, or a new suite of drawing-room chairs with their insides gushing out.[67]

This account can be read in many ways: it implies that Western things either malfunctioned because of the Indian climate or were mishandled by Indians, or symbolizes that the imported civilization, as a whole, never worked in India. There is frustration in Forster's description that what he viewed as familiar and regular was simply unable to endure the environment. There is also helplessness: as the Maharajah's secretary, Forster found it futile to attempt to ameliorate the situation.

This catalogue of broken instruments was likely to be the source material for an important scene in the penultimate chapter in *A Passage to India*, which opens with the description: 'All the time the palace ceased not to thrum and tum-tum'.[68] It is remarkable that, when music foreign and unsettling to Western ears in Gokul Ashtami is represented as at its most lingering and affective, it is a broken piano in the European Guest House, 'played' by Aziz, that resounds in the middle of the chapter. Knowing that Fielding is out on a boat with his family to see the celebration of Gokul Ashtami, Aziz intentionally chooses that moment to visit the Guest House. Once inside, he finds two letters on a piano and, out of vindictiveness, opens them. One letter is from Ronny to Fielding, with several references to Ronny's half-brother, Ralph Moore; the other is from Adela to Stella, Ronny's half-sister and now Fielding's wife. Both letters are written with ease:

---

[67] Letter to his mother (1 April 1921). *HD*, p. 32.   [68] *PI*, p. 294.

68   E. M. Forster and Music

> It was all 'Stella and Ralph', even 'Cyril' and 'Ronny' – all so friendly and
> sensible, and written in a spirit he could not command. He envied the easy
> intercourse that is only possible in a nation whose women are free. These
> five people were making up their little difficulties, and closing their broken
> ranks against the alien. Even Heaslop was coming in. Hence the strength
> of England, and in a spurt of temper he hit the piano, and since the notes
> had swollen and stuck together in groups of threes he produced a
> remarkable noise.
>   'Oh, oh, who is that?' said a nervous and respectful voice; he could not
> remember where he had heard its tones before. Something moved in the
> twilight of an adjoining room. He replied, 'State doctor, ridden over to
> inquire, very little English,' slipped the letters into his pocket, and to show
> that he had free entry to the Guest House struck the piano again.
>   Ralph Moore came into the light.[69]

This 'remarkable noise' emphatically drives the plot forward, bringing Aziz
to meet Ralph, an encounter which harks back to Aziz's first meeting with
Mrs Moore in the mosque and foreshadows the reconciliation between
Aziz and Fielding at the end of the novel. If the broken piano stems from a
fictionalization of Forster's personal experience, given the scene's importance to the plot, how are we to interpret the sounds produced by piano
keys 'stuck together in groups of threes'?

This 'noise' challenges the conventional notion of tonal harmony in
Western musicology. A unit of three consecutive piano keys combines
two minor seconds and one major second. Played together, the unit does
not belong to any traditional chords in the Western tonal system; it does
not belong to a diatonic scale but is part of a chromatic one; it is neither
concordant nor stable. If a major or minor second is regarded as 'imperfect' compared to the 'perfect' fourth, fifth, and octave, this unit is
doubly, or triply, 'imperfect'. Yet given that there are multiple units of
three keys stuck together, it is likely that what Aziz produces is a
discordant sound but with concordant possibilities between individual
notes, inexplicable at its first strike but suggestive of potential chromatic
chords. It is possible, then, that Forster attempts to evoke a sound that is
simultaneously foreign to the traditional Western notion of harmony and
resonant with contemporary concepts of chromaticism.[70] Another

---

[69] *PI*, pp. 298–99.

[70] 'Based on an octave of 12 semitones', a chromatic scale is 'opposed to a seven-note diatonic scale'
and 'consists of an ascending or descending line that advances by semitones'. In studies of harmony,
'chromatic' is 'applied to notes marked with accidentals foreign to the scale of the key in which the
passage is written'. Chromaticism flourished in the nineteenth century, with the works of Schubert
and Chopin and, most famously, Wagner's *Tristan und Isolde*, as representative examples. George
Dyson and William Drabkin, 'Chromatic', *Grove Music Online*, www.oxfordmusiconline.com
[accessed 10 May 2018].

possibility is the effect of overtones: when more than two consecutive piano keys are pressed together, each key's fundamental frequency overlaps and produces a sensation of amplified harmonic sonority.[71] The 'noise' might also be read as the effect of quarter-tones, a pitch a piano usually cannot create. When pressed together long enough, two neighbouring piano keys bring forth a pitch between the two fixed pitches and form an interval of half a semitone.[72] Whichever way we interpret the 'noise', it is evident that it is characterized by an uncertain tonality and produces an effect strangely jarring and alarming, if not instantaneously repulsive, to listeners familiar with what is commonly known as Western music.

The tonal ambiguity of the 'noise' echoes Forster's own puzzle when he listened to indigenous music in India. Like numerous contemporaries, Forster felt shocked, confused, and uncomfortable when hearing the flexible intonation of Indian music, especially Indian singing, for the first time.[73] In his description of a performance of Nautch, for example, Forster noted that 'the musicians seemed out [of] tune and playing in different keys'.[74] The account reveals his inability to pin down the tonality of Indian music and suggests an experience of recognizing something but hesitating to clarify his recognition. This sense of hovering between knowing and unknowing also recalls his description of Godbole's song, which has 'the illusion of a Western melody' that particularly baffles its English and Muslim listeners.[75] With its indeterminable intervals and unconventional chord construction, the 'noise' of the broken piano creates a similar tonal effect and seems to suggest an Indianization of the Western instrument. Given that Aziz, who becomes more and more explicitly nationalistic towards the end of the novel, is the person who 'plays' the piano, it is possible to offer a political reading of the scene and the 'noise'. Approaching the instrument, which epitomizes the malfunctioning of Western civilization in a colonial environment, Aziz uses it to make a strong and assertive response to British colonization. Compared to chapter 2, where Aziz informed Mrs Moore that he was not allowed to enter the English Club and could only hear sounds of an orchestra from

---

[71] Murray Campbell, 'Overtone', *Grove Music Online*, www.oxfordmusiconline.com [accessed 10 May 2018].

[72] Julian Rushton, 'Quarter-tone', *Grove Music Online*, www.oxfordmusiconline.com [accessed 10 May 2018].

[73] Zhou, 'Sublime Noise', pp. 165–67.

[74] Letter to his mother (6 November 1912). *SL*, I, p. 150. Brackets are the editors'.

[75] *PI*, pp. 71–72.

70   E. M. Forster and Music

outside, here in the novel's penultimate chapter, we see this once outsider having free access to the colonizers' interior space, making a sound himself with the piano under his control. The 'noise', then, not only problematizes Western understanding of music but also challenges the authority of the Empire. An example of the 'subaltern' being heard, Aziz's punch on the piano expresses sentiments akin to those of contemporary Indian nationalism, sending out a defiant note of Indian agency and autonomy.

Yet the novel's manuscripts reveal that Aziz's 'spurt of temper' was a late addition. Among the several drafts Oliver Stallybrass has identified, one draft close to the published version describes the 'noise' as 'amazing', while another, regarded by Stallybrass as an earlier fragment of the chapter, presents the scene significantly differently:

> He walked in, vaguely curious. <A> \The/ piano was open. He touched it and since the notes had stuck together in groups of two and three, produced a \most/ curious noise. '\Oh! Oh!/ <What do you want> \Do you speak English/?' said a voice that he knew – a nervous respectful voice: he could not think where he had heard it before.
>
> 'Vary vary slightly' he replied, thumping the piano with his fist, and turning round saw something move in the unlit room behind him. Mr Moore emerged, holding his chin, and apparently very sorry for himself.[76]

This fragment shows how the event would unfold if there were no letters involved; without being fuelled by his anger, Aziz would directly touch the piano keyboard. The punch on the piano would take place eventually, albeit deferred and for a different purpose. Perhaps because of Aziz's initial relative gentleness, the 'noise' is 'curious' rather than 'remarkable', but that Forster uses the adjective to describe both the subject (Aziz) as well as the object (the piano sound) is a curious choice itself. The repetition of the adjective can be read as an oblique allusion to *The Picture of Dorian Gray*, a text in which the term 'curious' recurs conspicuously. As Eve Kosofsky Sedgwick suggests, 'curious' in Wilde's novel connotes 'a built-in epistemological indecision or doubling', evoking 'the excess, "wrought" intensiveness of [a] knowledge-situation' where desire and impulse draw subject and object close to each other, and encapsulating 'the responsive, all but paranoid mutuality attributed to gay recognition'.[77] In this respect, the repeated term makes Forster's earlier version of the broken-piano scene a similar site of thrills and anxieties for the 'curious' player and his listener,

---

[76] *MSS-PI*, p. 542.
[77] Eve Kosofsky Sedgwick, *Epistemology of the Closet* (Berkeley: University of California Press, 1990), p. 174.

The Queering of Musical Instruments

the 'curious' sound infusing the encounter between Aziz and Ralph with a mixture of titillation and uncertainty. Both qualifications – the word 'vaguely' and the inserted 'most' – also suggest that Forster uses the word 'curious' to delineate an indefinably sensual and oddly affective experience where Aziz's body has transgressed beyond known boundaries. Certainly, Aziz comes to the European Guest House full of hatred for the British, but the evocativeness of the repeated 'curious' in the draft suggests that Forster first conceived the scene as another queer, highly homoerotic moment in the novel.[78]

From 'curious' via 'amazing' to 'remarkable', Forster's revisions do not erase homoeroticism but rather suggest it in the sound of the 'noise' itself. Tonally, the fact that the 'noise' comprises multi-chromatic chords and discords that remain unresolved echoes Susan McClary's contention that chromaticism 'takes on the cultural cast of "femininity"' and often becomes associated with emotive and erotic excess.[79] In its formal transgression and sensual affectivity, such excess, as recent theoretical work in queer musicology has informed us, can be read as a queer expression of desire.[80] Moreover, to describe the 'noise' as 'remarkable' is, in fact, to confess the failure to describe it, to admit that there is something about the sound that is worth being remarked upon but at the same time resistant to verbal description. The queerness of the 'noise' thus lies in its paradoxical remarkableness, in its creation of, in Philip Brett's words, 'an unspoken place' where 'the incoherencies and dramas of the closet may be played out in particularly revealing and suggestive ways simply because of the lack of rational verbal discourse'.[81]

As Sarah Hankins suggests, a queer relationship with music produces 'bodily arousal', 'a state in which we may be uniquely attuned to musical meaning'.[82] Wayne Koestenbaum also claims that 'to hear is metaphorically to be impregnated'.[83] In this way, then, the homoeroticism in the bonding between Aziz and Ralph can be interpreted as the result of their

---

[78] For a discussion of the novel's homoeroticism, see Joseph Bristow, *Effeminate England: Homoerotic Writing after 1885* (New York: Columbia University Press, 1995), pp. 83–91.

[79] McClary, *Feminine Endings*, p. 16.

[80] For an introductory article to the development of queer musicology, see Rachel Lewis, 'What's Queer about Musicology Now?', *Women & Music: A Journal of Gender and Culture*, 13 (2009), 43–53.

[81] Brett, 'Musicality, Essentialism, and the Closet', p. 18.

[82] Sarah Hankins, 'Queer Relationships with Music and an Experiential Hermeneutics for Musical Meaning', *Women & Music: A Journal of Gender and Culture*, 18 (2014), 83–104 (p. 85).

[83] Wayne Koestenbaum, *The Queen's Throat: Opera, Homosexuality, and the Mystery of Desire* (New York: Poseidon, 1993), p. 16.

72 E. M. Forster and Music

hearing of 'the remarkable noise', which not only brings them together but also stimulates the flesh of the two male bodies. Many details in Forster's description of their interaction obliquely allude to erotic, physical, even masochistic, pleasure. Aziz and Ralph are 'practically alone', one threatening and the other timid; the former finds the latter 'rather beautiful' and an 'extraordinary youth'; Ralph complains about how the bee stings 'throb' and, when being treated, Ralph describes Aziz's hands as 'unkind'; Ralph confesses that he minds not 'pain' but 'cruelty'; Aziz offers the 'magic ointment' and wishes to be remembered. And, finally, their gentle, understanding touch.[84] If the 'noise' propels Aziz and Ralph to bond intimately, its effect also seems to extend to the narrative voice. As Charu Malik comments, the representation of Aziz and Ralph's interaction is 'tentative, restrained, and considered', characterized by 'the narrative's undulating, sinuous movement of affection and gentleness'.[85] The ultimately indescribable 'noise' queers Aziz and Ralph's encounter, creating a sense of indeterminate tenderness that permeates the text.

The broken piano in the European Guest House could not be more different from the conventional piano in the nineteenth century, which was 'the ubiquitous and unrivaled instrument of the bourgeois home', 'function[ing] in sound and sight alike as an analogical referent to social harmony and domestic order'.[86] In its unplayable condition and 'remarkable noise', its peripheral existence at the margin of the Empire and its state of neglect, its futility in holding together a makeshift 'home' for the sightseeing Fieldings, its facilitation of the erotically charged encounter between Aziz and Ralph, and its enmeshment in colonial tension, this piano is queer. Forster's depiction of the instrument destabilizes the racial and sexual tenets of British colonization, resisting both the will to confine and the willingness to conform. The queered instrument brings forth alternatives; that which has been repressed, concealed, and contained is being exposed, shed light on, and unleashed. Although the novel never commits to anti-imperialism, here is an evocative demonstration of the potency of deviance.

***

In his discussion of the presence of everyday objects in *Howards End*, Henry S. Turner argues that the novel can be read as 'an extended

[84] *PI*, pp. 299–301.   [85] Malik, 'Masculine Desire', pp. 233 and 224.
[86] Richard Leppert, *The Sight of Sound: Music, Representation, and the History of the Body* (Berkeley: University of California Press, 1993), pp. 134 and 139.

The Queering of Musical Instruments

73

meditation on the difficulty of representing capital accumulation, in all its elusive and terrifying abstraction, as a total process'.[87] In representing the Schlegels' and the Wilcoxes' properties and investments, Henry Wilcox's company in Africa, Margaret's calling card, cousin Frieda's reticule, Leonard Bast's umbrella, and many other things, Forster illustrates not the relationship between production, labour, and commodification, but the 'relentlessness' of accumulation and its entailing 'cost' in the modern world: 'objects multiply and continue to multiply, they slip and jostle against each other, they resist the subject, they kill'.[88] For Turner, objects in *Howards End* are 'charged with symbolic or narratological significance and assume an independent motive force that drives the action of the plot', becoming 'the material hinges on which the narrative turns'.[89] They 'begin to spill over into places where they do not belong', 'draw[ing] characters into worlds either desired or feared'.[90] Some of them, like the Schlegels' overwhelming belongings when they have to move, the glass frame of Jacky's picture, and most things surrounding Leonard, are selected by Forster to be 'figures *for* loss and surplus', 'to bear the full brunt of the process' of ceaseless accumulation and 'to reveal its destructive power'.[91]

There are evident similarities to the ways Forster represents the three Western musical instruments in *A Passage to India*. Unwelcome, Ronny's viola falls under the pressure of the ideal of imperial masculinity and is made to retreat from sounding in public; unwanted, the harmonium strays into the car, exposing the contradictions among those on board or related to the instrument; unexpected, the broken piano creates a 'noise' full of indefinable resonances, leading up to the series of precariously formed reconciliation towards the end of the novel. In the language of Homi K. Bhabha, the inability of these musical instruments to fulfil their original function of producing 'standard' Western music reminds us of the colonial power's strategic use of 'mimicry' to characterize the 'other' as recalcitrant.[92] Yet, in these instruments, Forster encapsulates not only the abstract colonial will to civilize but also the emotional complexity of individuals. By dramatizing discrete improvisations and sensations in encountering these instruments, Forster suggests an excess that challenges the colonial power's attempt to contain, categorize, and normalize – an

---

[87] Turner, 'Empire of Objects', p. 329.   [88] Turner, 'Empire of Objects', pp. 338 and 341.
[89] Turner, 'Empire of Objects', p. 335.   [90] Turner, 'Empire of Objects', p. 336.
[91] Turner, 'Empire of Objects', p. 338.
[92] Homi K. Bhabha, 'Of Mimicry and Man: The Ambivalence of Colonial Discourse', in *The Location of Culture* (London: Routledge, 1994), pp. 121–31.

overflowing of deviant desires, a proliferation of meanings, and an emergence of different patterns of personal relations that circumvent, resist, and destabilize the racial, sexual, and cultural norms of the power structure of British India. The secret viola, the itinerant harmonium, and the dysfunctional piano thus demonstrate the concreteness of British colonialism but, at the same time, queer its contours as porous.

CHAPTER 3

From Literary Heritage to National Character

—O, well, said Mr Bartell D'Arcy, I presume there are as good singers to-day as there were then.

—Where are they? asked Mr Browne defiantly.

—In London, Paris, Milan, said Mr Bartell D'Arcy warmly. I suppose Caruso, for example, is quite as good, if not better than any of the men you have mentioned.

—Maybe so, said Mr Browne. But I may tell you I doubt it strongly.

James Joyce, 'The Dead'[1]

Frequently read by critics as an example of the short story's contemplation of the power of memory and the interdependence of the living and the dead,[2] the chapter epigraph from Joyce's 'The Dead' also shows that commentaries on musical composition and performances often draw attention to national and generational differences. This is evident, too, in the concert scene in *Howards End* during the lively discussion among the Schlegels and their relatives about Elgar's 'Pomp and Circumstance'. After a protest against Margaret's 'ugh! I don't like this Elgar that's coming', Mrs Munt's attempt to detain the Schlegels' German cousin Frieda and her fiancé Herr Liesecke 'to hear what *we* are doing in music' reveals a sense of confidence shared by many in Britain in the early twentieth century that Elgar's work could emulate, perhaps also challenge, Germany's long-celebrated supremacy in the art of music.[3] The irony here is that it is still Germans who are given the power to assess the merit of English music; one might also recall that, for all his links to English imperialism,[4] much of Elgar's contemporary fame came from the facts that his compositional style

---

[1] James Joyce, *Dubliners*, ed. Jeri Johnson (Oxford: Oxford University Press, 2000), pp. 138–76 (p. 157).

[2] John Scarry, 'William Parkinson in Joyce's "The Dead"', *Journal of Modern Literature*, 3.1 (1973), 105–7 (p. 107). Kevin Whelan, 'The Memories of "The Dead"', *The Yale Journal of Criticism*, 15.1 (2002), 59–97 (pp. 84–85).

[3] *HE*, p. 33.   [4] Fillion, *Difficult Rhythm*, p. 81.

75

was frequently aligned with those of Hector Berlioz and Richard Strauss and that his work was acknowledged and performed in Continental Europe.[5] Forster's depiction of the familial furore surrounding Elgar taps into the anxiety underlying English confidence in the perceived correlation between musical success and national prosperity at the time. For many in Europe and the United States in the early twentieth century, accomplishments in music intertwined with national history and international politics. An extreme would be the view of Cecil Forsyth, who claimed that England had previously sacrificed its development in music for 'the calls of Empire', whereas Germany, only having lately arrived at the colonial scene, had time 'to build up, brick by brick, an immense and noble artistic structure' but would have to give up some of its famous musicians in exchange for space in Africa.[6] Despite its illogical balancing of musical and imperial achievements, Forsyth's argument demonstrates that to write about the composition, performance, and consumption of Western art music was to negotiate existing perceptions of musical taste, sensibility, and knowledge as generationally and nationally specific.

This chapter considers Forster's alertness to these perceptions in his description of Donizetti's *Lucia di Lammermoor* in *Where Angels Fear to Tread*. It examines the opera scene's parodic allusions to nineteenth-century texts as politicized representations of literary history, which carried, as we shall see, considerable topical charge in debates on national character. The novel therefore coexisted alongside numerous contemporary delineations of national character, a majority of which built on Victorian discussions of Englishness as the nation's unique 'personality'.[7] Forster's portrayal of national character in the opera scene, however, is less concerned with uniqueness and more with the problem of generalization. Challenging previous interpretations of *Where Angels Fear to Tread* as one of Forster's 'suburban' novels,[8] the chapter argues that, through constructing a cross-national 'dialogue' that gestures towards economic and racial

---

[5] Meirion Hughes and Robert Stradling, *The English Musical Renaissance 1840–1940: Constructing a National Music*, 2nd ed. (Manchester: Manchester University Press, 2001), p. 63.

[6] Cecil Forsyth, *Music and Nationalism: A Study of English Opera* (London: Macmillan, 1911), p. 41.

[7] On the topicality of 'character' – individual as well as national – in Victorian England, see Stefan Collini, *Public Moralists: Political Thought and Intellectual Life in Britain 1850–1930* (Oxford: Clarendon, 1991), pp. 91–118. Additionally, Patrick Parrinder argues that the topicality of national character in the eighteenth and nineteenth centuries was intertwined with and indebted to the rise of the novel. Patrick Parrinder, *Nation and Novel: The English Novel from its Origins to the Present Day* (Oxford: Oxford University Press, 2006), pp. 21–22.

[8] In *E. M. Forster: A Literary Life*, Mary Lago separates Forster's novels into two groups: the Suburban Novels and the Indian Novel.

From Literary Heritage to National Character 77

conflicts between nations, the opera scene presents a much more complicated web of multinational relations of musical consumption, cultural appropriation, and touristic exploitation than the Anglo–Italian encounter on the surface. My approach thus differs significantly from Michelle Fillion's biographical reading. As Fillion suggests, the scene reincarnates Forster's personal experience in Italy in 1903, working his memory of the coloratura, Luisa Tetrazzini, into the after-effect of the opera on the novel's characters.[9] Much of her reading is valid, but it undercuts the fictionality of the scene and overlooks Forster's employment of the allusive power of musical representations for both stylistic and ideological purposes. Forster's parodic use of literary allusions and national stereotypes, as I shall be discussing, indicates his ambitions for the literary vision and political outlook of his first novel.

In examining the opera scene's many allusions to nineteenth-century texts, the chapter extends S. P. Rosenbaum's attempt to place *Where Angels Fear to Tread* contextually in literary history. Rosenbaum has drawn attention to the similarities between the novel and Henry James's *The Ambassadors* (1903) in terms of their plots and their representations of international encounters, but he has also noted that there are differences between the two works in narrative perspective and structure, characterization, and philosophy, and has suggested Forster's divergence from James.[10] Surprisingly, Rosenbaum's interpretation of the opera scene as 'part of [Forster's] unJamesean, even unBloomsburian satire of aestheticism' misses two obvious clues in tracing the novel's literary history.[11] For in choosing to write about a performance of Donizetti's *Lucia*, Forster's first novel continues a literary genealogy which can be traced back to Walter Scott's *The Bride of Lammermoor* (1819), on which the libretto by Salvadore Cammarano for Donizetti's opera is based, and Gustave Flaubert's *Madame Bovary* (1857), in which the opera plays a monumental role in Emma Bovary's adulterous life. Reading the opera scene's allusions to Scott and to Flaubert as highly self-referential, the chapter illustrates how Forster's positioning of his debut novel says as much about his departure from the styles of his literary predecessors as his homage to the cultural status they possessed. The chapter thus redresses the critical tendency to approach *Where Angels Fear to Tread* for its themes rather

---

[9] Fillion, *Difficult Rhythm*, pp. 24–38.
[10] S. P. Rosenbaum, 'Towards a Literary History of *Monteriano*', *Twentieth-Century Literature*, 31.2–3 (1985), 180–98 (pp. 183–85).
[11] Rosenbaum, 'Towards a Literary History of *Monteriano*', p. 185.

than its style. This is not to suggest that the novel displays the same degree of linguistic or narrative innovations as, say, *A Passage to India*. Rather, what the chapter seeks to demonstrate is that Forster's participation in the literary history surrounding Donizetti's opera suggests a writer adept in exploiting the quotability and malleability of the past (whether of literature or of music) for his own use.

This chapter thus continues the last chapter's inquiry into material culture by looking at another form of music's materiality – that is, the textual abundance of the musical industry. Whether copied and circulated among individuals or published and disseminated in the marketplace, the vast literature of, on, and around music – music printed (scores and songbooks); written about, commented on, and theorized (handbooks, guidebooks, pamphlets, treatises); described, imagined, and verbalized (concert programmes, reviews, and literary representations of music) – means that music has a textual existence. To write about music is to engage with existing writings about music, to appropriate them for a new context, and to alter their meanings for new audiences. The parodic allusiveness of Forster's opera scene, as we shall see, is particularly to the national dimensions of past and circulating representations of the stereotypes of opera audiences. Examining the way in which the opera scene's allusions evoke and question these national stereotypes, the chapter illustrates Forster's reflection on the inadequacy of generalizing about a nation's character. My own reading therefore resists previous interpretations that cast *Where Angels Fear to Tread* as a novel obsessed with national contrasts, arguing instead that it is the problem of contrasting nations that Forster explores in the novel. In this way, my reading complements Lauren M. E. Goodlad's assessment of the portrait of internationalism in *Where Angels Fear to Tread* as 'ethical': in 'cultivat[ing] an ethos of ongoing epistemological revision and embodied encounter', Forster, Goodlad suggests, delivers a vision of 'a contextualist attracted to the *frisson* of difference – a relationalist who asserts the power of affective ties to disclose the world rather than either perfect or preserve it'.[12] In many ways, my discussion in the previous two chapters has echoed Goodlad's argument, as we have seen how Forster's exploration of the protean meanings of rhythm and his representations of Western musical instruments are suggestive of his wariness of the limits of an English perspective in encounters with the racial other. What distinguishes this chapter from Goodlad's study is its

---

[12] Lauren M. E. Goodlad, 'Where Liberals Fear to Tread: E. M. Forster's Queer Internationalism and the Ethics of Care', *Novel*, 39.3 (2006), 307–36 (pp. 330 and 327).

From Literary Heritage to National Character 79

approach: instead of borrowing terms from current political and cultural theories, I pay attention to the textual, intertextual, and contextual nuances of the opera scene.

Flaubert and Scott

Donizetti's *Lucia di Lammermoor* (1835) was, and still is, perceived as a representative of Italian bel canto.[13] The melodramatic 'wronged bride' theme, the structured double arias and duets, and the demanding coloratura of Lucia's madness all ensure and sustain the popularity of the opera.[14] In nineteenth-century France, in particular, the opera enjoyed a sensational reception: its premiere in 1837 was received with 'enthusiasm [which] bordered on hysteria'.[15] Such fervour in France was augmented when, in 1839, Donizetti staged a French version of the opera, the French *Lucie*, which made a lasting impact on French culture thenceforth. In many respects, the famous opera scene in Gustave Flaubert's *Madame Bovary* resulted from, and contributed to, the popularity of the opera. Closing the novel's second part, Emma Bovary's attendance at a performance of Donizetti's *Lucie* with her husband, Charles Bovary, facilitates her downfall. Her rapturous, erotic, disturbed, and almost abandoned reactions to the opera, her fantasy about the leading tenor, her unexpected reunion with Léon, her subsequent adultery – all of these details became emblematic of the stereotypes about opera-box literature and adultery, and Emma Bovary's experience became *the* experience.[16]

Critics often reiterate, rather than investigate, Forster's allusions to Flaubert in the opera scene.[17] Compared to the farcical moment in *Where Angels Fear to Tread*, Emma Bovary's experience seems more

---

[13] For general discussion of the opera, see relevant subject entries in the *Grove*: William Ashbrook, 'Lucia di Lammermoor ("Lucy of Lammermoor")', and Mary Ann Smart, 'Donizetti, (Domenico) Gaetano (Maria): Biography', *Grove Music Online*, www.oxfordmusiconline.com [accessed 10 May 2018]. On the psychological depth of *Lucia*, for example, see Deirdre O'Grady, *The Last Troubadours: Poetic Drama in Italian Opera, 1597–1887* (London: Routledge, 1991), pp. 142–52. Recently, the opera particularly draws the attention of feminist musicologists: see e.g. Mary Ann Smart, 'The Silencing of Lucia', *Cambridge Opera Journal*, 4.2 (1992), 119–41.

[14] The phrase 'wronged bride' is from Jeremy Tambling, 'Scott's "Heyday" in Opera', in *The Reception of Sir Walter Scott in Europe*, ed. Murray Pittock (London: Continuum, 2006), pp. 285–92 (p. 290). 'Coloratura' is defined in the *Grove Music Dictionary* as '[f]lorid figuration or ornamentation' in vocal music. Owen Jander and Ellen T. Harris, 'Coloratura', *Grove Music Online*, www.oxfordmusiconline.com [accessed 10 May 2018].

[15] William Ashbrook, *Donizetti and His Operas* (Cambridge, UK: Cambridge University Press, 1982), p. 137.

[16] For a detailed discussion of Flaubert's description of the opera scene, see Cormac Newark, *Opera in the Novel from Balzac to Proust* (Cambridge, UK: Cambridge University Press, 2011), pp. 78–109.

[17] See e.g. Herbert Lindenberger, *Opera: The Extravagant Art* (Ithaca: Cornell University Press, 1984), pp. 156–66.

80 E. M. Forster and Music

appropriate and more 'normal', given the opera's content. Yet the very anomaly of Forster's opera scene is, I would suggest, deliberate: in *Where Angels Fear to Tread*, Forster revises, and meticulously as well as playfully subverts, the Flaubertian version of the opera. His revision, or subversion, can be understood as 'queering' Flaubert's text, partly because the hetero-sexual seduction between Emma and Léon is transformed into the homo-erotic touch between Philip and Gino.[18] As Fillion suggests, whereas Caroline 'escapes the display case of the "opera box"' and 'is freed to assume the position of subject rather than object of passion', Philip becomes the one, 'led by the seductive Gino, to occupy Forster's box'.[19] Yet it is also queering on a more comprehensive scale, or, in Michael Warner's definition of the term, a 'thorough resistance to regimes of the normal'.[20]

In every detail, Forster's opera scene is a complete inversion of Flaubert's text. Instead of a female spectator, Philip is at the centre of the narrative. The counterpart to Emma's unknowing husband is Philip's unknowing sister, Harriet. Whilst Emma relishes her fantasy by focusing on the tenor, Philip (as well as the narrator and thus the readers) sets his sight mainly on the prima donna, a characteristic identified by critics as particularly associated with male homosexuals.[21] Moreover, there are spatial and class inversions. Unlike Flaubert's urban setting, Forster's theatre is in a small town. Rather than an opera box, where Emma carries herself 'with the self-assurance of a duchess' and looks down at 'the crowd rushing to the right by the other corridor',[22] Forster's English characters are in the pit, unable to follow Baedeker's advice that British tourists should always reserve their seats in a box.[23] Unlike Flaubert's bourgeois 'subscribers', the rows of smiling businessmen whom Emma observes from afar,[24] Forster's English characters find themselves surrounded by Italian

---

[18] Margaret Goscilo, 'Forster's Italian Comedies: Que[e]rying Heterosexuality Abroad', in *Seeing Double: Revisioning Edwardian and Modernist Literature*, ed. Carola M. Kaplan and Anne B. Simpson (Basingstoke: Macmillan, 1996), pp. 193–214 (pp. 196–98); and A. A. Markley, 'E. M. Forster's Reconfigured Gaze and the Creation of a Homoerotic Subjectivity', *Twentieth-Century Literature*, 47.2 (2001), 268–92 (pp. 275–78). For a discussion of the homoeroticism in Philip and Gino's physical contact – Gino's inadvertent push in chapter 2 and the two men's fight in chapter 9 – see Bristow, *Effeminate England*, pp. 66–67.

[19] Fillion, *Difficult Rhythm*, p. 28.

[20] Michael Warner, 'Introduction', in *Fear of a Queer Planet: Queer Politics and Social Theory*, ed. Michael Warner (Minneapolis: University of Minnesota Press, 1993), pp. vii–xxxi (p. xxvi).

[21] Goscilo, 'Forster's Italian Comedies', pp. 197–98. See also Koestenbaum, *Queen's Throat*. pp. 101–2.

[22] Gustave Flaubert, *Madame Bovary*, ed. Margaret Cohen, trans. Eleanor Marx Aveling and Paul de Man (New York: Norton, 2005), p. 177.

[23] Karl Baedeker, *Italy: Handbook for Travellers: Second Part: Central Italy and Rome*, 13th ed. (Leipsic: Baedeker, 1900), p. xxiv.

[24] Flaubert, *Madame Bovary*, p. 177.

From Literary Heritage to National Character 81

locals who are clamorous and excited. Both texts use the narrative device of unexpected reunion, but while Emma receives Léon, who walks up to her box after the interval, Forster's Philip is taken by an arm, 'sho[oting] over the balustrade into [a] box'.[25] Class segregation in Flaubert's novel is transformed by Forster into utopian democracy, as the upper-middle-class Englishman is dragged upward to join Gino, a dentist's son, and his friends. The adulterous secrecy of Emma and Léon is substituted by public cordiality among young men. In terms of national identity, French sentimentalism is replaced by Italian passion, and French *liaison* by Italian comradeship. Philip's meeting with Gino thus rounds off, as well as embodies, all the inversions: the heterosexual encounter is homoeroticized, the spatial arrangement reversed, the class discrepancy defied, and hence the 'normal' Flaubertian version queered.

It is extremely intriguing, then, that when Forster's opera scene does explicitly allude to Flaubert's novel, it is a highly self-referential allusion. Describing Harriet's cluelessness at the opera, the narrator comments that she, 'like M. Bovary on a more famous occasion, was trying to follow the plot'.[26] This seems a typical Forsterian narrative voice that judges and satirizes the character, but its self-deprecation is evident in its comparative vocabulary, only deceptively so. Hidden within the novel's wholescale subversion of Flaubert's opera scene, the narrator's self-deprecating reference to *Madame Bovary* becomes an acknowledgement of, as well as a jibe at, the monumental work. It reveals a more flippant and less respectful attitude towards Flaubert compared to, for instance, Henry James's outlook in the 1870s: 'It is not in the temper of English vision to see things as M. Flaubert sees them, and it is not in the genius of the English language to present them as he presents them. With all respect to "Madame Bovary," "Madame Bovary" is fortunately an inimitable work'.[27] For Forster, not only was Flaubert's novel not 'inimitable'; it was open to subversion, too. The self-deprecating narrator is itself a playful subversion of the notable Flaubertian 'author', who 'must be like God in the universe, present everywhere and visible nowhere'.[28] The point of view of the Forsterian narrator is similar to Flaubertian omniscience, but the God-like detachment is replaced with intrusion and bias, both of which serve to

---

[25] *WA*, p. 97.   [26] *WA*, p. 95.

[27] Henry James, 'Charles de Bernard and Gustave Flaubert: The Minor French Novelists' (1876), in *Henry James: Literary Criticism*, ed. Leon Edel, 2 vols (Cambridge, UK: Cambridge University Press, 1984), II, pp. 159–83 (p. 168).

[28] Flaubert's letter to Louise Colet (9 December 1852), in *The Letters of Gustave Flaubert: 1830–1857*, ed. and trans. Francis Steegmuller (Cambridge, MA: Harvard University Press, 1980), p. 173.

82   E. M. Forster and Music

augment the elusiveness of the text.[29] Forster's text thus combines knowledgeable and playful reworkings of his Flaubertian source, paying homage to Flaubert's meticulousness in novel writing as well as emulating, challenging, and undercutting the very monumentality of the literary giant. It is worth stressing the fact that *Where Angels Fear to Tread* was Forster's debut novel. Using *Madame Bovary* as his literary material was therefore a deliberate strategy to align himself with those who conscientiously treated novel writing as a serious vocation. Yet the way he moulded Flaubert's opera scene into his comic version also suggests that Forster did not value Flaubert as much as he later valued other Continental novelists, such as Tolstoy, Dostoevsky, Turgenev, and Proust.[30]

If writing about *Lucia* meant a negotiation of Flaubert's opera scene, it also prompted Forster to glance back at another pre-eminent nineteenth-century novelist: Walter Scott. To many of Forster's contemporaries, Scott was the opposite of Flaubert: the sprawling plots of Scott's historical novels showed imaginative spontaneity and suggested a creative process different from Flaubert's scrupulous literary labour. Virginia Woolf, for example, commented on this difference between the two writers in her essay, 'Scott's Character' (1921):

> When it came to writing [Scott] had merely to turn on the tap and the accumulated resources rushed out. That this is not the way in which the works of Flaubert were produced is certain; but it is also probable that genius of a certain type must work unconsciously, like a natural force which issues unchanged, almost unnoticed by its possessor.[31]

Scott's 'unconsciously' creative process and Flaubert's highly conscious modulations of textual details were elsewhere seen by Woolf as the two different stages of literary genealogy: 'We may say that Scott is childish and Flaubert by comparison a grown man'.[32] Such an evolutionary evaluation of the two writers was conducive to Woolf's inheritance of, and resistance

---

[29] Paul B. Armstrong comments on the slipperiness of the Forsterian narrative voice: 'the narrator is not the author but a device that an anxious, proud writer can use to transform the contradictions he personally feels into socially useful games. It is then up to readers to play along with these games if they can and will.' Armstrong, *Play and the Politics of Reading*, p. 126.

[30] See *Aspects of the Novel* and 'Our Second Greatest Novel?' (1943), in *TCD*, pp. 216–19, for Forster's admiration for these European writers.

[31] Virginia Woolf, 'Scott's Characters' (1921), in *The Essays of Virginia Woolf*, ed. Andrew McNeillie (vols I–IV) and Stuart N. Clarke (vols V–VI), 6 vols (London: Hogarth Press, 1986–2011), III, pp. 301–4 (p. 303).

[32] Virginia Woolf, 'On Re-reading Novels' (1922), in *The Essays of Virginia Woolf*, III, pp. 336–46 (p. 343).

From Literary Heritage to National Character   83

to, her literary predecessors from 'that vantage ground'.[33] For early twentieth-century British novelists, if the works of Scott (as well as Flaubert) augmented their anxieties about literary precursors, there were also opportunities to use these works to delineate their own aesthetic aims.

For Forster, Scott represented not his aesthetic roots but a point of reference for his declaration of independence. In *Aspects of the Novel*, he delivers a relentless critique of Scott's fame: 'Scott is a novelist over whom we shall violently divide. For my own part I do not care for him, and find it difficult to understand his continued reputation. ... He is seen to have a trivial mind and a heavy style. He cannot construct'.[34] Calling Scott merely a 'story-teller' who reminded readers of their 'early happiness', Forster criticized Scott's lack of 'artistic detachment' and 'passion' and censured his stylistic negligence.[35] In particular, Forster considered *The Bride of Lammermoor* 'a novel that professes to be lean and tragic'.[36] It is possible to argue that his criticism of Scott's ponderousness, or the sheer length of Scott's novel, is embodied by the novella-like succinctness of *Where Angels Fear to Tread*; we might also suggest that the novel's representation of the proximity of vitality and death, or the mutability of human life, is the method that Forster adopts to convey a sense of the tragic. I do not wish, however, to state over-emphatically that *Where Angels Fear to Tread*, written more than two decades before his Clark Lectures, was conceived by Forster as a purposeful response to Scott's work. Rather, my contention is that in writing the opera scene, Forster's first novel invites a tracing of its lineage back to Scott.

Scott is explicitly referred to in the opera scene: playing down Harriet's concern about the notoriety of foreign theatres, Philip says, 'But this is an opera – *Lucia di Lammermoor* – Sir Walter Scott – classical, you know'.[37] The familiarity of Scott's name results in Harriet's assenting to join Philip and Caroline at the opera. With the three dashes, Philip's persuasion is structured in a syntactically ambiguous way. The three consecutive nouns linked by the dashes signal parenthetical apposition and suggest equivalence, but the dash between '*Lucia di Lammermoor*' and 'Sir Walter Scott' can also be construed as signifying merely the close relationship between the two nouns. What is more ambiguous is the adjective 'classical'. Linked by another dash to the three nouns, it appears to describe the opera: the 1835 opera is 'classical', or nineteenth-century, rather than contemporary or modern. The adjective can also be ascribed to Scott's name: Scott is

---

[33] Woolf, *Essays*, III, p. 343.   [34] *AN*, pp. 20–21.   [35] *AN*, pp. 21–22.   [36] *AN*, p. 23.
[37] *WA*, p. 92.

84 E. M. Forster and Music

'classical', or canonical, in comparison to twentieth-century writers. In either case, though, Philip's persuasion is knowingly misleading: as Harriet grows confused and wonders 'what ha[s] become of Walter Scott', Philip's enjoyment of the opera suggests his awareness that Donizetti's adaptation and Scott's original novel are not equivalent.[38] He is being mischievous, luring Harriet to associate 'classical' with 'classic', or even 'classy', while savouring the very ambiguity of the adjective inwardly. Perhaps the author himself is having fun as well, using 'classical' in this ironic sense to jibe at the obsoleteness of the opera and Scott's work. The adjective becomes a euphemism for outdatedness, a grand banner under which past, 'canonical' artworks are gathered and enshrouded. The self-referential irony of 'classical' mischievously dispatches Scott and his works to the past while associating *Where Angels Fear to Tread* with the current and the new. To demarcate Scott's work in this way suggests Forster's resistance to, and indeed challenge of, Scott's popularity and continuing relevance to the early twentieth century.

The allusions to Flaubert and Scott thus indicate Forster's familiarity with the literary history surrounding *Lucia di Lammermoor*, on the one hand, and his concern with *his* own style, on the other. What we have seen is not just a young novelist preoccupied with the significance of nineteenth-century literary heritage but a self-conscious writer acutely alert to his contemporary artistic landscape, to past literary trends and movements, and to the cultural arena in which he had to distinguish himself from others. Forster was searching for a suitable writing style as early as 1901, when his failure to 'invent realism', to 'imagine others equally commonplace', led him to 'hav[ing] a try at imagination pure & simple'.[39] Whether or not Forster's works did completely rely on 'imagination' thenceforth, it is evident that, at the very beginning of his career as a novelist, he was attentive to, and evaluative of, the style and form of his fiction. The subversion of the Flaubertian source and the resistance to Scottian canonicity in the opera scene articulate an irreverence towards past, celebrated fictional conventions and existing narrative models. The opera scene, that is, encapsulates Forster's knowledge of the literary history of the opera and reflects his intention to distance his novel from that history. Here, it may be tempting to argue for a reading of *Where Angels*

[38] *WA*, p. 95. Forster noted the differences between the opera and the novel in his Aldeburgh Festival lecture in 1948, commenting that 'Donizetti's *Lucia di Lammermoor* owns only the mildest obligations to Sir Walter Scott'. 'George Crabbe and Peter Grimes' (1948), in *TCD*, pp. 166–80 (p. 177).

[39] Letter to Goldsworthy Lowes Dickinson (15 December 1901). *SL*, I, p. 51.

Fear to Tread as a modernist text – that the novel's strategy to differentiate itself stylistically from literary traditions suggests a conscious rupture and expresses a desire for something new. This could be an attractive line of argument for those in favour of sealing Forster's modernist credentials because it suggests that his debut novel is not merely a study of social conventions but an experiment with form, thus moving the date of Forster's modernist career backward from the 1920s to the Edwardian years. However, modernism, as a category, has been frequently contested by critics as being too narrowly defined to be sufficiently inclusive, on the one hand, and for being so broadened as to become vague, on the other.[40] When applied here, the term 'modernism' becomes a distraction, the deployment of which risks giving *Where Angels Fear to Tread* an unnecessary stylistic label and aligning it with a form of cultural iconoclasm to which it does not commit. What is more important, then, is not naming but simply recognizing Forster's attempt at stylistic differentiation. The opera scene as a pastiche contra the styles of Flaubert and Scott signals Forster's parodic responses to the past and his distinction from that past. Rather than a pure homage to their cultural status, his allusions to Flaubert and Scott mark a moment of departure from them, exploiting their stylistic characteristics for his own ends, a strategy allowing him to carve out his own place as a new published novelist.

This transaction with literary heritage may seem incongruous with Forster's famous proposal in *Aspects of the Novel* to 'visualize the English novelists . . . as seated together in a room, a circular room, a sort of British Museum reading-room – all writing their novels simultaneously'.[41] When writing, writers are 'half mesmerized', not thinking about history or 'reacting against' someone specific.[42] After all, he concludes, the novel expresses 'human nature'; unless there is a change in the ways 'individuals manage to look at themselves' and thus an alteration in human nature, 'History develops, art stands still'.[43] First, there is a possibility that Forster's own perception of novel writing changed, or developed, from a contextualized enterprise to an ahistorical creation. As we have seen, Forster's work has often been perceived as gradually approaching modernist aesthetics; it is suggested that his pre–First World War output forms a transition between nineteenth-century social realism and twentieth-

---

[40] Ann L. Ardis's analysis of the relations between literary modernism and English studies, and how Wyndham Lewis's 'men of 1914' represented only a specific type of literary and aesthetic ideology in a contested cultural arena, is particularly illuminating. Ann L. Ardis, *Modernism and Cultural Conflict, 1880–1922* (Cambridge, UK: Cambridge University Press, 2002), pp. 78–113.

[41] *AN*, p. 5.   [42] *AN*, p. 5.   [43] *AN*, pp. 117–18.

86 E. M. Forster and Music

century modernism, which eventually led up to his approach to, but never arrival at, modernist formal and stylistic experimentation.[44] While using such a perception may help to accommodate the contradictions between Forster's earlier and later works, it is also possible that Forster's concept of creativity separates matter from method, content from form – or, to put it bluntly, what a novelist tries to say from how the novel says it. His words in *Aspects* certainly conceptualize the general act of novel writing as a demonstration of individual creativity, but it does not necessarily mean that, in terms of localized representations, there is no intertextual or contextual engagement. Perhaps Forster is being disingenuous in *Aspects*, denying influence and connection, and thus celebrating a Romantic perception of artistic creation as imbued with inspiration. As he writes in the essay 'Anonymity: An Enquiry' (1925) in the same vein of thoughts as in *Aspects*, 'the lower personality' is important to creative work: 'unless a man dips a bucket down into it occasionally he cannot produce first-class work'.[45] Another possibility is that Forster's discussion of creativity in *Aspects* is to counter what he calls 'pseudo-scholarship' and its interest in excavating a writer's biographical details to interpret a work.[46] By proposing an ahistorical understanding of novel writing, Forster separates art from life and thwarts the identificatory strategy of biographical criticism.

More importantly, though, the focus of *Aspects of the Novel* is specifically on 'English fiction', a detail which critics rarely consider:

> Can we, while discussing English fiction, quite ignore fiction written in other languages, particularly French and Russian? As far as influence goes, we could ignore it, for our writers have never been much influenced by the continentals. .... My subject is a particular kind of book and the aspects that book has assumed in English. Can we ignore its collateral aspects on the Continent? Not entirely. An unpleasant and unpatriotic truth has here to be faced. ... English poetry fears no one – excels in quality as well as quantity. But English fiction is less triumphant: it does not contain the best stuff yet written, and if we deny this we become guilty of provincialism.[47]

Forster's claim about the immunity of English novelists from Continental influence is coherent with his perception of novel writing as an ahistorical, independent occupation, but if we read it ironically, it becomes a satire on English fiction as isolated from and ignorant of parallel developments of its Continental counterparts. Is there a jibe at the insularity of English writers in the analogy of their writing simultaneously in the British Museum

---

[44] Such a view is explicit in Randall Stevenson's account of Forster's modernism.
[45] *TCD*, pp. 77–86 (pp. 82–83). [46] *AN*, p. 6. [47] *AN*, pp. 3–4.

From Literary Heritage to National Character 87

reading room? While 'provincialism', Forster goes on to explain, can be 'the chief source of [a novelist's] strength', as in Defoe's or Hardy's case, it is 'a serious fault' in criticism, against which Forster levels an accusation of wrongly regarding 'too many little mansions in English fiction ... as important edifices'.[48] *Aspects of the Novel*, as a whole, redresses this misjudgement: it is decisively not provincial; especially towards the later sections of the book, more and more Continental writers and their works are discussed in opposition to those who write in English (Dostoevsky as opposed to George Eliot in 'Prophecy'; Proust and Tolstoy in 'Rhythm' as opposed to Henry James in 'Pattern') to highlight the direction English novel writing may take and benefit from. His is therefore an informed exploration of the English novel as one particular strand of novel writing in Europe, acknowledging the importance of Continental exemplars and learning from them. Culturally, Forster's perception of England as part of Europe is evident. In a 1907 lecture 'Pessimism in Literature', Forster observed that 'One might compare Europe to a ship and England to a little boat, tugged in its wake. It is a very splendid little boat, but it does not come first'.[49] The opera scene's subversion of its Flaubertian source is a product of this widened purview of literary heritage; its playful appropriation of the Continental model is also a strategy to galvanize English fiction into innovation and variation. Forster's critical inheritance of the legacies of his literary predecessors should thus be viewed as intrinsically related to his nationality, and his parodic use of literary allusions, as I shall discuss, is interlinked with his concern with the issue of national character.

National Character

As Cormac Newark suggests, an opera outing in the novel often 'signal[s] narrative potential'.[50] In *Where Angels Fear to Tread*, the *Lucia* scene plays a crucial part in the unfolding of the plot. Although the narrator says, 'So this strenuous day of resolutions, plans, alarms, battles, victories, defeats, truces, ended at the opera', Forster's irony lies in that, instead of ending the eventfulness of the day, the opera scene sets future and imminent events in motion and even precipitates them.[51] The opera performance itself is punctuated with various incidents in the auditorium, culminating in the unexpected and, as we have seen, implicitly homoerotic reunion of Gino and Philip. On the one hand, this brings Philip a rosy illusion of

---

[48] *AN*, p. 4.   [49] 'Pessimism in Literature' (1907), in *AE*, pp. 129–45 (p. 132).
[50] Newark, *Opera in the Novel from Balzac to Proust*, p. 5.   [51] *WA*, p. 92.

88   E. M. Forster and Music

Gino and of Italy; on the other, the sight of the two men together
convinces Caroline that Philip alone cannot complete the task of 'rescuing'
the baby so she pays a secret visit to Gino the next morning. Her visit is the
starting point of a day where one thing leads to another, and an encounter
between any two of the characters further accelerates action: Caroline's
inability to find Gino at first, her fright after Gino's entrance, and her
observation of Gino bathing the baby are followed by Philip's visit, the two
men's short but cordial interaction, Harriet's abduction of the baby, the
Herritons' rash departure, the carriage accident, and the baby's death.
Gino's mourning, the two men's fight, and their subsequent reconciliation
via the mediation of Caroline conclude the day. The 'torrents of music'
that cause Caroline's insomnia after the opera performance seem also to
have released a narratological energy that drives forward the plot.[52]

The tragedy, death, and violence of these post-opera events are contrasted sharply with the comedy, liveliness, and friendliness at the opera.[53]
There, the exuberance of the atmosphere is characterized as specifically
'Italian'. The Italian listeners, as the narrator describes, attend to the music
'with tappings and drummings, swaying in the melody like corn in the
wind'; they 'hailed their brothers and sons in the chorus, and told them
how well they were singing'.[54] When Lucia sings, the audience 'murmured
like a hive of happy bees. All through the coloratura she was accompanied
by sighs, and its top note was drowned in a shout of universal joy'.[55] As the
opera unfolds, 'Violent waves of excitement, all arising from very little,
went sweeping round the theatre'.[56] The audience becomes riotous during
Lucia's mad scene: 'Now the noise became tremendous'.[57] When the
singer temporarily steps out of her character and flirts with young male
admirers while receiving applause, 'The house exploded', the narrator
reports.[58]

This portrayal of a relaxed, passionate, susceptible, noisy, even unruly,
local audience reiterates the idiosyncrasies of Italian musical traits. Previous
interpretations such as Alan Wilde's reading of the opera scene as 'Forster's
Italy at its best' and Suzanne Roszak's critique of Forster's 'inadvertently
patronizing' depiction of the Italian audience as 'unabashedly coarse'
overlook how Forster works prevalent stereotypes about Italian musical

---

[52] *WA*, p. 99.
[53] Richard Keller Simon describes the contrast as a 'moment of comic celebration' versus a 'moment of
melodramatic crisis'. Richard Keller Simon, 'E. M. Forster's Critique of Laughter and the Comic:
The First Three Novels as Dialectic', *Twentieth-Century Literature*, 31.2–3 (1985), 199–220 (pp.
204–5).
[54] *WA*, p. 94.   [55] *WA*, p. 95.   [56] *WA*, p. 95.   [57] *WA*, p. 96.   [58] *WA*, p. 96.

From Literary Heritage to National Character 89

sensibility into his text.[59] That is, the novel's 'Italian' audience recalls and echoes a long history of a variety of commentaries on Italian intoxication with music, especially with opera. Baedeker's 1900 edition of *Central Italy*, which Forster was likely to have been using while travelling around Italy in the early years of the twentieth century, cautioned British tourists that Italians 'seldom observe strict silence during the performance of the music'.[60] In a pseudo-official tone, Baedeker repeated a view widely publicized and accepted since the age of the Grand Tour: for a British tourist, to attend a performance in Italy was to be surrounded by noisy Italian people.[61] Hector Berlioz, once escaping from a house of clamorous Italian operagoers himself, attributed such a characteristic to Italians' imperviousness to 'the evocative, poetic side of music, as well as to any conception at all lofty and out of the common run'.[62] Italians, as Berlioz declared, enjoyed music 'solely for its physical effect' and treated music as nothing but 'a sensual pleasure'.[63] Compared to German listeners' interest in complex orchestration and well-designed harmony, Italian audiences showed an 'exclusive appetite for everything that dances and is gay and brilliant'.[64] In this regard, Italians were 'devoid of [the] faculty which to others makes the expressive variety of music'.[65] For Berlioz, there was no hope for improvement, partly because Italian composers continued to produce works that catered to Italian public taste, partly because such a distinct Italian musical trait was 'a natural and immutable consequence of the national physiology'.[66]

Berlioz's juxtaposition of Italian musical traits with those of the German national character was typical of nineteenth-century European commentaries on the differences between Northern and Southern musical cultures. As Emma Sutton has observed, the dichotomy of 'the Northern' and 'the Southern', of the sophisticated and cerebral 'playing North' and the spontaneous and visceral 'singing South', was prevalent in a variety of late nineteenth-century discourses on music; contemporary British writers, artists, and musicians employed, and sometimes parodied and critiqued,

---

[59] Alan Wilde, *Art and Order: A Study of E. M. Forster* (London: Peter Owen, 1965), p. 19. Suzanne Roszak, 'Social Non-Conformists in Forster's Italy: Otherness and the Enlightened English Tourist', *Ariel: A Review of International English Literature*, 45.1–2 (2014), 167–94 (pp. 188 and 187).

[60] Baedeker, *Central Italy*, p. xxiv.

[61] Jeremy Black, *Italy and the Grand Tour* (New Haven: Yale University Press, 2003), pp. 175–77.

[62] Hector Berlioz, *The Memoirs of Hector Berlioz*, ed. and trans. David Cairns (London: Victor Gollancz, 1969), p. 209.

[63] Berlioz, *Memoirs*, p. 209.   [64] Berlioz, *Memoirs*, p. 210.   [65] Berlioz, *Memoirs*, p. 210.

[66] Berlioz, *Memoirs*, p. 209.

E. M. Forster and Music

this dichotomy to define their own aesthetic leanings.[67] In *Where Angels Fear to Tread*, the cliché of the 'singing South' is best exemplified by the narrator's description of Gino's singing in the morning after the opera: 'The voice of [Caroline's] adversary was heard at last, singing fearlessly from his expanded lungs, like a professional. Herein he differed from Englishmen, who always have a little feeling against music, and sing only from the throat, apologetically'.[68] While critics often assume Gino to be singing from Donizetti's *Lucia* and emphasize the opera's lingering effect,[69] it is evident how the narrator relies on the stereotype of the 'singing South' to satirize the English's lack of musicality. Additionally, in the novel, the contrast between German and Italian musical characteristics is often filtered through a British – English, more accurately – perspective: 'Italians don't love music silently, like the beastly Germans', Philip tells Caroline before the opera.[70] The stereotype of noisy Italian listeners is juxtaposed with that of their serious, or uptight, German counterparts, a British cliché, too, in contemporary perceptions of German audiences. The widely acknowledged German musical supremacy was accompanied by perceptions of the seriousness, or the discipline, of German musical engagement. The adjective 'beastly' is indicative of Philip's preference for the 'Italian' manner: the animalistic connotation of the adjective marks 'the Germans' as brutish and unnatural, which, in contrast, suggests that he views Italians' noise during musical performances as a natural human reaction.

'The Germans', here and throughout the novel, are repeatedly referenced in a negative way. Gino's close friend, Spiridone, for example, mentions that a German smuggler was trying to bribe everyone in the custom house: 'Non era simpatico', he concludes.[71] Germans are represented as fastidious ('A German lady ... had given [a local girl] one [half penny] that very spring'), pedantic ('German research having decisively proved' that Giotto did not come to Monteriano), and ungraceful (Gino 'would take down his felt hat, strike it in the right place as infallibly as a German strikes his in the wrong place').[72] If these references suggest that the novel reflected the contemporary permeation of German stereotypes in England, it also reflected on them. For example, the characterization of Lilia is consistently associated with, but also defined against, 'the

---

[67] Sutton, *Aubrey Beardsley*, pp. 186–88. See also Emma Sutton, '"English Enthusiasts": Vernon Lee and Italian Opera', in *Exiles, Emigrés and Intermediaries: Anglo-Italian Cultural Transactions*, ed. Barbara Schaff (Amsterdam: Rodopi, 2010), pp. 375–402.

[68] *WA*, p. 101.   [69] For example, Goscilo, 'Forster's Italian Comedies', pp. 197–98.

[70] *WA*, p. 90.   [71] *WA*, p. 39.   [72] *WA*, pp. 83, 80, and 48.

From Literary Heritage to National Character 91

Germans'. As the narrator informs us, if Gino stands for 'the Latin man', Lilia represents 'the northern woman', and the conflict between the two is not only a clash of 'personalities' but also a 'struggle' of 'national' differences.[73] The personal encounter of the Italian youth and the English widow is thus elevated to an international level. Yet if Lilia's blond hair manifests her northernness, she is also often portrayed as an incomplete embodiment of 'German' qualities. The reception room where her piano is placed, for example, is devalued as insufficiently German: 'adorned with horsehair chairs, woolwork stools, and a stove that is never lit – German bad taste without German domesticity broods over that room'.[74] During Spiridone's visit, moreover, 'she played on the humming piano, very badly, and he sang, not so badly. Gino got out a guitar and sang too, sitting out on the loggia'.[75] Whilst this brief description alludes once again to the musical dichotomy of 'the Northern' and 'the Southern', Lilia's unaccomplished piano skill becomes an inferior version of Austro-German instrumental competence. On the one hand, the emphases on Lilia as not quite 'German' can be tied in with the novel's overall critique of the English middle class as culturally mundane and uninformed. On the other hand, they evoke the caricature of 'the English' as a bad parody of popular notions of German efficiency and progression. Given the mocking tone, Forster's description of Lilia's distinction from standard Germanness expresses not so much concern with the backwardness of English society in comparison to its German counterpart, a topical subject in contemporary discussions, as a jibe at these English obsessions with Germany as a symbol of foreign modernity.

That the novel repeatedly alludes to the German national character in its delineation of Italianness suggests that, if there was a spectrum between 'the Germans' and 'the Italians' at the time, 'the English' were placed closer to the German end. As Petra Rau suggests, 'writing about Germany' in the first half of the twentieth century 'was often a way of thinking about the condition of England': '[i]mages of German national identity are often uncertain projections of desired otherness to Englishness, projections that insist on alterity and myth in order to confirm a distinct difference between two nations strangely familiar with each other'.[76] Part of Philip's confidence in his knowledge of different national idiosyncrasies stems from his belief that he, instead of repeating popular notions about

---

[73] *WA*, pp. 50.   [74] *WA*, p. 31.   [75] *WA*, p. 42.
[76] Petra Rau, *English Modernism, National Identity and the Germans, 1890–1950* (Farnham: Ashgate, 2009), p. 10.

92 E. M. Forster and Music

Italy or Germany, grasps the nuances of the triangulated comparison of the English, the German, and the Italian character. For example, in his observation of the décor of the opera theatre:

> So rich and so appalling was the effect that Philip could scarcely suppress a cry. There is something majestic in the bad taste of Italy; it is not the bad taste of a country which knows no better; it has not the nervous vulgarity of England, or the blinded vulgarity of Germany. It observes beauty, and chooses to pass it by. But it attains to beauty's confidence.[77]

Philip's reliance on using 'the Germans' to highlight the unique foreignness – foreign for the English – of 'the Italians' is not different from the narrator's, but, by delving into the gradations between the three versions of 'bad taste', he perceives himself as sophisticated and insightful. Not completely resisting widely circulated stereotypes, Philip presents himself as a knowledgeable and perceptive outsider by being able to give an overview of and find faults with the three national characters. For him, his Italophilia is a result of an impartial survey that has not only admired 'the Italians', but also observed their foibles – hence a sense of superiority and a distancing of himself from English parochialism.

However, as James Buzard has noted, 'For all that he figures himself a "traveller" in touch with the people, not just the tourist attractions, of his favoured land, Philip clings to a shop-worn set of stereotypes about the Italians, whom he prefers to imagine in romantic and picturesque postures rather than in prosaic modern circumstances'.[78] Philip's Italophilia is likely to be informed by Lord Byron's portrayal of the country. Byron's *Childe Harold's Pilgrimage* (1812–18) is in the Herritons' family library: in chapter 1, after receiving the news about Lilia's engagement in Monteriano, Mrs Herriton 'looked up the place in *Childe Harold*, but Byron had not been there'.[79] As Barbara Schaff suggests, the nineteenth- and early twentieth-century English reception of Byron was influenced by, and intertwined with, that of Italy: while Byron's writing about Italy in his literary work and in his letters augmented his appeal to English readers and increased his popularity at home, Italy was Byronized and perceived as doubly exotic.[80] Contemporary tourism was quick in exploiting this link

---

[77] *WA*, p. 93.

[78] James Buzard, *The Beaten Track: European Tourism, Literature, and the Ways to Culture, 1800–1918* (Oxford: Oxford University Press, 1993), p. 310.

[79] *WA*, p. 11

[80] Barbara Schaff, 'Italianised Byron – Byronised Italy', in *Performing National Identity: Anglo-Italian Cultural Transactions*, ed. Manfred Pfister and Ralf Hertel (Amsterdam: Rodopi, 2008), pp. 103–21.

From Literary Heritage to National Character 93

between Byron and Italy. In another article, Barbara Schaff notes that, in the case of John Murray's *Handbooks to Italy*, Byron's texts were liberally incorporated into tips for tourists, which 'not only provided . . . cultured, elitist, anti-touristic gestures in the emerging age of mass tourism . . . but also appropriated, familiarised and marketed Italy as a product of English Romanticism'.[81] For Philip, his belief that 'Italy really purifies and ennobles all who visit her' echoes Bryon's description of Italy as 'Mother of Arts' whose 'hand / Was then our guardian, and is still our guide'.[82] Yet the echo was by no means idiosyncratic but a view that had been popularized – and thus made portable and conventional – by the dissemination of guidebooks for English tourists in the nineteenth century.

If Byron's work shapes Philip's Italophilia, Mark Twain's *A Tramp Abroad* (1880) – another book Mrs Herriton consults in the family library ('Nor did Mark Twain visit [Monteriano] in the *Tramp Abroad*') – is likely to have informed Philip's comment on German concert behaviour.[83] In Twain's novel, the American 'tramp' attends a performance of Wagner's *Lohengrin* in Germany, during which his reaction to the opera in the midst of German serious appreciation of the music produces the humour. As Emma Sutton suggests, the *Lohengrin* performance is represented as 'a microcosm of national traits and political relations', as a site where 'the national and racial self-image of the Anglo-American commentator is inherently vulnerable to the "foreign" qualities aroused by Wagner's late-Romantic affective music'.[84] Opposite this Anglo-American identity is the construction of 'the Germans': German psychological, aesthetic, and military traits are manifested in the tramp's depiction of the German audience around him.[85] The possibility that Philip has read Twain's novel augments the intertextuality of his description of German listeners as 'beastly': his use of the adjective can be read as alluding to the unnatural silence of the musically spellbound German audience Twain's tramp observed, or to their 'hurricanes of applause' under the influence of Wagner's music, or to their unreserved support for singers who have long

---

[81] Barbara Schaff, 'John Murray's *Handbooks to Italy*: Making Tourism Literary', in *Literary Tourism and Nineteenth-Century Culture*, ed. Nicola J. Watson (Basingstoke: Palgrave Macmillan, 2009), pp. 106–18 (p. 106).

[82] George Gordon Byron, *Childe Harold's Pilgrimage*, in *Byron: Poetical Works*, ed. Frederick Page (Oxford: Oxford University Press, 1970), Canto IV, XLVII, p. 233.

[83] *WA*, p. 11.

[84] Emma Sutton, 'Foreign Bodies: Mark Twain, Music and Anglo-American Identity', *Symbiosis*, 8.1 (2004), 109–19 (pp. 112 and 116).

[85] Sutton, 'Foreign Bodies', pp. 111–12.

94   E. M. Forster and Music

lost their once-renowned voice.[86] However, if there is allusion, the contrast between Philip's one-word critique of German musical characteristics and the tramp's pages-long clueless observation also suggests differentiation. The very succinctness of Philip's verdict on German listeners dissociates him from the tramp's artistic innocence, or ignorance. In this respect, Philip's oblique allusion to *A Tramp Abroad* evokes the cliché about American cultural vulgarity as a means of asserting his own sophisticated and superior musical sensibility. This contrast with 'the American' also demonstrates that Forster's description of the opera scene encapsulates a 'dialogue' between multinational musical stereotypes and presents a wider scope than its European setting.

That the novel touches on non-European national identity is further evidenced by an unobtrusive, so far undiscussed reference to music after the opera scene. When Caroline visits Gino the next day, she finds an empty room – the reception room 'sacred to the dead [Lilia]': 'A coon song lay open on the piano, and of the two tables one supported Baedeker's *Central Italy*, the other Harriet's inlaid box. And over everything there lay a deposit of heavy white dust, which was only blown off one memento to thicken on another'.[87] Whilst the Baedeker recalls Lilia's original role as a tourist who travels to Italy for 'a change of scene', Harriet's inlaid box reminds us of Lilia's tie to the Herritons, and to Harriet specifically, whose stiff patriotism provides much of the humour of the novel.[88] The most striking object here is the 'coon song'.[89] Extremely popular in America and in Britain in the late nineteenth and early twentieth centuries, coon songs, often sung by female 'coon shouters' in blackface performances, were a staple routine in contemporary theatre and music hall programmes. Borrowing ragtime elements of syncopation and anticipating American jazz, coon songs explored, exaggerated, and exploited every conceivable black characteristic; the lyrics of coon songs frequently incorporated, for comic use, imagined dialects and accents of African Americans, and delivered derogatory clichés of black people as ignorant, lazy, and promiscuous.[90] Explicitly racist, Lilia's songbook implies her unrefined taste and

---

[86] Mark Twain, *A Tramp Abroad* (New York: Penguin, 1997), p. 49.   [87] *WA*, p. 100.

[88] *WA*, p. 6.

[89] Carole Slade is the only critic to my knowledge who has noticed this passage, but she only discusses briefly the significance of the Baedeker and the inlaid box and does not comment on the reference to the 'coon song'. Carole Slade, 'E. M. Forster's Piano Players', *University of Windsor Review*, 14.2 (1979), 5–11 (pp. 8–9).

[90] Brandi A. Neal, 'Coon Song', *Grove Music Online*, www.oxfordmusiconline.com [accessed 10 May 2018]. For a detailed study of the 'coon song craze' in America between 1890 and 1910, see James

From Literary Heritage to National Character 95

artistic vulgarity, associating her with colonial power and highlighting her whiteness. Yet her interest in coon songs can also be a deliberate act, a way of defying the middle-class Herritons and the cluster of social and cultural values they have advocated. This is not to say that the Herritons are informed enough to reflect on the racism of coon songs. In fact, given the popularity of coon songs in early twentieth-century Britain, it would have been likely that the Herritons mingled with patrons from other social classes at a coon song performance. In interpreting Lilia's songbook as her resistance to middle-class conventions of English suburbia, I read the reference in relation to Philip and the others' attendance at Donizetti's opera. That is, Lilia's selection of an overtly 'low' musical entertainment contrasts sharply with the seemingly 'high' culture with which the rest of the Herritons are associated.

Like the harmonium in *A Passage to India*, Lilia's songbook, as well as the Baedeker and the inlaid box, are not indigenous but imported. Together, they present a suggestive tableau of the parallel between touristic and colonial consumption. The acquisitive nature of tourism – whether it is a souvenir, memory, or knowledge that a tourist is looking for – is a catalyst for the transformation of a tourist's destination, voluntary or involuntary; the more tourists there are, the more dependent on tourism a place becomes, and the more willingly locals adapt themselves to meet the expectations of tourists. The invasive influence of tourism on a place is specifically thematized in one of Forster's short stories, 'The Eternal Moment' (*c.* 1904), which, like *Where Angels Fear to Tread*, unfolds its plot around English, Italian, and German relations. In the story, Miss Raby, returning to the Italian town which inspired her first novel and which became popular among foreign tourists because of her novel, discovers that tourism has changed the town drastically: 'The whole population was employed, even down to the little girls'; 'Vorta had taken to the tourist trade'.[91] Tourism is, in the story's narrator's words, '[a] vast machinery' or, as James Buzard comments, '*systematic*' as 'each single tourist's or anti-tourist's failure to bridge the gap between intention and result' compounds the exploitation and misunderstanding of a place.[92] This portrayal of tourism in the short story exposes the industry's similarities with colonialism – a connection, I suggest, also reflected by the proximity of the coon song and the Baedeker. On the one side is the

---

H. Dormon, 'Shaping the Popular Image of Post-Reconstruction American Blacks: The "Coon Song" Phenomenon of the Gilded Age', *American Quarterly*, 40.4 (1988), 450–71.
[91] *MS*, p. 169. [92] *MS*, p. 174. Buzard, *Beaten Track*, p. 307.

96 E. M. Forster and Music

songbook, providing entertainment in the form of caricaturing and appropriating African American identity. On the other side is the Baedeker,
which, as its preface indicates, aims 'to aid [a tourist] in *deriving* enjoyment
and instruction from his tour in one of the most fascinating countries in
the world'.[93] Both are closely related to, as well as augmented by, imperial
expansion and colonial domination. The consumption of Italy within
British tourism is thus paralleled with that of African American culture
within the composition, performance, and dissemination of coon songs.

The tableau of the songbook together with the Baedeker was also
reflective of a centuries-long perception in Europe of 'the Italians' as a
different 'race'. Since the fifteenth century, 'the Italians' had been frequently associated with Africa, sometimes even physically portrayed as
Africanized; given the intermediate geography of the Italian Peninsula
between Europe and Africa, Italy was viewed by Western and Northern
Europeans not only as a location of classical antiquity but also as the
vestibule to the 'dark' exotic.[94] In *Where Angels Fear to Tread*, the narrator
and the characters are both symptomatic of this tendency to 'darken'
Italians. It is best exemplified by the skin colour of Lilia's baby with
Gino, as Gino exclaims: 'Who would have believed his mother was
blonde? For he is brown all over – brown every inch of him'.[95] This
hybrid brownness suggests a perception of 'the Italians' as black and
underscores the affinity between Italy and Africa. Forster's juxtaposition
of the songbook and the Baedeker further de-Europeanizes 'the Italians'
and associates the 'Italian' race with American blacks. Tellingly, in the
novel's manuscripts, Donizetti's opera is also described, through Philip's
free indirect speech, as 'the finest rag in the world'.[96] Among the multiple
definitions of the word 'rag', Forster's use of the term, given that it
describes the opera, is likely to refer to ragtime music. Perhaps its eventual
deletion suggests that Forster found it too mischievous a derision of
Donizetti's opera. This association of Italian opera with African
American music nonetheless 'darkens' Italian musical culture and characterizes 'the Italians' as racially foreign to the novel's English characters, and
to Western and Northern Europeans more broadly.

---

[93] Baedeker, *Central Italy*, p. v. My emphasis.
[94] As Nelson Moe notes, the *Mezzogiorno* (Southern Italy), in particular, became the object of exotic
fetishism. The cultural geography of the area was simultaneously represented as '"Africa" and *terra
vergine*, a reservoir of feudal residues, sloth, and squalor on the one hand and of quaint peasants,
rustic traditions, and exotica on the other'. Nelson Moe, *The View from Vesuvius: Italian Culture
and the Southern Question* (Berkeley: University of California Press, 2002), p. 3.
[95] WA, p. 111.   [96] WA, p. 165.

From Literary Heritage to National Character   97

Yet the novel's construction of 'the Italians' becomes unstable if we take account of the blackface convention in the performance of coon songs. Symbolically, a coon song on stage implies a knowing cultivation of the disjunction between appearance and content, which provides much of the performance's humour and caricature. However different Donizetti's *Lucia* and a coon song may be in terms of genre and reception, the textual proximity of the opera scene and the coon song reference in *Where Angels Fear to Tread* alerts us to the fact that Donizetti's opera similarly relies on a constructed spectacle of foreignness. This is evident in the description of the opera's opening scene: 'Harriet, meanwhile, had been coughing ominously at the drop-scene, which presently rose on the grounds of Ravenswood, and the chorus of Scotch retainers burst into cry'.[97] Just as a coon song, both in its lyrics and its performance, exploits the imagined characteristics of African Americans, the operatic adaptation of Scott's novel packages and consumes an imagined Scottish identity on stage.[98] Both involve geographical transmission and reflect concurrent imperial and colonial relations. These parallels not only highlight the consumption of otherness in the name of art and entertainment but also expose the nationalization of an appropriated foreign culture. The authenticity of the opera's manifestation of 'Italian' characteristics is being undermined.

The reference to the coon song also prompts us to contemplate the performative quality of the exuberance of the Italian audience at the opera, which is at odds with the opera's tragic content.[99] Berlioz, who perceived Italian music as 'always laughing', noted 'the admirable pathos' of Donizetti's *Lucia* to suggest that there existed another type of Italian music that 'sighs and wails' and 'goes [to] the other extreme'.[100] In the novel, the enthusiasm of the local audiences, recognized by Philip as quintessentially Italian, comes primarily from their familiarity with the conventions of the performance routine of the opera company. The 'clothes-horse' over which Lucia performs her aria, for example, is described as 'very ugly'; even

---

[97] *WA*, p. 94.

[98] Continental and English composers' interest in Scotland and construction of 'the Scottish' has a long tradition which can be traced back to the textualization and distribution of Scotch songs. While James Macpherson's 'translation' of the Ossian poems and Scott's *Waverley* novels both created high enthusiasm for Scottish legacies, the appeal decreased after improved transportation boosted Scottish tourism. The romance, then, died down once direct contact was made possible. See Roger Fiske, *Scotland in Music: A European Enthusiasm* (Cambridge, UK: Cambridge University Press, 1983).

[99] For a discussion of the style and innovation of Donizetti's *opera seria*, see Winton Dean, *Essays on Opera* (Oxford: Clarendon, 1990), pp. 187–203.

[100] Berlioz, *Memoirs*, p. 210.

98   E. M. Forster and Music

though 'most of the flowers in it were false', 'Lucia knew this, and so did
the audience; and they all knew that the clothes-horse was a piece of stage
property, brought in to make the performance go year after year'.[101] This
detail indicates that to perceive the audience's ebullient responses to the
opera as a reliable demonstration of the Italian national character is to
mistake particularity for commonality and to generalize about Italianness.
It brings us to note that, behind all the comedy and satire produced by the
national stereotypes we have seen, there is an awareness in the novel that
the very act of stereotyping and generalizing about a nation is problematic.
From this perspective, Alexandra Peat's reading of the opera scene as 'a rare
example of cultural translation and rapprochement' too readily implies that
the various national characteristics are authentic and stable markers of the
nationalities involved.[102] Forster's emphasis here, I suggest, is not on how
the opera provides a successful occasion for English–Italian communication, but on the illusion of capturing a nation's characteristics and the
inadequacy of applying such an illusion to actual personal relationships. By
deducing national character based on incidental musical traits while hint-
ing at the faults and limitations of such deduction, the opera scene calls
into question the convenience of generalization.

Generalization, Forster said elsewhere, should always be used 'cautiously'. In 1913, he read a paper, 'The English Character', to a group of
Indian students at Cambridge.[103] 'Having little knowledge of politics and
none of Economics or Science', Forster proposed 'psychology' as his main
subject, to which his – a novelist's – observation on English people might
be able to contribute.[104] What he wished to offer was 'in no sense a
lecture', but 'an information [sic] collection of notes':

> We are approaching the same subject though from different points of view.
> We are alike students of the English Character. What I have to say may help
> you, and what you say will certainly help me. Some people think that
> discussions of this sort are useless, because they must consist of generaliza-
> tions and one cannot generalize about a whole nation. I do not quite agree.
> Within limits one can. The generalization must be applied cautiously no

---

[101] WA, p. 95.

[102] Alexandra Peat, Travel and Modernist Literature: Sacred and Ethical Journeys (New York:
Routledge, 2011), p. 84.

[103] This is an early draft of 'Notes on the English Character' (1926), an article much better known
among Forster scholars nowadays, from which Forster's famous criticism of public-school spirit
and English insensitivity has been frequently quoted. Interestingly, Forster cut out the paper's
opening (quoted in length here) when he revised this 1913 paper into 'Notes on the
English Character'.

[104] 'The English Character' (1913), in AH, pp. 404–9 (p. 404).

From Literary Heritage to National Character 99

doubt. There are plenty of individuals whom it won't fit, and it will not exactly fit anyone. But it is better than nothing. It gives one a start.[105]

Forster's understanding of national character as a discursive subject is echoed by Peter Mandler's recent argument that the history of national character is characterized by its inconsistency and fluidity. As Mandler suggests, ideas of national character are contingent on and reflective of their specific contexts; discourses on national character are shaped to compete against other expressions and ideologies, and are modulated when time and place change.[106] In the preceding passage, Forster's modesty or caution reflects his alertness to the protean nature of national character, to the availability of multifarious approaches to the subject, and to the impossibility of defining – in his case – the English character. Yet his modest tone becomes more assertive when it comes to the ineluctability of generalization in discussing national character. As Perry Anderson observed in the early 1990s, such generalization, 'in principle so indefensible, yet in practice so unavoidable', causes the transition of critical focus from character to identity within studies of national politics.[107] This methodological weakness, however, is here described by Forster as a strength. If there is compromise in Forster's tentative approval of generalization, it results from having explored the individual enmeshed in but eager to communicate with the minutiae of the international world.

Like his allusions to Flaubert and Scott, Forster's allusions to Byron and Twain specifically, and to musical stereotypes about various nations more generally, are subversive in nature. Instead of simply subscribing to and imitating the popular conflation of musical and national characteristics of his time, Forster is parodying the popularity of stereotyping a nation's character according to its musical traits and sensibilities. In so doing, he offers a less defined picture of international encounter in *Where Angels Fear to Tread* than it first seems; the novel purposefully draws attention to its presentation of national contrasts, but the unfolding of its plot consistently resists being contained within or being explained away by such contrasts. What emerges from the opera scene is not an outright dismissal of but a cautious attitude towards national character.

---

[105] *AH*, pp. 404–5.
[106] Peter Mandler, *The English National Character: The History of an Idea from Edmund Burke to Tony Blair* (New Haven: Yale University Press, 2006), pp. 2–7.
[107] Perry Anderson, 'Nation-States and National Identity', *London Review of Books*, 9 May 1991, 3–8 (p. 6).

There is a sustained narrative to be made regarding Forster's conception of creation as differentiation at the beginning of his career. Explicitly acknowledging its literary heritage, *Where Angels Fear to Tread* expresses a confidence in writing after others as well as against others, as if coming after Scott, Donizetti, Byron, Flaubert, Berlioz, Twain, and many others, whether reputed or forgotten, emboldened him to take advantage of the material available to him. Such confidence also runs through his destabilization of national character, playing with musical stereotypes and exposing their superficiality. New to English novel writing, Forster's creativity as a debut novelist seems to have burgeoned around his parodic allusions to the cultural past he has inherited. If there is confidence, there is also wariness. As the opera scene reflects the connection between Forster's stylistic and ideological concerns, it illuminates his resistance to English insularity. Writing in the first decade of the twentieth century, Forster saw opportunities to write differently and was eager to make his work different, presenting his first novel as a version of international encounters distinct from those in the past.

***

In 'Sunday Music', an article Forster wrote in Egypt in 1917, he revisited the role of music in thinking about national character. It was another noisy occasion, where children of different nationalities chased after each other, adults read or chatted, and even sparrows chattered more vivaciously than usual: 'do not expect to hear', Forster said, 'Sunday music at San Stefano [a casino] is for the eye'.[108] The experience ended with a farce: the audience did not immediately realize that the music was 'only traversing a soft passage' in the middle of their applause.[109]

There are many parallels in Forster's description of the multinational gathering with that of the audience in the opera scene in *Where Angels Fear to Tread*. The noise and the visual enjoyment of music allude to the stereotypes about Mediterranean vivacity and vitality. Similarly, this vivid delineation of the 'Mediterranean' quality is juxtaposed with an invocation of Germanic characteristics. The details of the concert in Alexandria are compared to those of an opera performance Forster attended in Munich in 1905:

> Up in the Sanctuary if you think of that building as a church ... sat the band from the Kaiser's Imperial Yacht, performing with sailory precision

---

[108] 'Sunday Music' (1917), in *PT*, pp. 184–87 (p. 184).   [109] *PT*, p. 186.

From Literary Heritage to National Character 101

the Fire Music from *The Valkyrie*, and down in the auditorium sat squadron after squadron of awe-struck Germans, masticating silently, and among them sat I.[110]

The passage alludes to the seriousness of the German (musical) character, the cliché of German musical disposition, and the instrumental fineness of Austro-German traditions. As the explicitly military vocabulary indicates, they are immediately associated with German militarism and aggression. Forster recalled how he accidentally made a slight noise during the Munich performance: 'I might as well have dropped a bomb. Hisses broke out, scowls, exclamations of horror and rage. I had insulted Germany's Kaiser, her Navy, and her Art'.[111] Forster's satire cuts through all the German stereotypes encapsulated in this brief sentence; the 'bomb' is an imagined retaliation to the present German attacks in the First World War. His declaration that 'It is better to be inattentive with Latins and Levantines than to attend with Teutons' recalls Philip's Italophilia.[112] Here, the contrast between 'the Northern' and 'the Southern', between puritanical seriousness and epicurean spontaneity, is once again brought into play. Yet, like the other Egyptian articles we have discussed, 'Sunday Music' is also written in a scathingly ironic tone and prompts us to wonder how sincere Forster is. It seems that his preference for Mediterranean inattentiveness over Teutonic attentiveness is less an issue of making a musical judgement than of attacking German imperial expansion.

Most importantly, the music here is Wagner's. The work of Wagner was repeatedly linked to German military expansion in the late nineteenth and early twentieth centuries, and this link would become poignantly clear during the First World War.[113] Earlier in the war, Forster commented on the futility of banning German music: 'we at the outbreak of war tried to banish Beethoven and Wagner from our concert halls. We could do that, but we could not stop them from playing inside our heads whenever some chance sound reawoke their immortality'.[114] Whether linked satirically to German militarism or associated with the contest of cultural freedom back in Britain, Wagner was an important point of reference in Forster's commentary on music and nationality during the First World War. Yet this highly politicized status

---

[110] *PT*, p. 184.   [111] *PT*, pp. 184–85.   [112] *PT*, pp. 185.
[113] Sutton, *Aubrey Beardsley*, pp. 162–63.
[114] 'The Functions of Literature in War-Time' (1915), in *AE*, pp. 176–83 (p. 182).

of Wagner would only be made more problematic by the emergence of Nazism in the following decades. As the next chapter will discuss, at the outbreak of the Second World War, Wagner and his work became a thorny subject that Forster could not simply choose either to criticize or to advocate.

CHAPTER 4

The Problem of the Wagnerian Hero

I resent the power of Percival intensely[.]

Virginia Woolf, *The Waves*[1]

On 10 September 1940, Forster published *Nordic Twilight*, a pamphlet defending Britain's participation in the war as the only way to protect civilization. 'Hitler's Germany is the villain', Forster declared, not only because of its racial atrocities or military aggression, but also because of its cultural totalitarianism.[2] Its censorship of communication; its appropriation of artworks for governmental use; its establishment of centralized agencies to control artists; its destruction of Germany's and other nations' philosophical, artistic, and scientific legacies – all of these were regarded by Forster as the biggest threat to civilization and humanity. For him, these reinterpretations (and falsifications) of European cultures embodied and reinforced Nazi Germany's worship of the State, but they also revealed the deep sense of 'the Tragic' within German national culture. A belief that 'there must lie ahead for herself or for someone an irreparable disaster', was, Forster suggested, 'the mentality of Wagner':

> [P]erhaps the present war may be considered as a scene (we do not yet know which) out of the *Nibelung's Ring*. I listen to Wagner to-day with unchanged admiration and increasing anxiety. Here is a world in which someone must come to grief, and with the maximum of orchestration and scenery. The hero slays or is slain, Hunding kills Siegmund, Siegfried kills the dragon, Hagen Siegfried, Brunnhilde [*sic*] leaps into the flames and brings down the Halls of Earth and Heaven. The tragic view of the universe can be noble and elevating, but it is a dangerous guide to daily conduct, and it may harden into a stupid barbarism, which smashes at problems instead of disentangling them. It hopes to destroy; if it fails, it commits suicide, and

---

[1] Virginia Woolf, *The Waves*, ed. Michael Herbert and Susan Sellers, with research by Ian Blyth (Cambridge, UK: Cambridge University Press, 2011), p. 29. The speaker here is Louis.
[2] *NT*, p. 10.

103

E. M. Forster and Music

it cannot see that God may be wanting it to do neither. Göring, perched up in a castle with his drinking cups and plunder, and clamouring for Fate, is a Wagnerian hero gone wrong, an anachronism which has abused the name and the true nature of Tragedy.[3]

The violence and slaughter in Wagner's *Ring* cycle – the absence of compromise and the fetish of the extreme – were perceived by Forster as symptomatic of the inherent flaw of the German character. Continuing his Wagnerian analogy, Forster viewed Hermann Göring, the deputy director of Nazi Germany, 'not as Hagen but as Kundry: under a curse'.[4] The Nazis' abuse of Wagner's work was thus an extended manipulation of this innate tragic sense: 'Wherever they encounter variety and spontaneity the Nazis are doomed to attack'.[5] In Forster's opinion, the Wagnerian scenario of victory and death reflected and augmented the Nazis' totalitarianism.

It is intriguing, then, that this extended allusion to the *Ring* was completely deleted when, two weeks later, Forster revised the pamphlet into three radio talks. The pamphlet's title, with its explicit allusion to *Götterdämmerung*, was also changed into a matter-of-fact one: 'The Nazis and Culture'. What, we must stop to ask, was the rationale for such a revision? Perhaps Forster thought that the Wagnerian allusion was too long and complicated to fit into the script of the talks; the whole section was too cumbersome to be elaborated in spoken word, and the musical allusion too convoluted to be conveyed succinctly and properly on air. (Or was he presuming that the majority of his 'common' listeners might not be able to grasp the Wagnerian allusion?) It is also possible that the revision was to make his argument more concise as well as more precise. The main target of his criticism was the Nazis' governmental intervention in and exploitation of culture; without the essentialist reading of the tragic German disposition, his argument still worked.

Yet, all the practical considerations aside, could the revision also be political? Could the contentious and controversial status of Wagner in the 1930s and the 1940s have possibly influenced Forster's revision? Would it be possible that it was an intentional hush, a thoroughly conscious endeavour to hold back from referring to a composer whose name was almost synonymous with the Nazi regime? In comparison to the Edwardian years, during which Forster made numerous Wagnerian allusions in his works of fiction and non-fiction, the 1940s witnessed Forster's uncharacteristic

---

[3] *NT*, pp. 10–11. [4] *NT*, p. 12. [5] *NT*, p. 12.

The Problem of the Wagnerian Hero 105

silence about the subject: apart from *Nordic Twilight* and a passing reference to Wagner in 'The C Minor of that Life' (1941), a short essay mainly concerned with Beethoven's investment in the key, he seemed unusually reticent about referring to Wagner and Wagner's music in his writings until 1954, the year when he attended the Bayreuth Festival and subsequently made a radio broadcast, 'Revolution at Bayreuth'. Was Forster's silence about Wagner, then, a result of his alertness to, or a sign of paranoia about, the close link between Wagner and the Nazis? Hitler's admiration for the composer and his close relationships with Wagner's family were publicized and widely noted; the Third Reich's Nazification of Wagner's music and the Bayreuth Festival was also well known.[6] Although it has been contested and disputed by modern scholars in the past two decades, the theory that Wagner's music fuelled the Nazi project of racial cleansing was repeatedly endorsed by historians and musicologists immediately after the war.[7] Whilst some late twentieth- and early twenty-first-century critics have highlighted the incongruity between Wagner's work and Nazi ideology, for a contemporary British person the association of and similarities between the two might have seemed so overwhelmingly obvious that it obscured any such incongruity.

---

[6] For Hitler's admiration for Wagner's work and his attachment to the Wagners, see Ian Kershaw, *1889–1936: Hubris* (Harmondsworth: Penguin, 1999), pp. 20–23, 39–40, 41–43, 188–89, 251, 617, and 660; for Bayreuth in the 1930s, see chapter 5 in Frederic Spotts, *Bayreuth: A History of the Wagner Festival* (New Haven: Yale University Press, 1994); for the Nazification of German musicology during the wartime, see Pamela M. Potter, *Most German of the Arts: Musicology and Society from the Weimar Republic to the End of Hitler's Reich* (New Haven: Yale University Press, 1998); for the Nazification of a specific work of Wagner, see Thomas S. Grey, 'Wagner's *Die Meistersinger* as National Opera (1868–1945)', in *Music and German Identity*, ed. Celia Applegate and Pamela M. Potter (Chicago: University of Chicago Press, 2002), pp. 78–104; for Wagner's followers and their relations with National Socialism, see David C. Large, 'Wagner's Bayreuth Disciples', in *Wagnerism in European Culture and Politics*, ed. Large and Weber, pp. 72–133.

[7] For studies on the relationship between music and Nazism, see Hans Rudolf Vaget, 'Hitler's Wagner: Musical Discourse as Cultural Space', in *Music and Nazism: Art under Tyranny, 1933–1945*, ed. Michael H. Kater and Albrecht Riethmüller (Laaber: Laaber, 2003), pp. 15–31; for the Nazis' Germanization of music and their failure, see Pamela M. Potter, 'Music in the Third Reich: The Complex Task of "Germanization"', in *The Arts in Nazi Germany: Continuity, Conformity, Change*, ed. Jonathan Huener and Francis R. Nicosia (New York: Berghahn, 2006), pp. 85–110; for an investigation into Nazi control of music and theatre, see Alan E. Steinweis, *Art, Ideology, and Economics in Nazi Germany: The Reich Chambers of Music, Theater, and the Visual Arts* (Chapel Hill: University of North Carolina Press, 1993); for the counterpart projects regarding music and nationhood in Britain in the Second World War, see Robert Mackay's 'Safe and Sound: New Music in Wartime Britain' and Nick Hayes's 'More Than "Music-While-You-Eat"? Factory and Hostel Concerts, "Good Culture" and the Workers', both in *'Millions Like Us'?: British Culture in the Second World War*, ed. Nick Hayes and Jeff Hill (Liverpool: Liverpool University Press, 1999), pp. 179–208 and 209–35.

106   E. M. Forster and Music

The reception of Forster's last reference to Wagner before *Nordic Twilight* bore witness to this topical currency of the Wagner–Hitler connection. In January 1939, Forster was the first contributor to 'How I Listen to Music', a series of talks on the BBC. In his talk, later reprinted in *Two Cheers for Democracy* as 'Not Listening to Music', Forster discussed briefly how he once enjoyed Wagner's work:

> With Wagner I always knew where I was; he never let the fancy roam[.] In those days [music] was either a non-musical object, such as a sword or a blameless fool, or a non-musical emotion, such as fear, lust or resignation. ... I translated sounds into colours, saw the piccolo as apple-green, and the trumpets as scarlet. The arts were to be enriched by taking in one another's washing.[8]

The passage seems a parody of the transition of European artistic trends in the early twentieth century; its past tense indicates a change in Forster's musical taste. Yet for the art critic R. H. Wilenski, the series' second contributor, Forster's unguarded appreciation of Wagner's work was unscrupulous. As Wilenski suggested in his talk, when the composer was 'a crafty or threatening antagonist who is out to soothe, irritate or assault my nerves and senses and deprive my will and intellect of their control', extra caution was necessary. Wilenski called Forster's method of listening 'foolhardy' because Forster's consciousness 'will be scaled by the invader' and Forster the person will be transformed into 'the distressing spectacle of an intelligent adult head-nodding and foot-wagging without direction from his mind and will'.[9] With its patronizing tone, its metaphors of musical affectivity as pathologizing force and military invasion, and its alarmist emphasis on self-control and willpower, Wilenski's commentary reiterated the debilitating effects of Wagner's music delineated by numerous predecessors and contemporaries and revealed his own overlapping concern with the imminent war against Germany.[10] We do not know whether or how Forster reacted to this commentary, but it is evident that Wagner was, in the late 1930s, a highly contentious topic.

His silence about Wagner is particularly conspicuous when one considers the significance of music to Forster throughout the war and the diversity of his wartime musical activities. On the day when Britain

---

[8] *TCD*, pp. 122–23.
[9] R. H. Wilenski, 'How I Listen to Music', *Listener*, 2 February 1939, 281.
[10] See Sutton, *Aubrey Beardsley*, ch. II, 'The Pathology of Pleasure: Decadent Sensibility and Affective Art' (pp. 57–87), for an analysis of a variety of discourses on the debilitating effects of Wagner's music.

The Problem of the Wagnerian Hero

declared war on Germany, Forster played the adagio of Beethoven's Piano Sonata No. 28, Op. 101, and made the first entry in his unfinished Beethoven Notebook.[11] This project to annotate all of Beethoven's piano sonatas, to obtain 'a vision of Beethoven reached through playing him as well as listening to him', provided Forster with a diversion from the war, a symbolic retreat through which he could temporarily receive comfort and forget cruelty, although it was left incomplete after only a few entries.[12] At the same time, Forster was an ardent supporter of the National Gallery concerts and went to London regularly to listen to the chamber music performed by Myra Hess and many others. His participation in and advocacy of these wartime musical activities, in which German music had a prominent part, only highlight the absence of Wagner in his writing during and after the war.

To many of Forster's contemporaries, allusions to and evaluations of Wagner and his oeuvre were one of the means through which the national and racial myths constructed by the Nazis could be contested and dispersed. By claiming the right of interpretation, that is, anti-Nazi intellectuals, musicians, and writers reassessed the value of Wagner's music and criticized Wagner's anti-Semitism whilst challenging the Nazis' exploitation of Wagner's work over the years. Thomas Mann, for example, consistently formulated his polemics on German totalitarianism through evaluating Wagner's work during his exile in the United States.[13] Similarly, Virginia Woolf explored and critiqued contemporary dictatorship and militarism through structural and thematic allusions to Wagner's tetralogy in *The Years* (1937).[14] Also, Theodor Adorno's socialist and musicological study of Wagner, though published after the war, was first conceived in the late 1930s as an exploration of, as well as a resistance to, Nazism.[15] These examples demonstrate that 'Wagner', as a subject, was a

[11] Diary entry (3 September 1939). *JD*, II, p. 89.
[12] Letter to Forrest Reid (30 September 1940). *SL*, II, p. 182. For a discussion on the motivation and the timing of this Beethoven project, see Fillion, *Difficult Rhythm*, pp. 110–11.
[13] Thomas Mann decided to live in exile after his 1933 lecture, 'The Sorrows and Grandeur of Richard Wagner', commissioned by the Goethe Society of Munich for the fiftieth anniversary of the composer's death. The lecture caused an almost unexpected national controversy against Mann because of his criticism of Wagner's artistic dilettantism. This did not stop him from commenting on Wagner though, as he continued his scrutiny of Wagner in 'Richard Wagner and *Der Ring des Nibelungen*' (1937) and 'To the Editor of *Common Sense*' (1940). Thomas Mann, *Pro and Contra Wagner*, trans. Allan Blunden (London: Faber and Faber, 1985), pp. 91–148, 171–94, and 196–203.
[14] Sutton, *Virginia Woolf and Classical Music*, pp. 122–33.
[15] Theodor Adorno, *In Search of Wagner*, trans. Rodney Livingstone, with foreword by Slavoj Žižek (London: Verso, 2009). Žižek's foreword briefly discusses the background of Adorno's work, p. viii.

108   E. M. Forster and Music

point of contention between Nazism and anti-Nazism. If Forster had sought to establish his political ideology against Nazi Germany, uncovering the problematic national and racial elements in Wagner's music dramas would have been the shortcut to the goal. *Nordic Twilight* did exactly that, but the subsequent revision consciously renounced such a method and thus produced a hiatus in Forster's writing about Wagner.

This hiatus was, I would suggest, a considered decision, one in which Forster's decades-long rumination on heroism played an important part. Forster's denunciation of fascism in the late 1930s, especially in his famous 1938 essay, 'What I Believe', has been extensively discussed by critics; the statement about his anti-patriotic loyalty to friendships has also been much quoted and analysed in numerous critical studies. What demands to be emphasized here is that his championing of personal relationships is underpinned by his celebration of individualism, not as exceptionalism, but as a display of individualities. Whilst Forster's vision of individualistic engagement with music will be discussed in the next chapter, his general notion of individualism emphasizes freedom and idiosyncrasy, thus envisioning a community which embraces a spectrum of individuals. His anti-fascism is a rejection of uniformity, of the loss of the individual in a totalitarian regime. Even though a dictator is the utmost demonstration of individualism, a 'great man', as Rachel Bowlby notes, 'resemble[s]', rather than 'differ[s] from', every other: 'his greatness is a function of his life's proceeding not exceptionally or idiosyncratically, but along well-known, recognisable lines'.[16] Forster's notion of individualism, then, simultaneously celebrates the plurality of individualities and resists the replication of Great Men conventions.

It is exactly because of this distrust of 'Great Men', as Michelle Fillion suggests, that Forster's Beethoven Notebook project remained unfinished. As Fillion has observed, the project was abandoned because Forster's withdrawal into Beethoven's piano sonatas instead forced him to confront the heroic quality with which a century of criticism had symbolically endowed Beethoven and his music: in the rise of Nazism, Beethoven became 'an object of cautious love, but no longer a subject for criticism'.[17] Fillion's reading usefully unveils the contradictions and conflicts

---

[16] Rachel Bowlby, 'Jacob's Type', in *Feminist Destinations and Further Essays on Virginia Woolf* (Edinburgh: Edinburgh University Press, 1997), pp. 85–99 (p. 88).
[17] Fillion, *Difficult Rhythm*, p. 117. See also Zhou, 'Sublime Noise', pp. 1–4. For studies on Beethoven and heroism, see e.g. Scott Burnham, *Beethoven Hero* (Princeton: Princeton University Press, 1995); and Nicholas Mathew, *Political Beethoven* (Cambridge, UK: Cambridge University Press, 2013), pp. 17–58.

The Problem of the Wagnerian Hero 109

underlying Forster's project, but its depiction of the Notebook as 'doomed from the start' risks overstressing Forster's 'failure': it implies a characterization of the project as an ill-fated attempt which faltered when the association of the perceived heroism of Beethoven with the Nazi form of hero-worship became overwhelming.[18] To avoid such a disabling characterization, I find John Lucas's evaluation of Forster's polemical writings in the 1930s as '*deliberately* frail' and 'quietly devastating' particularly stimulating.[19] Arguing for Forster's 'enabling modesty', Lucas observes how Forster's language 'refuses to shift towards the rhetoric of public occasion [and] remains steadfastly that of the private conversationalist'.[20] The significance is therefore twofold: stylistically, Forster 'resists the rhetorical flourish that will either aggrandise or demonise'; ideologically, Forster kept himself at a slight angle to any political causes and campaigns.[21] It is this refusal to adopt the enemy's weapon to counter-attack, this quiet resistance to the permeation of divisive politics and public grandiosity, this constant wariness of the sectarian and dogmatic nature of political movements, that enables us to read the incompleteness of the Beethoven Notebook not as a failure but as Forster's restraint. The unfinished Notebook, I suggest, marks Forster's discreet decision not to participate in, and therefore not to augment, the topicality of heroism in a decade where newspaper headlines were dominated by 'Great Men'. In so doing, Forster did not resort to the easy distinction between heroism and anti-heroism, and remained independent from the multifarious concurrent 'isms' of political ideology.

Forster's silence about Wagner sends out similar implications. This chapter explores how Forster resisted hero-worship and attempted to redefine the 'heroic' in the first half of the twentieth century through criticizing Wagner's characterization of Siegfried. The chapter examines the ways in which Forster searched for an alternative to the Wagnerian scenario of hero and villain, victory and defeat, transcendence and death – that is, as we have seen in *Nordic Twilight*, a less extreme ideology than the 'tragic' view represented in Wagner's tetralogy. Forster's Wagnerism suggests a negotiation of the Wagnerian hero, an enduring exploration of a

---

[18] Fillion, *Difficult Rhythm*, p. 109.

[19] John Lucas, 'E. M. Forster: An Enabling Modesty', *EREA*, 4.2 (2006), 34–44 (p. 35 and p. 42).

[20] Lucas, 'Enabling Modesty', p. 42.

[21] Lucas, 'Enabling Modesty', p. 36. Additionally, Paul B. Armstrong comments on Forster's indirect style as 'a way of acknowledging that his discourse is necessarily entangled in the workings of power it criticizes'. Paul B. Armstrong, 'Two Cheers for Tolerance: E. M. Forster's Ironic Liberalism and the Indirections of Style', *Modernism/modernity*, 16.2 (2009), 281–99 (p. 285).

E. M. Forster and Music

complex web of discourses on Wagner's anti-Semitism, posthumous reception, and links to the Nazis. These discourses, stylistically and ideologically protean and complicated, are themselves discursive topics with a diverse range of critical associations. The chapter concentrates, consequently, on Forster's combined attention to Wagner and heroism because the underlying Forsterian ideology is not just idiosyncratic, but in many ways representative too: it recurred at different points of Forster's life and influenced a younger generation of writers. Christopher Isherwood, for example, called Forster an 'antiheroic hero', of whose existence 'the vast majority of people on this island aren't even aware'.[22] My discussion is intended, then, as a close reading of a subject to which Forster himself repeatedly returned, reiterating some of his abiding beliefs while making new comments in response to different political situations. Through analysing a variety of Forster's fictional and non-fictional writings, the chapter illustrates how his consistent questioning of Wagnerian heroism as apocalyptical suggests his opposition to the exceptionalism celebrated and worshipped in Wagner's work.

The Heroic Cad and the Jewish Scholar

Wagner's music dramas are not wanting in heroes, and these heroes are staple figures consistently referred to and commented on within Wagnerism.[23] Above them all, Siegfried is the champion. In *The Perfect Wagnerite* (1898), for example, George Bernard Shaw regarded Siegfried as 'a born anarchist, the ideal of Bakoonin, an anticipation of the "overman" of Nietzsche'.[24] For Forster, however, Siegfried was never a hero. In 1905, when attending his first *Ring* cycle, Forster wrote to his Cambridge friend Arthur Cole from Dresden, comparing the character to an ill-educated college fellow who 'ought never to have got his fellowship': 'his subsequent achievements confer little credit upon the institutions from which he draws his salary. To insist on marrying your half-aunt on both sides and then totally to forget her – this, as far as I can make out, is all that Siegfried does after gaining the Ring, the Tarn cap, and the Sword'.[25]

This jibe at Siegfried is elaborated in 'Pessimism in Literature', a paper Forster read at the Working Men's College in 1906.[26] The paper's primary

---

[22] Christopher Isherwood, *Down There on a Visit* (New York: Farrar, Straus and Giroux, 2013), p. 162.
[23] I find Simon Williams's reading of Wagner's heroisms in *Wagner and the Romantic Hero* (Cambridge, UK: Cambridge University Press, 2004) insightful and particularly helpful.
[24] George Bernard Shaw, *The Perfect Wagnerite*, 2nd ed. (London: Constable, 1908), p. 48.
[25] Letter to Arthur Cole (11 April 1905). *SL*, I, p. 68.
[26] The paper was then published in the *Working Men's College Journal* in 1907.

The Problem of the Wagnerian Hero

concern is the absence of happy ending in contemporary fiction: 'the modern mind ... has detected the discomfort and misery that lie so frequently beneath the smiling surface of things'.[27] These idiosyncrasies of 'modern' literature are, Forster suggested, those of the *Ring* too: 'Wagner can give us tragedy, and the disquieting passion of human love', but he cannot give us 'the poetry of laughter – the laughter that once filled the earthly paradise of Olivia's garden'.[28] In some respects, this evaluation anticipates the previously quoted passage from *Nordic Twilight*, in which Wagner's predilection for the tragic in the *Ring* is criticized for its extremity. In the paper, Forster's focus is on Wagner's failure to conjure up joy on stage:

> I am thinking of a scene that is intended to be perfectly joyful – to present, on a heroic scale, the cheerfulness, the high spirits, the audacious laughter that are so splendid and magnificent in life. The scene in question is the opening scene of *Siegfried*. In life the youthful Siegfried would be quite an agreeable person. We should like to know him – at all events we should like to think of him at a public school. 'Boys will be boys', we should murmur, when he laughed and shouted, and bullied and jumped to and fro in the most distracting way. But the youthful Siegfried on the stage is intolerable. ... It is that he is a bounder in a more fatal sense – neither a hero nor a school boy, but a cad. ... In spite of the jolliest music, the youthful Siegfried will not do, and when, in accordance with the stage directions, he 'makes a long nose' our depression is complete. Wagner has failed ... [a]nd the failure is so grave that it does much to spoil the whole of the opera. We cannot believe in Siegfried as a hero. Siegmund was a hero, because he was unhappy. Hagen is a hero, though heroically evil. But Siegfried remains to the end an upstart boy, who marries a woman ten times better than himself.[29]

Forster's assessment of these Wagnerian heroes suggests a set of criteria based on the scale of the character's aspirations, emotions, and actions; it does not necessarily matter whether the character is good or evil. The reference to Siegmund's unhappiness suggests Forster's awareness of the stereotypes of the Romantic hero, including in this case those of the anti-hero, and perhaps there is a slightly satiric undertone in his emphasis on such emotional indulgence. Nevertheless, from this point onward, Forster showed an unflinching admiration for Siegmund: the character was described as a 'glorious' 'intruder' to Valhalla in 1905; five decades later, Forster found Siegmund sexually arousing in *Die Walküre* in Bayreuth.[30] In contrast, Siegfried is denounced as a character with unbearable

---

[27] *AE*, p. 142. [28] *AE*, p. 143. [29] *AE*, pp. 143–44.
[30] *SL*, I, p. 68. Diary entry (11 August 1954). *JD*, III, p. 123.

E. M. Forster and Music

immaturity, limited aspirations, and unbound violence. Forster's commentary associates Siegfried with the callow, boorish, and unrefined – or, more specifically, with the public-school type of insensitivity of which Forster was particularly critical.

Forster's use of the term 'cad' invites more discussion. The term comments on Siegfried's vulgarity in the scene specified in the previous passage: Siegfried – loud, uncivilized, and intimidating – bullies Mime the dwarf by forcing the latter to forge a sword and to reveal his parentage. The term also connotes sexual duplicity, implying male ill treatment of women and perhaps thus recalling Siegfried's betrayal of Brünnhilde in *Götterdämmerung*. Its class connotations are no less suggestive: originally applied contemptuously by Oxford collegians to low-class town people, the term found its way into the general vocabulary of suburban England, with its modern sense as an insulting or chiding appellation applied to those whose behaviour has brought disgrace to their social class.[31] It is in this sense that, in *Where Angels Fear to Tread*, Philip calls Gino a 'cad'.[32] The term can therefore be read as Forster's jibe at Siegfried for dishonouring his godly blood. Intriguingly, in *The Longest Journey*, a novel Forster finished around the same time as 'Pessimism in Literature', 'Cad' is what Forster names his fictitious countryside in rural Wiltshire. Moreover, Stephen Wonham, a 'hero' growing up in this 'Cad-' area, was once named Siegfried.[33] Forster specified this genesis of the Stephen character in 1960, although the name 'Siegfried' does not survive in the extant manuscripts; as Elizabeth Heine suggests, Forster's 1960 recollection 'may have ... transformed intention into execution, or recalled some lost draft'.[34] This mythic model nevertheless opens up readings of the character's Wagnerian root and enhances discussions of the novel's extensive Wagnerian allusions.[35] Whilst the ways in which Wagner's Siegfried

---

[31] *OED.*   [32] *WA*, pp. 25, 55, 88, and 145.

[33] Forster mentioned that 'Stephen was at one time called Harold and at another Siegfried' in the introduction to the 1960 Oxford World's Classics edition of the novel. *LJ*, p. lxix.

[34] *LJ*, p. xiv. Elizabeth Heine also notes that, although passages in which Stephen appears as Siegfried cannot be found in the extant manuscripts, one of the discarded Harold chapters, marked as 'XIV', contains a fantasy adventure of the character, in which he runs naked through fields and at one point communicates with different animals. P. N. Furbank suggests that this particular episode recalls the forest scene in *Siegfried*, in which Siegfried understands the forest bird's song. See Furbank, *Forster*, I, p. 263.

[35] As several critics have noted, *The Longest Journey* is replete with Wagnerian allusions. Elizabeth Heine provides an introductory discussion of the novel's Wagnerian allusions and symbolism – see *LJ*, pp. x–xv. Several critics have attempted to read the Wagnerian 'model' behind the novel. See e.g. Tony Brown, 'E. M. Forster's *Parsifal*' and Judith Scherer Herz, 'This is the End of Parsival'. Michelle Fillion traces Forster's attendance at Wagner's music dramas and provides a detailed

The Problem of the Wagnerian Hero 113

contributes to Stephen's characterization as the archetypal, though also problematic, hero have been analysed,[36] the link between Forster's word-play of 'cad' and Stephen's ambiguous heroic quality has been overlooked.

Throughout *The Longest Journey*, Stephen is bestowed, even though sometimes ironically, with the epithet 'heroic'; as the narrator announces in chapter 12, he is 'not to be distinguished from a hero'.[37] Whether Stephen is a hero or not is a topic diegetically commented on by other characters. In chapter 11, Rickie and his fiancée, Agnes Pembroke, are on their visit to his aunt, Mrs Failing. At this point, Stephen's background as Rickie's half-brother is not yet disclosed: Rickie thinks of Stephen as an anomalous farmhand who has been living in the house through some unknown connection of Rickie's late uncle while Agnes, though curious, does not act inquisitively. One day, after Rickie reluctantly goes for a ride with Stephen, Mrs Failing shows Agnes around, 'point[ing] out the various objects of interest' in the surroundings (the River 'Cad', 'Cadbury Rings', 'Cadchurch', 'Cad Dauntsey', 'Cadford', and 'Cadover'), to which Agnes jokes, 'A terrible lot of Cads'.[38] The hostess then asks what her guest thinks about Stephen:

> 'Very nice', said Agnes, laughing.
> 'Nice! He is a hero.'
> There was a long interval of silence. Each lady looked, without much interest, at the view. . . . 'A hero?' [Agnes] questioned, when the interval had passed. Her voice was indifferent, as if she had been thinking of other things.
> 'A hero? Yes. Didn't you notice how heroic he was?'
> 'I don't think I did.'
> 'Not at dinner? Ah, Agnes, always look out for heroism at dinner. It is their great time. They live up to the stiffness of their shirt-fronts. Do you mean to say that you never noticed how he set down Rickie?'
> 'Oh, that about poetry!' said Agnes, laughing. 'Rickie would not mind it for a moment. But why do you single out that as heroic?'
> 'To snub people! to set them down! to be rude to them! to make them feel small! Surely that's the life-work of a hero?'
> 'I shouldn't have said that. And as a matter of fact Mr Wonham was wrong over the poetry. I made Rickie look it up afterwards.'

reading of the gender, ideological, and structural connotations of the Wagnerian allusions in the novel. Fillion, *Difficult Rhythm*, pp. 5, 21–22, 39–49, and 51–55.

[36] See e.g. Heine's introduction, *LJ*, pp. xiii–xiv, and Fillion, *Difficult Rhythm*, pp. 49–51.

[37] *LJ*, p. 115. In chapter 31, for example, Stephen 'stood, not consciously heroic, with arms that dangled from broad stooping shoulders, and feet that played with a hassock on the carpet'. *LJ*, p. 252.

[38] *LJ*, p 101.

114 E. M. Forster and Music

'But of course. A hero always is wrong.'

'To me', she persisted, rather gently, 'a hero has always been a strong wonderful being, who champions—'

'Ah, wait till you are the dragon! I have been a dragon most of my life, I think. A dragon that wants nothing but a peaceful cave. Then in comes the strong, wonderful, delightful being, and gains a princess by piercing my hide. No, seriously, my dear Agnes, the chief characteristics of a hero are infinite disregard for the feelings of others, plus general inability to understand them.'

'But surely Mr Wonham—'

'Yes; aren't we being unkind to the poor boy. Ought we to go on talking?'[39]

A discreet conversation about 'the hero' on the verge of turning into a gossip about a particular 'hero', this passage sees Mrs Failing slyly luring Agnes into commenting on Stephen. It recalls Rickie's warning before he leaves for the ride about his aunt's tendency to instigate a greater scale of 'family breezes';[40] it also anticipates the narrator's announcement of Stephen's heroic status in the following chapter. If the conversation has such narrative significance, it is, too, an unusually explicit, seemingly out-of-context debate about definitions of heroism. Two delineations of the hero are juxtaposed here: for Mrs Failing, a hero is a maverick against and outside social norms; for Agnes, a hero stands for an ideal, romanticized form of masculinity. However, it is exactly the context in which the conversation takes place that gives this generic debate a specific Wagnerian focus: the textual proximity of 'cad' and 'hero', when read with the knowledge of Forster's previous commentaries on Siegfried, indicates Forster's concern with Wagner's hero. Mrs Failing's exposure of the adversarial and confrontational elements within heroism, of the clichéd heterosexual reward at the end of a heroic quest, of the extreme individualism of the hero, is underpinned by Forster's scepticism about Siegfried. The analogue of Mrs Failing to a dragon thus not only questions the normative rite of passage of the hero and recounts it from the opposite perspective; it also offers a reflection on Siegfried's killing of the dragon, into which the giant Fafner has transformed, in Act II, scene ii, in *Siegfried*. This reinterpretation of a scene of heroic bravery as an insensitive intrusion emphasizes the unnecessary violence involved in the Wagnerian tradition of hero making, challenging the motivation of an act emblematic of Siegfried's heroism.

[39] *LJ*, pp. 102–3.   [40] *LJ*, p. 100.

The Problem of the Wagnerian Hero 115

It is important, then, to a reading of the novel's Wagnerian elements that the wordplay of 'cad' is included and considered, not just as an ironic detail of Stephen's characterization, but also as an indicator of Forster's preoccupation with Siegfried's status as the hero. The rural English landscape of the 'Cad-' area, on the one hand, transforms symbolism into reality, importing the metaphysical subjects of the *Ring* into an Edwardian environment.[41] On the other hand, it undercuts – and parodies – the mythology of Siegfried, sustaining Forster's wariness of hero-worship and his debunking of romanticization throughout the novel. Perhaps it is because of this fictional landscape that the name Siegfried was eventually dropped: an examination of the Siegfriedian caddishness does not need such an explicit allusion as to name the character after Wagner's hero. Another possibility behind the renaming is that the German name might not be appropriate to a character whose attachment to the English countryside is important to the plot.[42] Either way, Forster's inquiry into the 'heroic' stems from and revolves around his criticism of Siegfried: by situating Mrs Failing and Agnes's conversation in this 'Cad-' area, Forster reviews a truncated portion of Wagner's tetralogy, measuring Stephen's qualification as a hero through a reflection on Siegfried's characteristics and actions.

In the novel, this delineation of the 'heroic' Stephen is contrasted with that of the 'unheroic' Stewart Ansell:

> Ansell was in his favourite haunt – the reading-room of the British Museum. In that book-encircled space he always could find peace. . . . There he knew that his life was not ignoble. It was worth while to grow old and dusty seeking for truth though truth is unattainable, restating questions that have been stated at the beginning of the world. Failure would await him, but not disillusionment. . . . He was not a hero, and he knew it.[43]

A fervent philosopher, who tends to neglect people around him if he finds them unworthy of his attention, Ansell, Rickie's closest friend at Cambridge, has been read as the opposite of Stephen: Wilfred Stone, representatively, regards Ansell and Stephen as 'the intellectual and physical halves of Rickie's estranged soul'.[44] What critics rarely discuss is that

---

[41] Elizabeth Heine's introduction, *LJ*, p. xiv.
[42] P. N. Furbank suggests that Stephen's 'heroic' vitality is indebted to his affinity with the English countryside. Furbank, *Forster*, I, p. 119.
[43] *LJ*, p. 177. There is also a notable echo in their first names: 'Stephen' versus 'Stewart' – perhaps another reason for the name change?
[44] Stone, *The Cave and the Mountain*, p. 209.

116   E. M. Forster and Music

Ansell is, among other things, Jewish. On the level of the novel's plot and characterization, Ansell's Jewish background generates significant implications for his cultural ideal, career choice, artistic taste, and sexual identity. Yet, more importantly, Ansell's Jewishness also participates in contemporary racial and evolutionary discourses, especially those related to Wagner. Forster made, to my knowledge, no direct comment on Wagner's anti-Semitic essays, but he was likely to have known the existence of these texts, given that Wagner's anti-Semitism – especially in *Judaism in Music* (1850) – influenced contemporary debates about and perceptions of Jewishness and remained highly controversial in the subsequent decades.[45] Ansell's Jewish identity and his marked contrast with the Siegfried-like Stephen therefore make a suggestive critique of Wagner's ideology. And Ansell's actions in the novel, especially those after his acknowledgement of his ineligibility as a 'hero', can be read as a counter-narrative to the hero-driven plot in Wagner's tetralogy.

The Ansells are the sole explicitly Jewish characters in Forster's work.[46] This representation of Jewishness reflects both parallels with and differences from centuries-long stereotypes of Jews, prevalent in literary texts and multifarious accounts, as a 'race' distinct from Europeans.[47] Before the narrator reveals that Ansell has a 'lean Jewish face' in chapter 7, the depiction of the Ansells in chapter 3 delicately alludes to their Jewish background.[48] With Ansell's father being 'a provincial draper of moderate prosperity', the family is, as the narrator says, a 'plebeian household':

> To be born one thing and grow up another – Ansell had accomplished this without weakening one of the ties that bound him to his home. The room above the shop still seemed as comfortable, the garden behind it as gracious, as they had seemed fifteen years before, when he would sit behind Miss Appleblossom's central throne, and she, like some allegorical figure, would send the change and receipted bills spinning away from her in little

---

[45] Sutton, *Aubrey Beardsley*, pp. 20–21 and 109–16. See also Marc A. Weiner, *Richard Wagner and the Anti-Semitic Imagination* (Lincoln: University of Nebraska Press, 1995).

[46] Two of Forster's 1930s essays specifically addressed Jewishness in response to the Nazis' widely reported project of racial cleansing: 'Jew-Consciousness' (1939) and 'Racial Exercise' (1939), in *TCD*, pp. 12–14 and 17–20. See Armstrong, 'Two Cheers for Tolerance', pp. 286–87 and pp. 289–92, for a discussion of Forster's emphasis on racial heterogeneity.

[47] For discussions of representations of Jewishness in British fiction in the nineteenth and early twentieth centuries, see Bryan Cheyette, *Constructions of 'The Jew' in English Literature and Society: Racial Representations, 1875–1945* (Cambridge, UK: Cambridge University Press, 1993); *Modernity, Culture, and 'the Jew'*, ed. Bryan Cheyette and Laura Marcus (Cambridge, UK: Polity, 1998); Jonathan Freedman, *The Temple of Culture: Assimilation and Anti-Semitism in Literary Anglo-America* (Oxford: Oxford University Press, 2000).

[48] *LJ*, p. 62.

The Problem of the Wagnerian Hero 117

boxwood balls. At first the young man had attributed these happy relations to his own tact. But in time he perceived that the tact was all on the side of his father. Mr Ansell was not merely a man of some education; he had what no education can bring – the power of detecting what is important. Like many fathers, he had spared no expense over his boy – he had borrowed money to start him at a rapacious and fashionable private school; he had sent him to tutors; he had sent him to Cambridge. But he knew that all this was not the important thing. The important thing was freedom.[49]

An example of social mobility, the nature and nurture of Ansell alludes to the perception of Jewish people as a group outside the 'normal' social, and implicitly racial, hierarchies. That such mobility is secured and enabled by the family business associates the Ansells with worldly commercialism; this association reiterates the stereotype about Jewish adroitness in commercial activities, alluding to the cliché of the acquisitiveness – or, as it is frequently caricatured, greed – of Jews. This is not to say, however, that Forster's representation of the Ansells is predetermined as anti-Semitic. The ambivalence lies in the fact that both the narrator and Rickie celebrate the Ansells' family wealth: the narrator says, 'there was a curious charm in the hum of the shop, which swelled into a roar if one opened the partition door on a market-day', while Rickie exclaims, 'Listen to your money!', and describes the Ansells' income as 'alive'.[50] This portrayal of money as vital not only emblematizes the importance of commerce to modern capitalistic society but also conceptualizes wealth as the driving force behind Ansell's social mobility.[51] The philistine background of Ansell, then, alludes to the association of Jews and material affluence, but such economic privilege also means the possibility of his cultural refinement.[52]

Ansell's alignment with culture is his primary characteristic in the novel. His interest in metaphysics (as shown in the Apostolic debate in chapter 1), his ambition for a Cambridge fellowship, his worship of his alma mater throughout the novel – all these details indicate that the 'not ignoble' life he envisions in the British Museum is a cultured life, and the 'freedom' he emphasizes is an intellectual and spiritual freedom. Yet this quest for culture is driven by a certain social motivation; culture is the 'key' for Ansell to his assimilation into Western society. That is, his intellectual career reveals anxieties about the conception of 'the Jew' as the other in Western civilization as well as aspirations for a redefined cultural identity

---

[49] *LJ*, pp. 30 and 29. [50] *LJ*, p. 31.
[51] For discussions of Forster's attitude towards money, see e.g. Wilfred Stone, 'Forster on Love and Money', in *Aspects of E. M. Forster*, ed. Stallybrass, pp. 107–21; and Delany, 'Islands of Money'.
[52] Cf. Leonard Bast in *Howards End*.

118 E. M. Forster and Music

for assimilating Jews.[53] His research on German philosophy – a subject that 'lies behind everything' – also reinforces this reading: his focus on Schopenhauer and Hegel can be read as an attempt to trace his cultural genealogy back to the philosophical tradition of Western high culture, and as a strategy to study, and perhaps also to contest, monumental texts in which the alterity of 'the Jew' was established.[54]

Although it is debatable whether this portrayal of Ansell suggests Forster's empathy with Jewish assimilation, Ansell's study of German philosophy echoes discrete turn-of-the-century intellectual projects of numerous Jewish scholars who attempted to revise previous discourses on Jewishness. Given the notoriety of Wagner's anti-Semitism, it should come as no surprise that Wagner was frequently critiqued by many of such attempts. Among these was Max Nordau's *Die Entartung* (1892).[55] Published in English as *Degeneration* in 1895, Nordau's book 'centralized Wagnerism, Wagner, and Wagner's work in debates about decadence and cultural degeneration for the remainder of the decade'.[56] By identifying the 'degeneracy' of Wagner and many other artists as the source of cultural 'degeneration', Nordau's pseudo-medical 'diagnosis' of the *fin de siècle* was, too, a redefinition of Jewishness. As Jonathan Freedman notes, using 'the avant-garde artist' 'to replace the Jew as arch-degenerate', Nordau's criticism of Wagner and degeneration was underpinned by his Zionist belief.[57] As a Zionist activist, Nordau argued against anti-Semitic stereotypes by proposing the concept of 'the muscle Jew'. First mentioned in 1898 and repeatedly elaborated thenceforth, 'the muscle Jew' was an idea mediated through a matrix of contemporary discourses on cultural decay, social reform, eugenic research, and Jewish nationalism.[58]

Forster's description of Ansell's engagement with music was informed by these discourses on degeneration, Wagnerism, and Zionism. This is not to say, however, that Forster in any way polemically echoed or refuted Nordau's idea in his portrayal of Ansell, for there is no mention in the novel of Ansell reading Nordau and, in biographical terms, we do not

---

[53] Freedman, *Temple*, p. 54. Freedman's analysis of the constructions of, and the responses to, 'the Jew' in nineteenth-century Anglo-American conceptions of 'culture' is particularly illuminating, pp. 37–54.

[54] *LJ*, p. 29. As Jonathan Freedman has observed, Hegel's construction of 'the Jew' in *The Spirit of Christianity* (1799) exercised a significant influence on later delineations of Jewishness. Freedman, *Temple*, pp. 39–40.

[55] Max Nordau, *Degeneration*, trans. anon. (Lincoln: University of Nebraska Press, 1993).

[56] Sutton, *Aubrey Beardsley*, p. 52.   [57] Freedman, *Temple*, p. 126.

[58] Todd Samuel Presner, *Muscular Judaism: The Jewish Body and the Politics of Regeneration* (London: Routledge, 2007), pp. 1–4.

The Problem of the Wagnerian Hero 119

know whether Forster had read any of Nordau's writings, although Nordau's work was undoubtedly accessible to him and his contemporaries. Nonetheless, Ansell's reactions to music, and to Wagner's music especially, create resonances with Nordau's Zionist ideology. At first glance, Ansell, though cultured, seems unmusical. Both Elizabeth Heine and Michelle Fillion suggest that Ansell lacks musical knowledge and has little Wagnerian sensibility; they use the discussion between Rickie and Ansell in chapter 1 about the tonality of the Rhinemaidens' glorious leitmotif in *Das Rheingold* and the epistolary exchange in chapter 9, during which Rickie and Ansell allude to Wagnerian female characters, to support their readings.[59] Under closer scrutiny, however, Ansell's engagement with music, especially with Wagner's music, is more ambivalent than a sheer lack of musical knowledge and sensibility. Heine's and Fillion's readings unintentionally overlook Ansell's cynicism in their examples. What they regard as Ansell's lack of interest in music is, I believe, his knowing disinterestedness: given his wry interruption of Rickie's fantasizing and his ability to participate in the cultural game of Wagnerian allusions, Ansell is not unmusical but knowledgeable about as well as critical of Wagner's music. In fact, Rickie, more than tellingly, exclaims in their discussion about *Das Rheingold*: 'oh, of course, you despise music';[60] surely, to 'despise' something is to have some knowledge, or preconception, of the thing one is against? Here, Ansell's attitude towards music produces a suggestive narrative: to be antagonistic to music, to undercut or refute Rickie's Wagnerian allusions, is to dissociate himself from the 'inflammability' of Wagner and Wagnerism, and thus from aesthetic and cultural 'degeneration'.[61] Such an attempt reflects his awareness of, and anxiety about, contemporary perceptions of intellectuals, homosexuals, and Jews as alienated, unfit, and exotic – that is, as 'cases' of otherness in concurrent discourses on decadence and eugenics. The fact that Ansell is a combination of these roles, and that the connotations and associations of each of these roles are often interlinked, augments such awareness and

---

[59] For Heine's interpretation, *LJ*, pp. 408 and 416–17. Fillion, *Difficult Rhythm*, pp. 44–45 and 48–49. What might also support these interpretations of Ansell's lack of musicality is a painting in the Ansells' home: 'a harp in luminous paint' with the inscription 'Watch and Pray' (*LJ*, p. 31). Whilst the painting can, of course, be simply read as indicative of the Ansells' practice of Judaism, the image of the sacred harp, as Jonathan Freedman notes, was a prominent symbol in nineteenth-century denigrations of Jewish musical accomplishment. Freedman, *Temple*, pp. 109–11. Rickie's visceral reactions to the painting have also been linked to the novel's homoerotic undercurrent. See Anke Johannmeyer, '"For Music Has Wings": E. M. Forster's "Orchestration" of a Homophile Space in *The Longest Journey*' (unpublished MA thesis, Uppsala University, 2009), pp. 11–12.

[60] *LJ*, p. 16.   [61] The term 'inflammability' is from Sutton, *Aubrey Beardsley*, p. 86.

120   E. M. Forster and Music

anxiety, and endows his dissociation with added urgency.[62] His antagonism to music can thus be read as one of the strategies in a broader project of resistance to any association with 'degeneration'.

If Ansell 'despises' music in order to distance himself from being labelled as a 'degenerate', he is also more actively cultivating an image of his Jewish body as healthy and able. In chapter 9, for example, Ansell's physical domination over Rickie during their 'frolics' is punctuated by his remark: 'I wish I wanted to bully you'.[63] An expression of tenderness, playfulness, and surreptitious homoerotic sadism, Ansell's remark also emphasizes his physical strength. Whilst this emphasis on his own able-bodiedness is, in part, an intended contrast with Rickie's disability, it can also be read as Ansell's physical demonstration of anti-degeneration. Just as his intellectual endeavour, as I have suggested, is related to his Jewish identity, so is his physical strength suggestive of his concern with contemporary perceptions of the Jewish body. In chapter 20, his response to Widdrington, a fellow Cambridge scholar, who laments 'the curse of being a little intellectual', more directly challenges the anti-Semitic notion of the Jewish body as weak and deformed:

> 'But we are bloodless brutes. ... Two philosophic youths repining in the British Museum! What have we done? What shall we ever do? Just drift and criticize, while people who know what they want snatch it away from us and laugh.'
> 'Perhaps you are that sort. I'm not. When the moment comes I shall hit out like any ploughboy.'[64]

Whilst Widdrington's words reiterate the perceived degeneracy of intellectuals, Ansell's reply resists it. The comparison of himself to a ploughboy connects him with Stephen (Stephen is once described by Rickie as 'a kind of cynical ploughboy'), but it also resonates, resoundingly, with Nordau's ideal of 'the muscle Jew'.[65] In a 1905 pamphlet, Nordau argued that Zionism was 'to make' those who are 'all divorced from nature ... once more familiar with the plough and with nourishing Mother Earth'.[66] In Ansell's response, the invocation of a return to Nature is simultaneously a delineation of the 'healthy' Jew. The parallel between Ansell's resistance to

---

[62] For the homoerotic undertone of the characterization of Ansell, see e.g. Joseph Bristow, '*Fratrum Societati*: Forster's Apostolic Dedications', in *Queer Forster*, ed. Martin and Piggford, pp. 113–36 (pp. 121–25). Bristow, elsewhere, discusses the intersection of homoeroticism, eugenics, and masculinity in the novel: Bristow, *Effeminate England*, pp. 68–71.

[63] *LJ*, p. 65.   [64] *LJ*, p. 180.   [65] *LJ*, p. 192.

[66] Max Nordau, *Zionism: Its History and Its Aims*, trans. Israel Cohen (London: English Zionist Federation, 1905), p. 19.

social perceptions of him and Nordau's Zionist revisions of Jewishness becomes striking.

A musical instrument has an intriguingly prominent role in the moment when Ansell does 'hit out'. In chapter 27, when he discloses Stephen's parentage to Rickie in front of all the boarders at the Sawston School during a Sunday dinner, Ansell, standing 'by the harmonium', 'put one foot on a chair and held his arms over the quivering room. He seemed transfigured into a Hebrew prophet passionate for satire and the truth'.[67] A shock to Rickie and a scandal for Agnes, Ansell's decisive act is significant in many ways. In the novel, the school harmonium is explicitly associated with the imperial ideal of *esprit de corps*: 'over the harmonium to which [the school] sang the evening hymns was spread the Union Jack'.[68] Ansell's defiance thus disrupts the unity of imperial patriotism, and his Jewishness diffuses the Christian religiosity so frequently conjured up in proclamations of the Empire's 'missions'. Additionally, the students' disharmonious singing of the school anthem, presumably accompanied by the harmonium, is elsewhere described by the narrator as in 'the style of Richard Strauss'.[69] While the ironic reference to Strauss might simply indicate Forster's disparagement of late Romantic tonal discordance and excessive chromaticism, the association of the harmonium with a composer who was widely regarded as the inheritor of Wagner's musical legacy lends added significance to Ansell's search for a rejuvenated Jewish identity.[70] Here, we see Ansell take control of the harmonium while radiating an inspired Jewishness that disperses any vestiges of associations with 'degeneration'. If his self-manifested aversion to music is a strategy of defence, he is enabling his Jewish identity to confront not just music but a particular style of music. By denying the instrument the chance to sound, Ansell's action can be read as a Jewish triumph, secured after overcoming Wagner's (and Strauss's) 'degenerate' musical affectivity.

Forster's juxtaposition of the Siegfried-like Stephen with this self-proclaimed unheroic Jewish intellectual, then, makes a parodic divergence from the novel's Wagnerian source. Ansell's confession of not being a hero now seems ironic, since his disclosure of Stephen's parentage, as we have seen, is described as an emotionally heightened moment, and it is his 'heroic' act that moves the plot forward and facilitates the reunion of the two brothers. Interestingly, it is indeed described as an 'act'. In the chapter

---

[67] *LJ*, pp. 223 and 224–25.   [68] *LJ*, p. 222.   [69] *LJ*, p. 158.

[70] Bryan Gilliam and Charles Youmans, 'Strauss, Richard', *Grove Music Online*, www.oxfordmusiconline.com [accessed 10 May 2018].

E. M. Forster and Music

before his action, Ansell, alone in the garden where he has just encountered Stephen, is deep in his own thoughts, as described by the narrator: 'Ansell prepared himself to witness the second act of the drama; forgetting that all this world, and not part of it, is a stage'.[71] Given the novel's extensive Wagnerian allusions, the paraphrased Shakespearean line also alludes to the Wagnerian stage. Ansell's subsequent prominent role on this Wagnerian stage thus demonstrates how Forster's narrative is driven by this unheroic figure and how it, consequently, differs from Wagner's hero-packed tetralogy. Replacing conquest and violence with restraint and self-deprecation, mocking the 'hero' as a cad while placing the assimilated Jewish scholar under the spotlight, *The Longest Journey* critiques Wagner's conception of heroism. It is through the same strategy of juxtaposing the heroic and the unheroic that Forster contested Wagner's heroism in the late 1930s.

'V Stands for Vulgarity'

In a letter to Cecil Day-Lewis on 30 October 1938, Forster wondered about the possibility of a war:

> Either we yield to the Nazis and they subdue us. *Or* we stand up to them, come to resemble them in the process, and are subdued to them that way. Your poems, particularly the long one, offer the possibility of heroic action, and many will be satisfied by that; but not you nor I.[72]

Forster's statement is a firm refusal to adopt heroism, regardless of its broad topicality, as an option with which Britain could curb the aggression of Nazi Germany. It is, in part, a reiterated pacifist critique of the 'soldier hero': back in the First World War, Forster told Malcolm Darling not to 'indulge in Romance' because '[t]he newspapers still talk about glory but the average man, thank God, has got rid of that illusion'.[73] The statement is a response to Nazism, too. Forster perceived the Nazis as a political oligarchy: the reference to Hermann Göring in *Nordic Twilight* is an example; also, in 'A View without a Room' (1958), the fictional postscript to *A Room with a View*, Forster directly identifies Nazism as 'Hitlerism', which was 'an enemy of the heart as well as of the head and the arts'.[74]

---

[71] *LJ*, p. 218. [72] *SL*, II, pp. 161–62.

[73] Letter to Malcolm Darling (6 November 1914). *SL*, I, p. 214. The phrase 'soldier hero' is from Graham Dawson, *Soldier Heroes: British Adventure, Empire and the Imagining of Masculinities* (London: Routledge, 1994), p. 1.

[74] 'A View without a Room' (1958), in *RV*, pp. 210–12 (p. 211).

The Problem of the Wagnerian Hero

This identification of individual figures as the target of his criticism indicates Forster's opposition to 'Great Men'. His dismissal of wartime heroism was, then, informed and augmented by these perceptions of Nazi Germany; for him, to refuse to adopt heroism was to prevent British democracy from turning into Nazified authoritarianism. This strategy of differentiation, however, put him in a difficult situation: ultimately, the Nazis had to be thwarted, but how? Forster's resistance to heroism – his pacifism as well as his anti-Nazism – made it difficult for him to envision Britain's role and course of action against this adversary. 'What I Believe' and 'Post-Munich', two of the essays Forster wrote in the months leading up to the war, address this difficulty. Though different in tone, both essays dismiss heroism whilst searching for an alternative solution to the political crisis. More importantly, Wagner's *Ring* cycle provides the means through which both essays negotiate these issues.

'What I Believe' was, as is widely agreed, a Forsterian manifesto against disparate concurrent political causes in the 1930s, in which Forster articulates the central tenets of his ideology, including humanism, liberty, democracy, sensitivity, and individualism.[75] Many parts of the essay have been scrutinized, but a half-paragraph-long allusion to the *Ring* has received little attention within Forster scholarship. In his discussion of democracy, Forster acknowledges the necessary existence of state force but argues that it is human beings' responsibility to keep it in check, as 'all the great creative actions, all the decent human relations, occur during the intervals when force has not managed to come to the front':

> Consider [the strong people's] conduct for a moment in *The Nibelung's Ring*. The giants there have the guns, or in other words the gold; but they do nothing with it, they do not realize that they are all-powerful, with the result that the catastrophe is delayed and the castle of Valhalla, insecure but glorious, fronts the storms. Fafnir, coiled round his hoard, grumbles and grunts; we can hear him under Europe today; the leaves of the wood already tremble, and the Bird calls its warnings uselessly. Fafnir will destroy us, but by a blessed dispensation he is stupid and slow, and creation goes on just outside the poisonous blast of his breath. The Nietzschean would hurry the monster up, the mystic would say he did not exist, but Wotan, wiser than either, hastens to create warriors before doom declares itself. The Valkyries are symbols not only of courage but of intelligence; they represent the human spirit snatching its opportunity while the going is good, and one of them even finds time to love. Brünnhilde's last song hymns the recurrence

---

[75] Originally titled as 'Two Cheers for Democracy', the essay was published on 16 July 1938 for the series 'Living Philosophy' in the New York political magazine *Nation*. *TCD*, pp. 65–73.

of love, and since it is the privilege of art to exaggerate she goes even further, and proclaims the love which is eternally triumphant, and feeds upon freedom and lives.[76]

Though principally a discussion of the confrontation between the giant and the gods, the passage subtly critiques Siegfried. Forster's disapproval of the 'Nietzschean' reiterates his doubt about Siegfried, criticizing Wagner's hero, as Mrs Failing does the intrusive dragon slayer, for the hazardous action which instigates greater scale of violence and destruction. That Siegfried is the key character not explicitly named here displaces the narrative focus of the *Ring* cycle and divorces the tetralogy from an environment of hero-worship. Given the widely reported close relationship between Bayreuth and the Nazis, such divergence from Wagner's hero-mythology becomes a declaration of anti-Nazism in the form of celebrating Brünnhilde's redemptive role as the ultimate ideal of 'love'. But such idealism is characterized by a distinct consciousness of a world on the verge of war; the optimism underpinning his celebration is undercut by poignant fatalism, expressed by phrases such as 'catastrophe', 'will destroy us', and 'doom'. Forster's allusion to the tetralogy, then, combines his criticism of Siegfried with expressions of his mixed feelings towards the current international situation. Whether optimistic or pessimistic, idealistic or practical, his avoidance of Siegfried and emphasis on Brünnhilde dismiss counteractions and uphold a pacifist view. This view is self-consciously and purposefully idealistic, if not merely escapist: 'I look the other way until fate strikes me. Whether this is due to courage or to cowardice in my own case I cannot be sure'.[77]

Forster could no longer be idealistic, however, after the Munich Agreement, which was signed on 30 September 1938.[78] In 'Post-Munich', an essay exploring the prevalent uncertainty in Britain in the first half of 1939, Forster not only remarks on the futility of heroic action but also abandons his faith in 'love':

> The decade being tragic, should not our way of living correspond? How can we justify trivialities and hesitations? Ought we not to rise to the great dramatic conception which we see developing around us? ... Ought we not, at such a moment, to act as Wagnerian heroes and heroines, who are

---

[76] *TCD*, p. 68.   [77] *TCD*, p. 68.

[78] For a contextual discussion of Forster's and other contemporaries' responses to 'The 1939 State', see Steve Ellis, *British Writers and the Approach of World War II* (Cambridge, UK: Cambridge University Press, 2014).

raised above themselves by the conviction that all is lost or that all can be saved, and stride singing into the flames?

To ask such a question is to answer it. No one who debates whether he shall behave tragically can possibly be a tragic character. He may have a just sense of the stage; he may discern the scene darkening and the powers of evil marching and the ravens gathering; he may feel the first breath of the tempest as it lifts him off his feet and whirls him backwards. But he is not properly cast as an actor; there will be something petty in him – perhaps something recalcitrant – which mars the aesthetic unity. He will not even pay the tribute of unalloyed terror. He will be half frightened and half thinking about something else on the very steps of the altar, and when the sacrificial knife falls he will perish an unworthy victim, a blemished and inferior lamb, of little esteem at the banquet of the gods.[79]

Forster finds the *Zeitgeist* in 1939 in stark contrast to that in 1938. For him, people in 1938 either support pacifism or urge military action. Continuing his Wagnerian allusion, Forster compares the pacifists to Brünnhilde and militarists, i.e. those who 'prepared to fight – with what weapons and against what they did not stay to consider', to Siegmund.[80] But the year 1939, for Forster, is a moment when 'certainties and heroisms' no longer exist, and neither 'cowardice' nor 'bravery' can clarify the complexity people have to live in and confront.[81] Under these circumstances, Forster suggests extra sensitivity: only by being sensitive can 'we' sharpen our blunted emotions and attempt to survive this decade in which 'the Crisis . . . has become a habit, indeed almost a joke'.[82]

Compared to 'What I Believe', 'Post-Munich' alludes to the *Ring* cycle in a less dramatic manner. The changed attitude towards Brünnhilde questions the relevance and applicability of her redemptive suicide to the present world, rehearsing Forster's criticism of the 'tragic' sense of Wagner and German national culture in *Nordic Twilight*. The differentiation of life from theatre and the biblical analogue of the lamb both remove the collective 'we' from Wagner's 'tragic' scenario of violence and death, love and sacrifice; instead, 'we' in this post-Munich era are characterized by 'trivialities and hesitations'. Such deflation of 'tragic' heroism, combined with the emphasis on the shared mundanity, not only underlines Forster's pacifism but also suggests his resistance to simplification and sectarianism. His replacement of the heroic with the mundane, that is, simultaneously refrains from fuelling or accelerating the actual conflict with individual actions and rejects the 'either-or' logic of contemporary political conflicts.

---

[79] 'Post-Munich' (1939), in *TCD*, pp. 21–24 (p. 21).   [80] *TCD*, p. 22.   [81] *TCD*, pp. 22–23.   [82] *TCD*, p. 24.

It indicates a moderate approach to political contingencies; though caught between the aggressive justification of fighting and the eschewing of violence, the indecisive, sensitive 'we' are allowed to have discerning musings about the complexity of 1939. That is why sensitivity is underscored and endowed with such significance at the end of 'Post-Munich'. Echoing his delineation of the 'aristocracy of the sensitive' in 'What I Believe', Forster's emphasis on sensitivity in 'Post-Munich' permits and encourages lingering thoughts on the complicated political dynamics between Nazism and anti-Nazism: 'Sensitive people are having a particularly humiliating time just now. Looking at the international scene, they see, with a clearness denied to politicians, that if Fascism wins we are done for, and that we must become Fascist to win'.[83] Demolishing the dichotomized perception of Germany and Britain, the last sentence is the main reason why Forster resisted heroism so strongly and resisted joining or exploiting the topicality of heroism in the late 1930s. For Forster, to come to war with Germany, which would inevitably happen, was to thwart Nazism on the one hand, but also to accept, aggravate, and aggrandize the Wagnerian scenario of extremity, where glory and death are intertwined, on the other. His interpretation of Wagner's heroes as irrelevant in 'Post-Munich' reiterates his refusal to counter-attack and anticipates his consequent silence about Wagner in the coming years.

During the war, Forster made numerous critiques of heroism in his private writings. In a diary entry made two months after the outbreak of the war, for example, Forster mentioned how his life remained in unexpected serenity: 'I have even found comforts and beauties and wish I had the force to write about them'. He did give a list of his observations on things around: 'the search lights from the roof of my flat', 'the finely contrived entrances to the public buildings', 'the freedom from aeroplanes', and many more. However, he realized that '[b]eneath this fantasy the usual meanness and bullying must be burgeoning, but don't yet show'. Another twist of mood followed, as he wrote, resolutely and emphatically, that 'I would rather notice all this than contemplate Heroism[.] . . . War is <u>not</u> best tackled by regarding it as the antithesis of peace'.[84] It is evident, then, that Forster, in his own way, upheld his resistance to heroism, which is also a resistance to propaganda, during the war. In another diary entry, Forster wrote what would have been controversial if he had stated in public:

[83] *TCD*, p. 23.   [84] Diary entry (13 November 1939). *JD*, II, p. 90.

The Problem of the Wagnerian Hero   127

> I want Germany to lose but not England to win, I take no interest in news
> except when the names of places are mentioned, listen to no speeches, and
> scarcely read newspapers. This is partly war-weariness and sadness, partly
> propaganda-reaction: I know that I am being got at: frankness is used to lull
> suspicion and make us uncritical of the next lie.[85]

Like this intentional avoidance of public discourses on the war, Forster's
unfinished Beethoven Notebook and his silence about Wagner were
similar strategies of restraint, a way of remaining critical of the politicization of the work and status of the two composers.

Amidst this negotiation of heroism, the recurrence of the term 'vulgarity' in Forster's wartime writings is too conspicuous to be ignored. By no
means randomly applied, 'vulgarity' was used by Forster as a synonym of
and a substitute for heroism. The emphasis on Britain's 'heroic' mission
against Nazi Germany, on fighting this war for a righteous cause,
prompted Forster to exclaim: 'And the vulgarity of it all. Deeper than
the cruelty and the deceit, the vulgarity'.[86] This alignment of heroism with
vulgarity recalls Mrs Failing's assessment of the hero in *The Longest
Journey*; it reminds us, too, of Forster's description of Siegfried as a 'cad'.
In 1943, when Mussolini was overthrown and imprisoned by the Italian
government, Forster wrote: 'If we were not a nation of cads, if all nations
were not cads, we should see that the rescue of Mussolini [by Hitler's
order] was the one heroic achievement of the war'.[87] Whether Forster was
being controversial or satiric, the remark plays with the old pairing of
cad and hero, and destabilizes the notion of the heroic. When victory
was foreseeable, Forster's identification of heroism with vulgarity increased
in volume:

> Italy gave in on the 6.0. news. No happiness or hope felt. This sort of good
> news cuts ice with me no longer. Pleased however when they put on the 5th
> Symphony, although they doubtless did so because V stands for vulgarity.[88]

Forster's bitter condemnation of the capitalized 'V' targeted the 'V for
Victory' campaign, which had been propagated by the BBC appropriating
the connection between the rhythm of the opening notes of Beethoven's
symphony and the letter V in the Morse code in their programmes
broadcast to Europe. A trenchant response to his nation's and other
Allied countries' recourse to violence for the aim of victory, Forster's

---

[85] Diary entry (31 August 1941). *JD*, II, p. 94.   [86] Diary entry (23 May 1940). *JD*, II, p. 92.
[87] Diary entry (15 September 1943). *JD*, II, p. 98.
[88] Diary entry (8 September 1943). *JD*, II, p. 98.

128 E. M. Forster and Music

'V stands for vulgarity' reiterated his alertness to and anxieties about the increasing politicization of the perceived heroism of Beethoven's music.

Like the ironic characterization of Ansell's heroic quality in *The Longest Journey*, Forster's wartime writings challenge the concept of the mundane as the unheroic. This attempt to reconfigure mundanity is implicit at the end of 'Post-Munich': 'The world won't work out, and the person who can realize this, and not just say it and lament it, has done as well as can be expected of him in the present year'.[89] Common people, daily routines, private relationships, and trivial decisions were commended for their value in this time of crisis on their own terms. On 8 September 1940, Forster made a diary entry titled 'London Burning':

> I watched this event from my Chiswick flat last night with disgust and indignation, but with no intensity though the spectacle was superb. . . . This is all that a world catastrophe amounts to. Something which one is too sad and sullen to appreciate. Perhaps we are really behaving heroically[.][90]

Forster's description captures the destructive violence and the aesthetic excitement of the spectacle of a city ablaze.[91] The application of the adverb 'heroically' to the endurance of the collective 'we' uncouples the idea of heroism from individual decisive action and exceptional deeds. More importantly, the use of the term simultaneously diminishes wartime heroics, indicates Forster's admiration for the mundane, and centralizes the great public's experience in perceptions of and accounts about the war. Like the descriptions of Ansell, this diary entry elevates the status of the common and the self-acknowledged insignificant individuals and redefines heroism.

'Siegfried Should Be Bearable'

Wagner remained a highly contentious – and indeed controversial – subject in the aftermath of the war. Forster would certainly have been aware that the Nazified Wagner was a taboo in these years of denazification; he would have almost certainly heard Wagner criticized in lurid language in the Harvard symposium he attended in 1947. The symposium was dominated by anti-Wagnerian scholars: one of them, the American composer and music critic Roger Sessions, unequivocally claimed in his

---

[89] *TCD*, p. 24.   [90] *JD*, II, p. 94.
[91] For a perceptive reading of other descriptions of the flaming London in the Blitz, see Leo Mellor, *Reading the Ruins: Modernism, Bombsites and British Culture* (Cambridge, UK: Cambridge University Press, 2011), pp. 62–84.

The Problem of the Wagnerian Hero 129

speech that he and several others in attendance found Wagner's music 'distasteful' and 'repulsive'.[92] Such prevalent anti-Wagnerism also might have contributed to the fact that, in Forster's lecture, 'The *Raison d'Être* of Criticism', he made only one passing reference to Wagner – not even in his words but simply a quotation from the English humorist 'Beachcomber'.[93] Whether a coincidence or a calculated detail, whether a personal judgement of Wagner's irrelevance to his topic or a strategic evasion from controversy in the symposium, the lecture's lack of Wagnerian allusions continued Forster's silence about the composer.

Not until 1954 did Forster reopen his discussion of Wagner. In that year, Forster attended the annual Bayreuth Festival and wrote 'Revolution at Bayreuth' for a BBC broadcast talk. A focused study of Wagner's music dramas, Forster's talk expressed mixed feelings about his Bayreuth experience, casting doubt specifically on the Wagner grandsons' attempt to dilute Wagner's distinct Teutonism by augmenting the composer's 'universal' appeal through abstraction.[94] One of the books which Forster was reading before his trip to Bayreuth and which was likely to have informed his reception of the Bayreuth production of Wagner's work was *The Cult of the Superman* by the American critic and playwright Eric Bentley. Forster, in his diary, considered it a 'good book'.[95] In his *Commonplace Book*, he gave a brief appraisal of the book's individual chapters: 'Many such readable remarks are in the book, which has the more solid merit of an intelligible account of Nietzsche. The section on Wagner also v. good Carlyle and Stefan George less so'.[96] It is worth speculating which parts of Bentley's interpretation of Wagner's ideology might have garnered Forster's praise. At a broader level, Forster might be approving of Bentley's approach to the controversial subject of Wagner and heroism in the aftermath of Nazism. As Bentley said in the foreword to the book, people in the 1940s 'are not in a frame of mind to listen to praise of Bismarck, Frederick the Great, and the Germans', but he found it necessary to tease out the nuances of previous ideas of heroism, not only because they could not be 'dismissed as Hitlerism' but also because we 'need [not]

---

[92] Roger Sessions, 'The Scope of Music Criticism', in *Music and Criticism: A Symposium*, ed. Richard F. French (Cambridge, MA: Harvard University Press, 1948), pp. 35–51 (p. 48).
[93] *TCD*, p. 110.
[94] For a discussion of the radio broadcast, see Tsung-Han Tsai, '"Worse than irritated – namely, insecure": Forster at Bayreuth', in *Wagner and Literature*, Special Issue of *Forum for Modern Language Studies*, ed. Michael Allis, 50.4 (2014), 466–81.
[95] *JD*, III, p. 118.   [96] *CB*, p. 194.

130   E. M. Forster and Music

adopt a patronizing attitude to these critics of democracy'.[97] Forster might therefore have valued Bentley's study for its subject matter and its ideological aim.

It is also possible that, on a specific note, Forster was in accord with Bentley's reading of Siegfried. Bentley regarded Siegfried as 'the iconoclast', but disparaged the character's action in the tetralogy as 'too loud, too violent, too arrogant: an unregenerate pagan devoid of compassion'.[98] The parallel between Bentley's and Forster's readings of Siegfried is evident, and Bentley's words might have thus informed Forster's comment on Siegfried in 'Revolution at Bayreuth'. In the radio broadcast, Forster was, as he had been throughout the first half of the century, focused on Siegfried's prominence in the tetralogy. Focusing on the forging of the sword *Nothung* in Act I, scene i, in *Siegfried*, Forster described the scene as 'a heroic romp':

> Siegfried in a patch of ruddy light, Mime in a greenish patch, did their bests, hiss went the blade, crash the anvil, topple the pot, and there stood the dubious hero armed. It does not do to think earnestly about Siegfried. Bayreuth started him off with a rush and a crash and stopped one thinking. I have never objected to him less. It is essential to one's enjoyment of 'The Ring' that Siegfried should be bearable, that his caddishness should be accepted as boyishness and his infidelity as hallucination. He is an awkward customer, but he got pulled through.[99]

The passage demonstrates that Forster again assessed the heroic quality of Siegfried in his evaluation of the character. Siegfried's status as the hero is accepted here thanks to the live performance. The passage highlights, semi-satirically, the fact that the fast-paced action and the visual and auditory sumptuousness provided entertainment but no pause for thought. Read alongside his diary entry on *Siegfried*, in which he unreservedly declared that 'Act I was splendid – only physical action but they did act and the making of a hero is always heroic',[100] Forster's description of Siegfried as 'bearable' in 'Revolution at Bayreuth' indicates a qualification of his admiration and suggests a probing into the factors behind his admiration. Perhaps there is homoeroticism in Forster's immediate praise of the 'physical' part of the performance, although we can only speculate in what way the acting or the appearance of the renowned tenor Wolfgang

---

[97] Eric Bentley, *The Cult of the Superman: A Study of the Idea of Heroism in Carlyle and Nietzsche, with Notes on Other Hero-Worshippers of Modern Times* (London: Hale, 1947), pp. xi–xii, vii, and xvi.
[98] Bentley, *Cult*, p. 153.   [99] 'Revolution at Bayreuth' (1954), in *PT*, pp. xi–xii, vii, and xvi.
[100] Diary entry (12 August 1954). *JD*, III, p. 123.

The Problem of the Wagnerian Hero   131

Windgassen as Siegfried might have inspired Forster to suspend momentarily his distrust of the character.[101] The preceding passage is therefore also an example of the effect of Wagner's music on the audience: only through writing retrospectively without the excitement of the live performance can Forster retain his critical judgement on Siegfried as a 'dubious hero'.

At the end of his time in Bayreuth, Forster wrote in his diary: 'My last Bayreuth evening. I never shall, do not even wish to come back, but a gap in my inexperience has been filled'.[102] Ambivalently, Forster rounded off his Wagnerism. 'Revolution at Bayreuth' can thus be read not only as a personal account or a travelogue but also as a symbolic end of his decades-long engagement with Wagner – with Wagner's music, ideology, and hero-worship. From his early reactions to Siegfried's caddishness, to his characterization of Stephen and Ansell, to his pre–Second World War Wagnerian allusions, to his silence about Wagner and disgust with the 'vulgarity' of the war, and, finally, to his Bayreuth pilgrimage, we see a critical process through which Forster reflected on Siegfried's heroic quality and formulated his own ideas of heroism. Such a process considers not only the Wagnerian heroism but also, as I have suggested, the political repercussions Wagner and his work generated. Yet whatever contingent discourses informed his reflection, Forster's personal, sometimes idiosyncratic, commentaries on Siegfried suggest the centrality of subjectivity to his evaluations of Wagner. For Forster, Wagner's work was always art. His silence on Wagner during and after the Second World War exemplifies this belief in Wagner's aesthetic significance; 'I listen to Wagner to-day with unchanged admiration and increasing anxiety', he declared in *Nordic Twilight*. Forster's lifelong engagement with Wagner's music, then, consistently prioritizes the value of individualistic opinions; the freedom conferred by being a musical 'outsider'; and the importance of personal, direct aesthetic experiences.[103] And just as he favoured the mundane in response to the topical worship of heroes during the war, so Forster endowed musical amateurism with added significance in the wake of professionalization in the early decades of the twentieth century, to which we will now turn.

---

[101] It is possible to listen to a recording of Joseph Keilberth, who was a staple conductor in Bayreuth in the 1950s, conducting the *Ring*, with the cast Forster would have heard, though the now famous Keilberth Bayreuth *Ring* recording on the Testament label dates from 1955.

[102] Diary entry (16 August 1954). *JD*, III, p. 125.

[103] The term 'outsider' is from 'Revolution at Bayreuth'. *PT*, p. 176.

CHAPTER 5

Amateurism, Musicology, and Gender

> Here stood the great piano, its keyboard open under the light of the
> french window opposite the door through which she came. Behind
> the great closed swing doors the girls were talking over their *raccom-
> modage*. Miriam paid no attention to them. She would ignore them
> all. She did not even need to try to ignore them. She felt strong and
> independent. She would play, to herself.
>
> Dorothy Richardson, *Pointed Roofs*[1]

Forster's short story, 'The Celestial Omnibus' (1908), describes a boy's
aesthetic and cultural enlightenment. It is a curiously fanciful story in
Forster's oeuvre, with its fairy-tale conventions of children's adventure, its
humanistic reimagining of the Dantean *Paradiso*, and its supernatural,
dark, slightly moralistic ending. Its fantastical elements are further
endorsed by Wagnerian mythology: like *The Longest Journey*, which
Forster completed just a few months earlier in 1907, the story contains
extensive allusions to Wagner's *Ring* cycle, most explicit in the description
of the boy's first omnibus ride. Conducted by Sir Thomas Browne, the
journey is almost identical to the gods' entrance to Valhalla in the final
scene of *Das Rheingold*. The thick fog that the omnibus goes through; the
peal of thunder that sounds like 'the noise of a blacksmith's forge'; the
rainbow bridge unveiled from the 'shattered' cloud amidst growing mur-
murs;[2] the glorious precipice in the morning sunshine; the 'three maidens'
down in 'an everlasting river', playing with 'something that glistened like a
ring' and singing to those on the bridge – all of these details bear striking
resemblance to their Wagnerian sources.[3] The effects of these spectacles
and sounds are also those of Wagner's music dramas, as the excited – if not
debilitated – boy cannot decide whether he should watch, listen, or sing

---

[1] Dorothy Richardson, *Pilgrimage*, 4 vols (London: Virago, 1979), I, p. 56.
[2] Peter E. Firchow has studied the importance of the mythology of the rainbow bridge to Forster.
Firchow, 'Germanic Mythology', pp. 60–68.
[3] 'The Celestial Omnibus', in *MS*, pp. 29–44 (p. 36).

132

Amateurism, Musicology, and Gender   133

along. Such experiences are combined with the boy's instantaneous familiarity with Wagner's music: on his second ride on the omnibus, he sings the Prelude to *Das Rheingold* without knowing anything about the tune. Compared to the death of his awestruck travel companion, Mr Bons, who is too 'knowledgeable' to appreciate the adventure, the boy's unconscious enjoyment, his unassuming character, and his non-discriminatory attitude towards the people he meets are rewarded with aesthetic refinement.[4] Forster's delineation of the boy's acquisition of a Wagnerian sensibility thus privileges direct stimulation and close observation over formal training and extensive background knowledge. That such a dawning moment takes place during a personal experience through the most direct contact with the artwork suggests the centrality of the individual in Forster's vision. That is, Forster's story prioritizes all forms of individualistic, sometimes even idiosyncratic, engagement with music.

This figure of the individual is, among other things, an amateur. Throughout his life, Forster repeatedly emphasized his role as a musical amateur, with the following words from 'The *Raison d'Être* of Criticism' as the representative example: 'I have no authority here. I am an amateur whose inadequacy will become all too obvious as he proceeds'.[5] Such self-abasement also appears in the essay, 'The C Minor of that Life':

> I have battered my head against [whether tonalities have special qualities] for years – a head untrained musically, and unacquainted with any instrument beyond the piano. Perhaps, like many amateur's problems, it is no problem, but one of those solemn mystifications which are erected by ignorance, and which would disappear under proper instruction.[6]

Forster's usual apologetic tone is evident, but another dimension of his musical amateurism is also clear here: underlying his self-acknowledged inadequacy is a wariness of instruction, or educational prescription, from outside. The adjective 'proper' reveals Forster's reservation about training and scholarship, about a standardized and systemized approach to musical works, about excessive emphasis on knowing rather than feeling. Such reservation is explicitly expressed in 'The *Raison d'Être* of Criticism': 'training may sterilize the sensitiveness that is being trained; that education may lead to knowledge instead of wisdom, and ... that spontaneous

---

[4] Nicole duPlessis notes that the contrast is further complicated by the fact that the short story eventually separates the boy from society. Nicole duPlessis, 'Transcendence, Transformation, and the Cultural Economy of Literacy in E. M. Forster's "The Celestial Omnibus" and "Other Kingdom"', *LIT*, 21.2 (2010), 81–100 (p. 85).

[5] *TCD*, p. 105.   [6] 'The C Minor of that Life' (1941), in *TCD*, pp. 119–21 (p. 119).

134 E. M. Forster and Music

enjoyment ... may be checked because too much care has been taken to direct it into the right channel'.[7] This wariness of instruction, at times, amounted to defiance against professional opinions. Forster's claim that he 'lost [his] Coriolanus' because the overture was 'spoiled' by Wagner's 'right' analysis, that the music 'remains, but the sounds have been vulgarised and hardened', indicates not just his opposition to fitting programmes to music but also his resistance to expert intervention.[8] In another example, when writing to the writer E. H. W. Meyerstein in 1944, Forster declared that, in terms of the first movement of the 'Appassionata' Sonata, 'I'm disposed to think everyone is wrong except myself'.[9] His 'subjective reactions' to Beethoven, Forster said to Meyerstein, 'were well worth recording' because they were, as he said elsewhere, the result of his 'physical approach to Beethoven which cannot be gained through the slough of "appreciation"'.[10] This odd, slightly unexpected twist of the Bunyanesque metaphor suggests that Forster perceived 'appreciation' as a lack of discernment.[11] His 'physical' approach to Beethoven's music as a pianist, in contrast, was active, his subjectivity endowed with a certain freshness and dissociated from amateurish reverence. His playing of Beethoven's music became an existential evidence; to uphold it against circulated interpretations became a way of asserting his individuality and of remaining independent from external influences. In insisting on such direct engagement with music, Forster looked forward to 'infection', to a 'sense of cooperation with a creator', to a transformative experience through which one is 'rapt into a region near to that where the artist worked'.[12]

The study of music, not as performance but as a system of knowledge, was being professionalized and socially stratified at the turn of the twentieth century. As the rapid professionalization of society brought forth an increasing emphasis on expertise and credentials in a diverse range of musical activities, musicology gradually transformed from an amateur pursuit to a serious academic discipline in universities.[13] The establishment of music professorships, the reforms of curricula and examinations,

[7] *TCD*, p. 106.   [8] *CB*, pp. 111–12.
[9] Letter to E. H. W. Meyerstein (24 November 1944). King's College Archive Centre, Cambridge: The Papers of E. M. Forster, 18/378/18/Meyerstein.
[10] *TCD*, p. 125.   [11] From John Bunyan's *Pilgrim's Progress*: 'the Slough of Dispond'. *OED*.
[12] *TCD*, pp. 113–14.
[13] This theme runs through Meirion Hughes and Robert Stradling's book *The English Musical Renaissance*. For the establishment of musicology in the United States, see Joseph Kerman, *Musicology*.

the development of theories and analytical tools – all of these contributed to shaping and consolidating the scholarship of musicology.[14] In this respect, Forster's acknowledgement of being an amateur in 'The *Raison d'Être* of Criticism' was prompted by and responsive to the presence of musicologists, academics, and professional musicians in the Harvard symposium. There is certainly a degree of self-awareness of inadequacy, of his inability to use 'the proper language of the professional', in his acknowledgement.[15] However, Forster also gestured deliberately towards themes he deemed beyond critical dissection and differentiated his lecture from musicological – and perhaps, for him, more technical – studies. Forster's manifestation of his amateur status was formed within this historical context; his perception of his musical knowledge as insufficient but nevertheless unique was informed and augmented by the growing population of musical scholars.[16]

In a recent collection of essays on the relationship between music and institutions in nineteenth-century Britain, Paul Rodmell notes that, whilst 'the means of institutionalisation became increasingly diverse and complex', 'music(ians) benefited from being organised': '[T]he tendency ... to professionalise and move away from some of the patriarchal structures of previous periods', he observes, helped 'music and musicians escap[e] the patronage system which had previously sustained them'.[17] While Rodmell correctly unpacks the implications of the liberation of Western art music from exclusive hands, he overlooks that what we understand as 'professional' today is itself a constructed and contested idea. This is not to question his account of Western music's improved social status, but to suggest that, for music to shape itself into 'musicology' and to become a subject worthy to be studied within a contentious intellectual arena, it involved a self-gendering as masculine. To become professional, as David Trotter argues, is to lay claim to virtues such as idealism and abstraction,

---

[14] See e.g. Lisa Parker, 'The Expansion and Development of the Music Degree Syllabus at Trinity College Dublin during the Nineteenth Century', in *Music and Institutions in Nineteenth-Century Britain*, ed. Paul Rodmell (Farnham: Ashgate, 2012), pp. 143–60.

[15] Stephen Benson, *Literary Music: Writing Music in Contemporary Fiction* (Aldershot: Ashgate, 2006), p. 3.

[16] For a discussion of the frictions between and anxieties shared by amateurs and professionals in late nineteenth-century England, see Paula Gillett, 'Ambivalent Friendships: Music-Lovers, Amateurs, and Professional Musicians in the Late Nineteenth Century', in *Music and British Culture, 1785–1914: Essays in Honour of Cyril Ehrlich*, ed. Christina Bashford and Leanne Langley (Oxford: Oxford University Press, 2000), pp. 321–40.

[17] Paul Rodmell, 'Introduction', in *Music and Institutions in Nineteenth-Century Britain*, ed. Rodmell, pp. 1–9 (p. 9).

136   E. M. Forster and Music

through which the expert dissociates the discipline from 'mass' experience.[18] Rather than a sudden, neutral emergence, the establishment of musicology was a process through which gender denominators were used as a means of producing the symbolic capital of its expertise – and thus a means of ensuring its professionalism. As Philip Brett eloquently argued, 'seeking to detach itself from performance in order to attain academic respectability', musicology in the last century was characterized by

> a steady emphasis on a rational scientific basis to both music history and theory; the search for fact at the expense of critical judgment; the avoidance of emotion or of the use of musicological studies to develop emotional maturity as opposed to power through knowledge; an escape from the gendered and dangerous present into the distant past, particularly a glamorized 'Renaissance,' with its aristocratic and male values; the recourse to formalism and immanent criticism in music analysis; an insistence on the autonomous, universal, and transcendent qualities of 'music,' a category usually left unmarked but referring exclusively to European high art music; and a denial of the subjective basis of all scholarly activity. All the considerable apparatus of a rational male scholarly discipline, together with an assumed heterosexuality, was deployed to ward off the evil spirit of femininity and the worse threat of effeminacy that lay beyond.[19]

Ian Biddle further extends Brett's queer criticism of musicology by exposing that the discipline is not only 'patrilineal' but also 'stubbornly white'.[20]

It is within this context that this chapter places Forster's portrayals of scholarly women in musicology. Examining how Forster's representations of musical scholarship are underpinned by his championing of amateurism and resistance to professionalism, the chapter analyses their implications for our understanding of Forster's conception of gender. Critical opinion has long been divided over Forster's representations of women: his women characters have been read as typical and as unconventional, as complex New Women and as gay men in travesty, as facilitators to homosocial bonding and obstacles to male desires.[21] This chapter focuses on his

---

[18] David Trotter, *Paranoid Modernism: Literary Experiment, Psychosis, and the Professionalization of English Society* (Oxford: Oxford University Press, 2001), especially pp. 7–11.

[19] Philip Brett, 'Musicology and Sexuality: The Example of Edward J. Dent', in *Queer Episodes in Music and Modern Identity*, ed. Sophie Fuller and Lloyd Whitesell (Urbana: University of Illinois Press, 2002), pp. 177–88 (pp. 179–80).

[20] Ian Biddle, *Music, Masculinity and the Claims of History: The Austro-German Tradition from Hegel to Freud* (Farnham: Ashgate, 2011), p. 12.

[21] Jane Goldman, 'Forster and Women', in *The Cambridge Companion to E. M. Forster*, ed. Bradshaw, pp. 120–37.

portrayals of musical women, yet not those who listen to or perform music. Previous criticism has produced extensive discussions of Helen Schlegel's listening to Beethoven's Fifth in *Howards End* and Lucy Honeychurch's playing of Beethoven's Piano Sonata Op. 111 in *A Room with a View*, commenting on the significance of music to the formulation of their sexual, gender, and social identity.[22] Like Miriam Henderson in *Pilgrimage*, as we saw in the chapter epigraph, music-making creates a site of solipsistic pleasure and becomes an expression of subjectivity for these characters. What has not been examined is Forster's characterization of women's intellectual engagement with music. The chapter brings into critical focus two women characters who are scholars of music, discussing the ways in which Forster writes about their study and expertise. Focusing on the portrayals of Vashti in 'The Machine Stops' and Dorothea in *Arctic Summer*, the chapter asks whether Forster's championing of amateurism and his distrust of musicology as a professionalized discipline are delineated at the expense of women. The chapter asks why his satire of musical professionalism targets women professionals, and whether his ironic depictions of women's musical scholarship specifically, and women's intellectualism more generally, suggest misogyny. What the chapter seeks to demonstrate, then, is not just Forster's negotiation of the increasingly widened gap between professional and amateur; it also poses questions about Forster's attitude towards women, considering the uneasy resonances generated by his representations of women's intellectual pursuit in the discipline of musicology.

In a chapter on musical amateurs, some words need to be said regarding the failure of Leonard Bast's self-education in *Howards End*. Bast's awkward and anxious concert and post-concert experiences alongside the Schlegels have been the subject of many critical analyses, several of which have condemned Forster's characterization of Bast as reflective of his (Forster's) class prejudice and sense of superiority. Jonathan Wild, for instance, suggests that 'Forster and his ilk actually believed in the logic of a permanent intellectual caste system, a system which could

---

[22] See, representatively, Weatherhead, '*Howards End*', pp. 251–63; Björkén-Nyberg, 'Music and Gender', pp. 89–102; Michelle Fillion, 'Edwardian Perspectives on Nineteenth-Century Music in E. M. Forster's *A Room with a View*', *19th-Century Music*, 25.2–3 (2001–2), 266–95; Fillion, *Difficult Rhythm*, pp. 60–78 and 83–92; Zhou, 'Sublime Noise', pp. 78–133; Regula Hohl Trillini, *The Gaze of the Listener: English Representations of Domestic Music-Making* (Amsterdam: Rodopi, 2008), pp. 201–5; and Sutton, *Virginia Woolf and Classical Music*, chapter 2, 'Killing the Pianist in the House', pp. 48–68.

138   E. M. Forster and Music

conveniently dismiss from its circle those of more limited intellectual capacity'.[23] However, as Gemma Moss suggests, if the concert scene in *Howards End*, in its depiction of each of the individuals' free response to Beethoven's symphony, illustrates 'the democratic potential of the music', it also highlights that 'this freedom is incredibly limited' as 'the playing field is already extremely uneven'.[24] The salient point here is that Forster's version of amateurism is preconditioned by this limitation if 'love' is what Forster perceives as the prerequisite for being an amateur and total immersion is the only course of action.[25] Bast's failure to gain culture via music says more about Bast's lack of money (and thus time and access) and less about his lack of intelligence. In a novel which registers the material limitations (or possibilities) of one's circumstances, as demonstrated by the intrusive narrator's famous announcement about 'the very poor' as 'unthinkable',[26] Forster's portrayal of Bast does not necessarily perpetuate the boundary between the privileged and the deprived, but it does recognize that the attitude towards culture as an end rather than a means is something that only money can afford. Forster's preference for musical amateurism seems not a protest against monetization of the subject or against competition from working class's participation, as in the history of the professionalization of other amateur activities or fields of study. Nonetheless, it does suggest an ideal of pure intent free from financial worries and unconcerned with additional material benefit. It is not a guarded ideal against social inclusivity, but the case of Leonard Bast suggests that Forster's vision of the individualism and independence of an amateur's pursuit very much depends on external factors beyond one's intent, interest, or passion.

Arguably, in his fictional writing, Forster finds it easier to voice his celebration of musical amateurism not by writing about an amateur's attempt to engage with music but by writing against the professional. Both 'The Machine Stops' and *Arctic Summer* satirize musical scholarship

---

[23] Jonathan Wild, *The Rise of the Office Clerk in Literary Culture, 1880–1939* (Houndmills: Palgrave Macmillan, 2006), p. 116.

[24] Moss, 'Music in E. M. Forster's *A Room with a View* and *Howards End*', p. 502.

[25] After the declaration of his amateur status in 'The *Raison d'Être* of Criticism', Forster decidedly returned to 'Love': 'However cautiously, or with whatever reservations, after whatsoever purifications, we must come back to love' (*TCD*, p. 118). William Roerick, with whom Forster revised the lecture the day before the event, reminisced that Forster gave him the liberty to restructure the lecture but demanded 'Love' be mentioned 'at the beginning, in the middle and at the end'. William Roerick, 'Forster and America', in *Aspects of E. M. Forster*, ed. Stallybrass, pp. 61–72 (p. 65).

[26] *HE*, p. 43.

in its institutional form, exposing the professional's control of a powerful set of gendered rhetoric, concepts, and assumptions to suppress or to regulate the individual. Issues of gender – like those of money, class, and ethnicity – are thus inevitable in reflecting on the construction of professionalism. Forster's characterization of his musical scholars as women only complicates the issues.

'The Machine Stops'

'The Machine Stops' was Forster's sole attempt at science fiction. Written in 1908, the story was first published in *The Oxford and Cambridge Review* in 1909 and subsequently included in Forster's second collection of short stories, *The Eternal Moment and Other Stories*, in 1928. Intended as a response to Wellsian optimism about progress and technology, the story is set in a future world where every human being is designated a subterranean cell, and every aspect of human life is sustained and controlled by the intelligent and omnipotent 'Machine'. As critics have noted, the story provides an extraordinarily prophetic exploration of the crisis of humanity under the influence of science. It has been read in relation to Forster's belief in personal relationships and tied in with discussions about Forster's notion of intimacy and homosexual desire.[27] It has also been contextualized within the genre of science fiction: acknowledged as a precursor of later dystopian fictions, it has been regarded as a prescient portrayal of late twentieth- and early twenty-first-century cyber networks.[28]

However, the prominence of music in the story has never been discussed. Music plays a multifaceted role in Forster's future world. First and foremost is its ambivalent part in the Machine regime's programme of mass control. At the opening of the story, when the narration begins by delineating the main character's cell, sounds of music can be heard: 'There are no musical instruments, and yet ... this room is throbbing with melodious sounds'.[29] This description of disembodied music conjures up an evidently modern soundscape. It echoes the effect of Wagner's hidden

---

[27] Ralph Pordzik, 'Closet Fantasies and the Future of Desire in E. M. Forster's "The Machine Stops"', *English Literature in Transition*, 53.1 (2010), 54–74.

[28] See e.g. Douglas Mao, 'The Point of It', in *Utopianism, Modernism, and Literature in the Twentieth Century*, ed. Alice Reeve-Tucker and Nathan Waddell (Basingstoke: Palgrave Macmillan, 2013), pp. 19–38; Tom Moylan, *Scraps of the Untainted Sky: Science Fiction, Utopia, Dystopia* (Boulder: Westview, 2000), pp. 111–21 and 159; Brooks Landon, *Science Fiction after 1900: From the Steam Man to the Stars* (New York: Routledge, 2002), pp. 11–21; and Silvana Caporaletti, 'Science as Nightmare: "The Machine Stops" by E. M. Forster', *Utopian Studies*, 8.2 (1997), 32–47.

[29] *MS*, p. 87.

140   E. M. Forster and Music

orchestra at the Bayreuth *Festspielhaus*. It also recalls the development of sound recording at the turn of the century, which overturned the centuries-long perception of musical sound as irrevocable. Most importantly, the modernity of the music is also manifested in its transmission through a worldwide broadcast system, which anticipates, uncannily, the operation of the BBC more than a decade later. The reliance on such a far-reaching communication network, however, gives music in the short story a sinister presence. This future broadcast system is characterized as thought controlling and linked specifically to state surveillance: 'Under the seas, beneath the roots of the mountains, ran the wires through which [human beings] saw and heard, ... and the hum of many workings clothed their thoughts in one garment of subserviency'.[30] What underlies this advanced civilization of technophilia is, then, the menacing authoritarianism of the Machine. Writing in the late Edwardian years, Forster might not have foreseen that this critique of the association between media and state control would work reflexively as an ironic footnote to his own engagement with the BBC after the 1920s. Or perhaps we could say that his entire career as an active broadcaster – and as an important national voice after the Second World War – was prompted exactly by this alertness to the power of media and an intention to take good advantage of it.[31] In this respect, music, transmitted through such a broadcast system, seems to be one of the tools of mass control used by the Machine. And since subsequent depictions of music in the story show that the same tracks are played repeatedly ('the symphonies of the Brisbane school', which will be discussed later), the music's melodiousness seems to produce a hypnotic effect on its listeners.

This portrayal of music as a potentially hypnotizing, sedative device in the Machine world was informed by the topicality of musical affectivity within turn-of-the-century formulations of crowd theory: the crowd was often defamiliarized as foreign and characterized as feminine and susceptible to music's effect.[32] In the story, the characteristics of the 'audience' at the receiving end of the broadcast system are associated with those of the crowd: they are anonymous, featureless ('People were almost exactly alike all over the world'), and impressionable ('No one could mistake the

---

[30] *MS*, pp. 114–15.

[31] For an insightful discussion of Forster as a BBC broadcaster, Peter Fifield, '"I often wish you could answer me back: and so perhaps do you!": E. M. Forster and BBC Radio Broadcasting', in *Broadcasting in the Modernist Era*, ed. Matthew Feldman, Erik Tonning, and Henry Mead (London: Bloomsbury, 2014), pp. 57–77.

[32] Sutton, *Aubrey Beardsley*, pp. 104–6.

Amateurism, Musicology, and Gender 141

reverent tone in which [a lecture on religion] had concluded, and it awakened a responsive echo in the heart of each').[33] Although the story never specifically describes whether music lends its power to the Machine's dominance over human beings, Forster's depictions of the music's pervasiveness, recurrence, and melodiousness imply that music plays a part in sedating its listeners and contributes to transforming human beings into a conglomeration of senseless creatures.

The association between music and mass control, however, is made ambiguous by the previously quoted word 'throbbing', which endows the hypnotic melodiousness with a heartbeat-like energy. This bodily pulse of the music recalls the vitalistic associations of the term 'rhythm' and contradicts the assumption that music is used as mass sedation, as it embodies a certain corporeality which the Machine cannot diminish. Such a conceptualization of music as an organic entity recurs in part III of the story when signs of the Machine's failure appear. Vashti, the main character, complains to her friend about the 'trouble' lately with the music broadcast: there have been 'those curious gasping sighs that disfigure the symphonies of the Brisbane school. They sound like someone in pain'.[34] Her personification of these auditory 'defects' sends out multiple implications for the role music plays in the story.[35] On a thematic level, the music here is endowed with senses and emotions and thus placed in opposition to the Machine, which lacks – and attempts to subdue – those qualities. Metaphorically, the 'sighs' can be read as an expression of agony about the condition of human beings under the surface of comfort and convenience. The 'sighs' also suggest a symbolic moment when human beings start to break free from the control of the Machine; they announce the imminent collapse of the system and seem to anticipate the liberation as well as the survival of humanity after the Machine stops. If music in the story is being used by the Machine, it also plays a subversive role in the technophile world.

Vashti is a 'lecturer' on music. In Forster's future world, lecturing – or, more precisely, broadcasting – is the occupation for intellectuals. They lecture on a wide range of subjects; Vashti's 'expertise' lies in 'Music during the Australian Period':

> She opened with a humorous account of music in the pre-Mongolian epoch, and went on to describe the great outburst of song that followed

---

[33] *MS*, pp. 96 and 110. As Emma Sutton observes, 'audience' and 'crowd' were two of the terms that were developed by various texts of crowd theory and were 'identified as distinct entities laden with ideological meaning'. Sutton, *Aubrey Beardsley*, p. 105.
[34] *MS*, p. 112.   [35] *MS*, p. 113.

142   E. M. Forster and Music

> the Chinese conquest. Remote and primaeval as were the methods of
> I-San-So and the Brisbane school, she yet felt (she said) that study of
> them might repay the musician of to-day: they had freshness; they had,
> above all, ideas.[36]

These references to Australia are meant to be ironic, presenting Vashti as devoted to something contemporary English readers would find odd and absurd. In biographical terms, we know little of Forster's attitude towards Australia; he made no explicit remarks on Australia in his published and private writings. It is unclear whether Forster had in mind any specific musical works composed in Australia or by Australians; in fact, we do not know whether Forster was familiar with or knowledgeable about Australian musical culture. It is also unclear whether the text is referring to Aboriginal Australians' music or music imported from Europe. It seems that Forster might have simply selected 'Australia' for its otherness, using its relatively short white history to poke fun at Vashti's antiquarian interest. Although, at the turn of the century, social and political changes in Australia started to obtain wider publicity in Britain and such a myth of Australia as 'the lost Arcady' no longer existed, the wild landscape, the unique fauna and flora, the transportation of convicts, and the gold rushes still contributed to shaping the British cliché of Australia as an exotic 'down under'.[37] The fictitious 'Australian' music thus produces much of the irony of Vashti's lecture. From a postcolonial perspective, Forster's satire of Vashti's intellectualism hides a Eurocentric sense of humour.

It would be wrong, though, to dismiss Forster's representations of 'Australian' music simply because of his problematic national imagining; details in Vashti's lecture reflect Forster's critique of musical revivalism. The Brisbane school, according to Vashti, was concomitant to a musical trend during which 'the methods of I-San-So' were popular. Whilst 'I-San-So' seems Forster's coinage of a three-character East Asian name, it can also be 'I sang so' and thus implies a singing practice that constitutes a formulaic refrain or recalls, even more specifically, the Tonic Sol-fa method of teaching singing. Read alongside the detail that the Brisbane school took place after 'the great outburst of song', music from this fictitious Australian period seems to have a distinct vocal legacy and is embedded in a culture marked by its oral tradition. Vashti's backward, antiquarian exploration of these musical cultures can be read as an allusion

---

[36] *MS*, p. 91.
[37] Coral Lansbury, *Arcady in Australia: The Evocation of Australia in Nineteenth-Century English Literature* (Carlton: Melbourne University Press, 1970), pp. 154–58 and 167.

to the interest in English folksong collecting in Edwardian society. By 1910, English folksong had been a subject of extensive attention from musicians, composers, and academics, among others, whose observations were often underpinned by anxieties about the future of English music and intertwined with their delineations of nationhood. For example, Charles Villiers Stanford, in 1889, identified folk music as the key to the establishment of a national school of music in England.[38] In 1905, Edward Elgar similarly underlined the importance of folk music, encouraging young musicians to 'draw their inspiration more from their own country' in order to 'arrive at having an English *art*'.[39] While the concept of 'folk' in the English folk revival will be discussed further when we turn to *Arctic Summer*, what I wish to emphasize here is the similarities between Vashti's lecture and remarks made by these early twentieth-century folk enthusiasts. Like the latter, Vashti's words attempt to glorify the past by emphasizing its conceptual significance to the present. Whilst Stanford, Elgar, and others looked for 'inspiration' from English folksong, Vashti stresses that those early musical works have 'ideas'.

The worship of 'ideas' in the story is a satiric exaggeration of excessive (and false) intellectualism. Whatever the subject is, a lecture in the Machine world always concludes on a note about obtaining 'ideas'. This is more a blank catchphrase than a meaningful anticipation: 'ideas' are only invoked in the lectures but never discovered or reified. This intoxication with 'ideas' is a product of technophilia: the genesis of the Machine civilization is a simple wish to free human beings from manual work. However, while the 'soul' does receive more attention after 'bodies' have been released from labour, it is an undue attention.[40] 'Ideas' are thus allowed to form, but they form without originality or individuality, since acquired information is privileged over first-hand experiences in the Machine civilization: 'First-hand ideas . . . are but the physical impressions produced by love and fear'.[41] Forster's future intellects gather and reiterate information that no longer has any bearing on their epistemology of the world. Their lectures, instead of being instructive, endorse the Machine's intermediation in everyday life. They are successors of 'master brains', but they have surrendered to science and become 'a generation absolutely colourless' – hence the featureless crowd we have seen.[42]

---

[38] Hughes and Stradling, *English Musical Renaissance*, pp. 32–33.
[39] Edward Elgar, *A Future for English Music and Other Lectures*, ed. Percy M. Young (London: Dobson, 1968), p. 51.
[40] *MS*, p. 94.   [41] *MS*, p. 109.   [42] *MS*, pp. 111 and 110.

144   E. M. Forster and Music

Vashti's emphasis on 'ideas' is particularly significant, given that music is her subject. Her declaration that music has 'ideas' and, at the same time, her complete neglect of the physicality of musical sensibility allude obliquely to late nineteenth-century characterization of musical effect as intellectually processed and the argument that listening to music is a cerebral rather than physical act.[43] Moreover, Vashti's worship of 'ideas' firmly aligns her with 'mind' in opposition to 'body', differentiating her from women's traditional role as performer of music. As Lucy Green observes, for centuries, the main aim of women's music-making, whether vocally or instrumentally, was to display her feminine body, both to allure and to be gazed at and thus consumed, whereas composing was deemed improper for women and beyond women's capability: those who composed were perceived as a threat to 'the transcendent male ego' because, by composing, a woman demonstrated that 'she also has a mind'.[44] The dualism of mind and body is therefore also one of knowledge and practice, Art and Craft, creative and reproductive, and masculine and feminine. Though not a composer, Vashti's pursuit of 'ideas' adopts the masculine language and criteria of criticism, foregrounding not her body but her critical apparatus and prowess of logic and thoughts, and thus delineating her departure from the women's traditional role in musical performances.

However, Vashti's approach to music is being satirized: the story's ironic portrayal of the Machine civilization reveals that Forster's sympathy lies with the perception of the body as central to musical sensibility. Vashti *knows*, but never *feels*, the music on which she lectures; the problem, as we have seen Forster caution against in 'The *Raison d'Être* of Criticism', is that excess focus on knowledge and instruction results in blunted sensitivity and lost intuition. This ironic portrayal of Vashti's musical scholarship is suggestive on two levels. First, it suggests Forster's critique, as an amateur, of the professionalization of musicology. The absurdity and emptiness of Vashti's lecture is a way of discrediting the authorial figure, of parodying as well as deflating the grandiosity of public dissemination of 'expertise' and

---

[43] Sutton, *Aubrey Beardsley*, pp. 74–75. Many critics have documented and commented on the interdependence of music and science in the late nineteenth and early twentieth centuries, noting music's influential role in the development of various sub-disciplines in sciences – such as psychology, physiology, neurology, and sexology – and have also explored the ways in which newly formulated scientific hypotheses and theories fed into perceptions of music. See e.g. Phyllis Weliver, *Women Musicians in Victorian Fiction, 1860–1900: Representations of Music, Science and Gender in the Leisured Home* (Aldershot: Ashgate, 2000), especially the chapter 'Harmony and Discord in the Self: Music, Mesmerism and Mental Science', pp. 59–97.

[44] Lucy Green, *Music, Gender, Education* (Cambridge, UK: Cambridge University Press, 1997), p. 113.

Amateurism, Musicology, and Gender 145

'knowledge'. The satire of Vashti's intellectualism delivers a quiet endorsement of the pre-eminence of the body in all forms of engagement with music. Forster's is therefore a strategy of recuperating subjectivity and individuality through undercutting the credibility of the professional. Second, the portrayal of Vashti expresses Forster's critique of masculinity. Vashti's interest in the rational and cerebral aspects of musical effect, her revivalistic exploration of past musical cultures, and her subscription to the abstract and conceptual significance of music can be read as Forster's caricatures of the gendered self-delineations of the emergent discipline of musicology in its attempt to define its uniqueness, respectability, and status in academia. By exposing the expert's unawareness of music's symbolic corporeality as a subversive power against the control of the Machine, Forster jibes at the masculine ideal of professional culture and underscores the importance of the physicality of musical effect, celebrating a form of musical sensibility traditionally marginalized and pathologized as feminine.

What demands our further consideration is that it is a woman who is the professional in 'The Machine Stops'. It is possible that Forster first conceived the character of Vashti as a mother. Vashti's maternal role has narratological importance in the short story, as it provides Kuno, her son, with the opportunity to tell his story about his adventure to the surface of the earth in part II. As parental responsibilities are rendered obsolete by the Machine, Vashti, as mother, is both close to and aloof from Kuno. She is repelled by Kuno's desire to escape, but also feels the need to accept his request to travel to see him in person; when told the outcome of his adventure, her mixture of shame and pity implies both her subjection to the Machine and her kinship with Kuno. Vashti, as a musical scholar and as a mother, thus allows Forster to unfold the collapse of the Machine. On the one hand, she stands for the system against which Kuno, who 'detest[s] music' and has 'a certain physical strength', rebels;[45] on the other, their blood tie is why Kuno takes her into his confidence and appears at the end of the story to reassure her of the continuance of humanity.

Yet there are other implications of Forster's choice of a woman as a music scholar. By the first decade of the twentieth century, although women had garnered increasing visibility in musical performance and entered several other different areas in English musical culture, women music scholars were still rare.[46] One might argue that Forster is therefore a

---

[45] *MS*, pp. 113 and 100.
[46] Paula Gillett, *Musical Women in England, 1870–1914: "Encroaching on All Man's Privileges"* (New York: St Martin's Press, 2000).

146 E. M. Forster and Music

women's writer, granting this character the public prominence and author-itative status rarely seen in reality, but the irony in his characterization immediately undermines this celebratory reading and points to another possibility that Forster is simply misogynistic in his negative portrayal of Vashti's professionalism. This is particularly uncomfortable, as it shows Forster as resorting to the entrenched perception of women's role in music as performer, mocking and denouncing women's ability to engage with music intellectually. However, Forster's portrayal of professionalism as a gendered discourse suggests an alertness to the fact that women, in order to define their social standing in a highly professionalized society, are required to adopt masculine values to enter the intellectual coterie. In this respect, his portrayal of Vashti suggests not women's ineligibility for scholarly work but their participation in, if not complicity with, patriarchy. If Forster's privileging of the physical, the spontaneous, and the individualistic over the intellectual, the trained, and the systematic is established at the expense of one woman, his satirizing of Vashti's musical scholarship criticizes not the specific woman but the reproduction of professional norms and the domination of patriarchy. By emphasizing the body as beyond the grasp of the professionalized discipline of musicology, the representations of music in 'The Machine Stops' suggest Forster's resistance to the gendered hier-archy of professional and amateur.

Arctic Summer

Like 'The Machine Stops', *Arctic Summer* provides an examination of the professionalization of musical scholarship, especially its antiquarianism, but its allusions to contemporary musical and political trends are more specific than those in the short story. Begun in 1911, *Arctic Summer* was drafted, laid aside, continued, abandoned, significantly revised, and again abandoned before Forster's first trip to India in September 1912. He revisited the fragments in 1951; he revised and read the first five chapters at the Aldeburgh Festival. After that, *Arctic Summer* was put aside and left unfinished.[47] Like much of Forster's fiction, the novel revolves around two men: as Elizabeth Heine elegantly describes, the novel is 'to join the

---

[47] Thanks to Elizabeth Heine's editorial work, the novel's manuscripts are presented as three texts: the main version, with its first five chapters revised in 1951 and about four remaining chapters unrevised, plus a note for the Aldeburgh reading in which Forster explained why he could not finish the novel; the 'Tripoli Fragment', presumably an inceptive draft written in 1911; and the 'Radipole version', a wholescale revision of the novel in summer 1912. Heine's discussion of Forster's writing of the novel is particularly illuminating. *AS*, pp. xi–xxv.

Amateurism, Musicology, and Gender   147

physical courage of the thoughtlessly chivalric hero with the moral tolerance of the civilized man, to re-educate the one and revitalize the other'.[48]
On the one side is Martin Whitby, whose ideal is an arctic summer, where
there is 'to have no dawn' as 'Dawn implies twilight, and we have decided
to abolish them both', and thus there 'will be time to get something really
<great> \important/ done'.[49] Opposite Martin stands Clesant March, 'a
Knight errant born too late in time who finds no clear issue to which to
devote himself'.[50] Martin dedicates himself to work, looking forward to a
modernized and ameliorated society, whereas Clesant abides by tradition,
emphasizing honour, family, and established social order. Around Martin
and Clesant are several minor characters (perhaps not coincidentally,
mostly women), one of which is Dorothea Borlase, Martin's sister-in-
law. Dorothea is an educationalist, an active campaigner for women's
suffrage, a socialist like her sister Venetia, and an English folksong collector. Dorothea does not appear in person in the first five chapters; she is
only briefly mentioned, in Martin's thoughts, as the sister who has 'the
finer mind'.[51] For the audience at Aldeburgh, then, without any knowledge of the remaining four chapters, Dorothea would only have a faint
presence compared to Venetia, whose character is more extensively delineated in the pages Forster read. Moreover, they would not know of
Dorothea's involvement in folksong collecting because the only reference
to it in the first five chapters was deleted by Forster during revision.
Whether this deletion was to give a more focused presentation of
Martin's character in the Aldeburgh reading or suggests that Forster in
1951 thought of the English folk revival as a dated movement, this original
aspect of Dorothea's characterization reflects Forster's awareness of the
popularity of folksong collecting when he was drafting the novel in the
early 1910s.

As we have seen in the previous section, many scholars and musicians in
the Edwardian years dedicated themselves to retrieving and reviving past
musical cultures, proposing that the future of English music lay in the
recovery and dissemination of folk music. One of the most famous pro-
ponents of English folksong was Cecil Sharp, whose field work, influence,
and legacies have been extensively discussed by critics.[52] In 1908, Forster
attended one of Sharp's folksong lectures, after which he wrote

[48] *AS*, p. xii.   [49] *AS*, p. 125. Quotations from *Arctic Summer* retain Heine's editorial marks.
[50] Letter to Forrest Reid (2 February 1913). *SL*, I, p. 187.   [51] *AS*, p. 132.
[52] Hughes and Stradling, *English Musical Renaissance*, chapter 5, 'Crusading for a National Music',
pp. 164–214.

148   E. M. Forster and Music

appreciatively about the way Sharp lectured on the subject.[53] Sharp might
have contributed to Forster's characterization of Dorothea, although it is
also possible that Forster modelled her on contemporary female folksong
collectors, such as Lucy Broadwood and Maud Karpeles. Whoever provided the source for Dorothea's musical work, her characterization is not
just a reflection of a popular musical activity but also suggestive of Forster's
view on folksong collecting as entwined with social and political elitism. As
we shall see, Forster's text anticipates the insights of late twentieth-century
criticism that English folksong collecting was methodologically flawed and
politically conservative.

The antiquarianism we have seen in Vashti's backward glance at musical
pasts recurs in Dorothea's interest in English folksong, yet it is given a
more specific institutional form. Dorothea's antiquarianism is set in a
scholarly environment where there is an established collective effort to
work on English folksongs in an active and systematic way. She works 'at
the Conservatoire', as well as travels – like her 'colleagues' – to different
parts of England to collect songs.[54] She notates the singing, identifies the
tonality, and compares different variants of songs:

> [Dorothea] began singing a folksong in scholarly fashion; she had collected
> half a dozen variants of it already:
>
> "'Oh he did whistle and she did sing sing—'"
>
> 'Who are he and she?' asked Venetia, looking over her shoulder.
> 'Joseph and Mary. That's from Hereford. Now listen to this. Kent.
>
> "Oh he did whistle and she did sing
> And all the bells of earth did ring
> For joy that Jesus Christ was born
> On Christmas day in the morning."
>
> Now for Wiltshire. The mode's Doric. "Oh he did—'"
> 'They sound to me very much alike,' said her sister, passing out with
> the breakfast things.[55]

Indicating to Dorothea that the nuances between different variants of a
song are unnecessarily complicated for non-professionals, Venetia's words
mock the excessive scrupulousness of this rigorous analysis of English folk
music. What underlies Dorothea's tendency to analyse (or overanalyse)
English folksongs is an assumption – or, for the collectors themselves, a

---

[53] Diary entry (26 March 1908). *JD*, I, p. 162.   [54] *AS*, pp. 182 and 183.   [55] *AS*, p. 183.

Amateurism, Musicology, and Gender

149

belief – that English folksong deserves such scrutiny. Dorothea collects folksongs because 'they are beautiful'.[56] Compared to Vashti's wish to obtain 'ideas', Dorothea's expectation of finding something no less intangible echoes the sentiment of contemporary folk enthusiasts. Ralph Vaughan Williams, for example, claimed:

> this music is not mere clownish nonsense, but has in it the germ of all those principles of beauty, of expression, of form, climax and proportion which we are accustomed to look for in the highly developed compositions of great masters.[57]

The word 'germ' is crucial, as folk revivalists dwelled on a vision of a musically endowed 'Merrie England', long lost and in need of being revived, which reveals their ambition as well as anxiety. As we saw in Chapter 3, English music was perceived as lagging behind its Continental counterparts; contemporary folksong collectors were not merely concerned with the belatedness of the development of English music but also anxious that England did not have a corpus of a recorded folk culture that promised future blossoming. As Vaughan Williams cautioned, '[w]e have been rather late in the day in England in doing what other nations have long considered their duty'.[58] In this respect, if Dorothea's admiration for the 'beauty' of English folksongs expresses a national ambition to emulate other European musical cultures, her pedantic approach also betrays the shared anxiety about the quality of England's 'folk' output.

Such a preoccupation with the quality of the songs determines the way Dorothea works:

> Dorothea opened her notebook, the companion of many a country tramp. In it were her gleanings of English song. Her enthusiasm, cold and steady, had led her among queer places and rough men. There were entries in it such as 'Mr Lodge, Imber in the Down. Only when drunk.' 'Mrs Tarr, Blandford Workhouse.' Some of the verses were unprintable. All that was beautiful and pure – and there was much – would be sifted out of the chaff, and resown.[59]

That Dorothea is portrayed not only as a collector but also as an editor suggests Forster's alertness to the many problems inherent in the motives and methods of the English folk revival that modern criticism has targeted. His description of Dorothea's 'sift[ing]' anticipates modern critiques of

---

[56] *AS*, p. 185.
[57] Ralph Vaughan Williams, *English Folk-Songs* (London: English Folk Dance and Song Society, 1966), p. 8.
[58] Vaughan Williams, *English Folk-Songs*, p. 4.   [59] *AS*, p. 183.

E. M. Forster and Music

folksong collectors' regular omission, manipulation, and bowdlerization of the material they had gathered to serve their bourgeois and intellectual ends. His awareness that English folksong was far from a creation of 'the people' and that folk promulgators justified themselves as 'rescuing' a 'waning' culture ('the old people were dying out', as Dorothea believes)[60] attends to the constructedness of the whole movement.[61] What motivates her to devote her time to this 'work', as Dorothea's telling use of the word 'resown' indicates, is her educational ideal.[62] Dorothea edits the songs because she will later have what is 'beautiful and pure' 'taught back in schools to the grandchildren of those who had known them instinctively'.[63] Based on an invented concept of 'the folk', her educational programme aims to recreate as well as to intervene.

Exposing Dorothea's 'interventionist intent',[64] Forster goes on to highlight that 'the folk' is often objectified, exoticized, and even pathologized by the English folksong collecting movement in the justification of its revivalism. Dorothea's notes on 'drunk' or 'rough' interviewees demonstrate that her work is a form of specimen collection, revealing both her consumption of her interviewees as anecdotal cases and her indulgence in thinking of her own condescension to places beyond her familiar middle-class environment as adventurous and well-meaning. That folksong collectors perceive their subjects as in need of help, at best, and diseased and contagious, at worst, is most explicit in the description of a brief encounter between Dorothea and a window cleaner who comes to sing her a song he knows: 'Pray that he's not full of fleas', Dorothea jokes before her visitor arrives.[65] After the window cleaner turns out to be 'a disappointment' – he knows no folksong and is 'difficult to get rid of' – Dorothea plays 'Pergolesi, to drive all interruption from her ears'.[66] In the early twentieth century, Pergolesi (1710–36) was one of the composers who received considerable attention from musical antiquarians: for example, Stravinsky's ballet *Pulcinella* (1920) used pieces that, at that time, were thought to be Pergolesi's compositions.[67] Dorothea's choice of Pergolesi,

---

[60] *AS*, p. 183.

[61] Dave Harker, *Fakesong: The Manufacture of British 'Folksong', 1700 to the Present Day* (Milton Keynes: Open University Press, 1985). See, also, Hughes and Stradling, *English Musical Renaissance*, pp. 210–11.

[62] *AS*, p. 183.   [63] *AS*, p. 183.

[64] I borrow the phrase from Georgina Boyes, *The Imagined Village: Culture, Ideology and the English Folk Revival* (Manchester: Manchester University Press, 1993), p. 4.

[65] *AS*, p. 184.   [66] *AS*, p. 187.

[67] Stephen Walsh, 'Stravinsky, Igor', *Grove Music Online*, www.oxfordmusiconline.com [accessed 10 May 2018].

Amateurism, Musicology, and Gender

then, underlines her antiquarian intellectualism, but the irony is that what she believes to have a cleansing power might as well be as inauthentic and impure as the disappointing sample sung by the window cleaner. This episode can be read as Forster's jibe at the futility of folksong collecting and his critique of its snobbishness and elitism.

Dorothea's obsession with cleanliness is both literal and metaphorical:

> Venetia was at Newnham, Dorothea lived at home, and was destined by her parents for a more domestic career. Both were in full revolt against their lot. Their war cry <amazed Martin at first. It> was 'Be tidy'. They wanted to help in tidying up the world. It is time. The age of discovery is over – there will be no new countries. It is time to arrange the old, and all men and women must turn to. Romance, whether in action or in thought, is a relic of the age of untidiness; it assumes the unknown, whereas we know, or at all events we know enough. Untidiness. The word caught. It ran like wildfire through Newnham[.][68]

The passage refers to many social and political trends at the time. The reference to Venetia's education at Newnham links the 'war cry' to what male students at Cambridge described as the 'agitation' caused by campaigns for degrees for Girton and Newnham students[69] and, more broadly, to women's suffrage, especially the suffragettes' protests in London. The phrase 'Be tidy' is an explicit allusion to British Fabianism. Popular around the time when Forster was drafting *Arctic Summer*, the Fabian society advocated an impersonal approach to social improvement and upheld the ideal of a scientifically planned, institutionally organized, and professionally operated society. Although frequently criticized by contemporaries for its focus on bureaucracy, its goal in putting social ills in order attracted many young intellectuals who believed in science, efficiency, and professional culture. Forster's tribute to Beatrice Webb in 1943 suggests that he was aware of Fabians' method of tackling social issues through institutional overhaul: Webb, he wrote, 'did not believe in a local and sentimental pity' but in 'Commissions of Enquiry and note-taking', because they truly could have 'cured' poverty and social injustice.[70] By aligning Dorothea with Fabianism, Forster makes her musical work and political leaning mutually explanatory. Her revulsion at the window cleaner's fleas becomes a caricature of the Fabians'

---

[68] *AS*, pp. 131–32.

[69] Rita McWilliams-Tullberg, *Women at Cambridge: A Men's University – Though of a Mixed Type* (London: Victor Gollancz, 1975), p. 133.

[70] 'Webb and Webb' (1943), in *TCD*, pp. 208–11 (p. 209).

E. M. Forster and Music

idiosyncratic preoccupation with tidiness. This intersection suggests that Forster's critique of folksong collecting as elitist can be applied to Fabianism, too. Although Ian Britain has argued that it is necessary to distinguish Fabian socialism from a sheer elitism that has 'no egalitarian ramifications' because Fabians' motivation 'was nothing if not benevolent',[71] Forster's depiction of Dorothea's insistence on personal and social tidiness suggests that he discerned in Fabianism the same conservative and elitist attitude in folksong collecting.

More specifically, Forster's characterization of Dorothea can be read as a response to Rupert Brooke, who was closely affiliated to the Fabian society at the time and whose obsession with cleanliness has been well documented.[72] On 24 November 1911, Forster wrote to Brooke: 'I have this moment decided to put all I can remember of your paper on art into a novel – and as I remember it'.[73] The paper Forster was referring to is Brooke's *Democracy and the Arts*. Read at the Cambridge University Fabian Society in 1910, Brooke's paper proposed that, in order to 'produce as large and appreciative a public as possible', 'Arts', especially contemporary art, need to be 'subsidized' because 'the living, them you can stir or warm and enable to work, and work at their best'.[74] Brooke's perception of the economic sustenance of an artist's life as inseparable from his or her creative work echoes Woolf's argument in *A Room of One's Own* (1929); his vision of state-subsidized art, however, would later be questioned by Forster in 'The Duty of Society to the Artist' (1942) as impractical because the artist and the State 'must disagree'.[75] What is pertinent to our discussion here is that, while emphasizing the importance of the vitality of contemporary art to society, Brooke dismissed cultural antiquarianism: 'It is no good going back to the Middle Ages and the great communal art of the Cathedrals and the folksongs'.[76] At first glance, then, the relation between Forster's unfinished novel and Brooke's paper seems straightforward: Forster's critical view of folksong collecting in *Arctic Summer* is a reflection of Brooke's privileging of the modern over the past. Yet I would suggest it is not a case of agreement only. Forster was not without

---

[71] Ian Britain, *Fabianism and Culture: A Study in British Socialism and the Arts, c. 1884–1918* (Cambridge, UK: Cambridge University Press, 1982), p. 230.

[72] For example, John Lehmann describes that Brooke was attracted to the actress Cathleen Nesbitt in 1912 because she seemed 'unspotted by the "uncleanness" which obsessed his mind in connection with his earlier friendships and emotional involvements'. John Lehmann, *Rupert Brooke: His Life and His Legend* (London: Weidenfeld & Nicolson, 1980), p. 77.

[73] *SL*, I, p. 126.

[74] Rupert Brooke, *Democracy and the Arts* (London: Rupert Hart-Davis, 1946), pp. 4, 22, and 27.

[75] *TCD*, pp. 94–98 (p. 97).   [76] Brooke, *Democracy*, p. 5.

Amateurism, Musicology, and Gender 153

reservations about Brooke's personality and ideology. In his sketch of Brooke immediately after Brooke's death, he wrote to their mutual friend Malcolm Darling that Brooke 'was serene humourous intelligent and beautiful – as charming an acquaintance as one could desire – and latterly most friendly. But he was essentially hard; *his hatred of slosh* went rather too deep and affected the eternal water-springs, and I don't envy anyone who applied to him for sympathy'.[77] The identification of Brooke's obsession with cleanliness as one of his defining characteristics and the association of this obsession with Brooke's tendency to be unsympathetic suggest Forster's decisive differentiation of himself from Brooke. In *Arctic Summer*, Dorothea at work is 'cold and steady', suggesting a scientific exactness and a temperamental hardness not different from Brooke's. Read in this way, Forster's characterization of Dorothea parodies Brooke's lack of sympathy, suggesting wariness of and resistance to Brooke's brand of socialism. Forster's incorporation of Brooke's Fabian ideas into *Arctic Summer* is more complicated than mere reproduction.

It becomes clear that Forster's uneasiness with folksong collecting and Fabianism is related to his emphasis on personal relationships. In his criticism of Brooke's personality, his reflection on Beatrice Webb's fascination with institutional reform, and his satiric portrayal of Dorothea, Forster casts doubt on the elitist desire to wield influence from above. An equal footing is necessary in facilitating change, as Forster suggests through the representation of another strand of Dorothea's public work: children's education. It is unclear whether this aspect of Dorothea's characterization was inspired by the renowned educationalist Dorothea Beale (1831–1906), Principal of Cheltenham Ladies' College, but the same initials (D. B.) are suggestive. In the novel, Martin comments that 'Most work is done indirectly. Educationalists like Dorothy admit as much. They try to drop knowledge into the subconscious stratum of the child's mind'.[78] Martin objects to this view, suggesting that 'A child ... is a sharper subject than you school-ma'ams suppose'; to pass on knowledge, 'One subconsciousness must call to another. Which is a clumsy way of saying that there must be affection'.[79] Martin's vision of a more equal relation between teacher and student and his celebration of mutual understanding in personal relationships are manifestly Forsterian. His word 'drop' is ironic, as it satirizes Dorothea's belief in placing the teacher high on an eminence, implying an unchallengeable omniscience with an unassailable commission

---

[77] Letter to Malcolm Darling (2 August 1915). *SL*, I, p. 227. My emphasis. [78] *AS*, p. 152.
[79] *AS*, p. 152.

154   E. M. Forster and Music

to teach and guide the young. Revealing how the enchantment with the Foucauldian power-knowledge runs through Dorothea's musical, political, and educational activities, Forster envisions a less patronizing and more understanding relationship between proselytizer and proselytized. As Forster specified in his plan for *Arctic Summer*, 'My motive should be democratic affection'.[80] In *Arctic Summer*, then, it seems that the Forsterian 'democracy' is positioned at the very opposite of Dorothea's work. That is, Forster forms (or, more accurately, half-forms) his vision against Dorothea's interest in the collective and the institutional, in knowledge and reform.

As critics have noted, the 'democracy' in *Arctic Summer* is exclusively male and explicitly homoerotic;[81] to these qualities of the novel's 'democracy' I would add the adjective misogynistic. On a biographical level, Martin's objection to Dorothea's educational ideas materializes Forster's personal bias against Christabel Meredith, the wife of Hugh O. Meredith, the friend Forster once adored during and after his Cambridge years.[82] An educationalist and a published author, Christabel Meredith's ideas of children's education were in line with some of the advanced pedagogical theories widely circulated in Continental Europe at the time.[83] In *The Educational Bearings of Modern Psychology* (1916), for example, Meredith opposed lecturing, punishment, and formalized curricula, contending that schooling should be a process of socialization through which a child can discover and develop his or her inner kindness and sensitivity; she proposed an educational scheme in which the teacher, instead of attempting to quench the students' impulses, works knowingly with their instincts.[84] For Forster, however, it seems that he never recovered from his depression

---

[80] Diary entry (19 December 1910). *JD*, II, p. 19.

[81] Joseph Bristow, for instance, observes that the disparate fragments of *Arctic Summer* reveal 'the enduring interest in brotherhood', suggesting an intention to 'broach the subject of homosexuality, to which fraternal love would be the key'. Bristow, 'Forster's Apostolic Dedications', p. 125. See also Vybarr Cregan-Reid, 'Modes of Silence in E. M. Forster's "Inferior" Fiction', *English Literature in Transition*, 56.4 (2013), 445–61 (p. 454).

[82] Hugh O. Meredith has been regarded as the model of Clive Durham in *Maurice*. See e.g. Philip Gardner's Introduction to the Abinger edition of the novel, *M*, pp. xv–xvi. Although P. N. Furbank suggests that Forster used Christabel Meredith as a model for his characterization of Venetia, it should be Dorothea who is modelled on her given the similarity between their work in children's education. Furbank, *Forster*, I, p. 208.

[83] For a discussion regarding women's contribution to children's education and educational policies in the Edwardian years, see e.g. Jane Martin, *Women and the Politics of Schooling in Victorian and Edwardian England* (London: Leicester University Press, 1999).

[84] Christabel M. Meredith, *The Educational Bearings of Modern Psychology* (Boston: Houghton Mifflin, 1916).

after learning about his friend's engagement in 1906.[85] In the years that followed, he wrote frequently in his diaries and letters – to his confidante, Florence Barger, who used to be Christabel's fellow educationalist but who had a different (much more traditional) view of family life – about the Merediths, recording every single row between the couple whilst censuring Christabel's insistence on working after marriage and her 'pernicious' methods of child-rearing.[86] Believing that Christabel's theories would never succeed when it comes to her own children, Forster wrote in his diary: 'Don't think I <u>could</u> see my eldest son's character and health spoilt by a dotty dirty sexless bluestocking'.[87] Unrequited love thus turned into hatred and bitterness; Forster's portrayal of Dorothea suggests a fictionalized stab, a release of anger.

We are therefore confronted with the same problem as we encountered in our discussion of 'The Machine Stops': Forster builds his irony around the figure of a woman musical scholar, and the meanings of a text come from reading against what the character stands for. Although *Arctic Summer* is an unfinished work, the biographical allusion to Christabel Meredith in the characterization of Dorothea suggests that women professionally working in public troubled Forster. It is also possible, however, that Forster was critical not of professional women per se but of the gendering of professionalism and professionalization. Dorothea's role as an English folksong collector sees her adopt the methodology of impersonality, aspire to the ideal of tidiness, devote herself to revive a 'past', and seek to reform 'the people' while distancing herself from them – all these align her with characteristics, concepts, and projects that are traditionally celebrated as masculine. It is useful here to quote from Virginia Woolf's *Three Guineas* (1938):

> we, daughters of educated men, are between the devil and the deep sea. Behind us lies the patriarchal system; the private house, with its nullity, its immorality, its hypocrisy, its servility. Before us lies the public world, the professional system, with its possessiveness, its jealousy, its pugnacity, its greed. The one shuts us up like slaves in a harem; the other forces us to circle, like caterpillars head to tail, round and round the mulberry tree, the sacred tree, of property. It is a choice of evils. Each is bad. Had we not

---

[85] Both P. N. Furbank and Wendy Moffat record Forster's depression after learning the engagement of Hugh and Christabel in 1906, Furbank, *Forster*, I, p. 141; and Moffat, *Forster*, p. 87.

[86] Letter to Florence Barger (10 November 1920). *SL*, I, p. 319. See also *SL*, I, p. 146, pp. 229–30, and 243; *SL*, II, p. 6; Furbank, *Forster*, I, p. 186; *JD*, II, pp. 12–13, 19, 26, and 58.

[87] Diary entry (30 September 1923). *JD*, II, pp. 70.

156   E. M. Forster and Music

better plunge off the bridge into the river; give up the game; declare that the whole of human life is a mistake and so end it?[88]

Like 'The Machine Stops', musical scholarship in *Arctic Summer* provides women with a public platform, while paradoxically acclimatizing them to gendered rhetoric and ideology that stand as 'professional' in a system shaped and dominated by male values.

***

Tchaikovsky's *Pathétique*, as widely agreed, plays an important part in *Maurice*. In this novel where Forster finally represents cross-class homosexual bonding between men and, in a way, materializes the 'democratic affection' that *Arctic Summer* is unable to achieve, both the composer and the symphony, as Michelle Fillion argues, are '*negative* models of masculine love and emblems of old ways to be rejected before Maurice can attain emotional and sexual maturity'.[89] This is most explicit in chapter XXXII, in which Maurice attends a concert where the symphony is performed and afterwards encounters Risley – the 'Wildean homosexual'.[90] That Maurice 'enjoyed the piercing and the tearing and the soothing – the music did not mean more to him than that' can be read as Forster's subversion of contemporary English professionals' alarmist gendering of Tchaikovsky's music as an 'attack' on 'English' senses.[91] Yet Maurice does not thus happily greet the knowing amateur he runs into: Risley's sneer at the audience and revelation of the homosexual sentiments of Tchaikovsky's, though unveiling what is not said publicly by professional views and capturing Maurice's interest, do not give Maurice what he is looking for. Consequently, it is worth noting that throughout Maurice's relationship with Alec, music has no place, as if the bodies of the two men needed neither mediation nor metaphor to convey the urgency of their desire.

What is often bypassed by readers and critics alike is that it is a woman, Violet Tonks, who provides Maurice with the ticket to the concert where he meets Risley. The ticket was originally for Kitty, Maurice's youngest sister, but she cannot use it. Kitty calls her friend from the Domestic

---

[88] Virginia Woolf, *Three Guineas* (Harmondsworth: Penguin, 1977), p. 86.
[89] Fillion, *Difficult Rhythm*, p. 96.   [90] Cole, *Male Friendship*, p. 65.
[91] Malcolm Hamrick Brown, 'Tchaikovsky and His Music in Anglo-American Criticism, 1890s–1950s', in *Queer Episodes in Music and Modern Identity*, ed. Fuller and Whitesell, pp. 134–49. Judith A. Peraino suggests that it was exactly the 'open secret' of Tchaikovsky's homosexuality that made his music appealing to the audience. Judith A. Peraino, *Listening to the Sirens: Musical Technologies of Queer Identity from Homer to Hedwig* (Berkeley: University of California Press, 2006), p. 82.

Amateurism, Musicology, and Gender 157

Institute a 'socialist', whom Clive's country estate 'won't impress'.[92] During the concert, Maurice develops 'a warm feeling of gratitude towards Miss Tonks' and very briefly entertains the idea that she might be able to turn him 'normal'.[93] What he does not know, and what the now-abandoned Epilogue hints at, is her lesbianism. In the Epilogue, we follow Kitty cycling in the countryside: 'Since Violet Tonks had married – that rather than her brother's disgrace had been the crisis – she had lost her vigour, no longer attended concerts, lectures on hygiene &c, or cared for the improvement of the world; but looked after her mother or helped the Chapmans wearily'.[94] Consequently, the novel's democracy is for Maurice and Alec only; women are not only excluded, but sacrificed in a way – their desire, professionalism, and socialist ideals lost either to marriage or to family ties.[95] How do we, then, read the concert ticket? Just as Clive, earlier in the novel, uses Tchaikovsky's symphony as a code to woo Maurice in Risley's room,[96] there is a possibility that Violet Tonks plans to use the concert to court Kitty. That the ticket initially fuels Maurice's illusion of a heterosexual courtship becomes ironic; Maurice subsequently senses the irony himself too: his comprehension of Tchaikovsky's sentiments makes him realize that marriage would only lead to 'disaster'.[97] As a plot device, the ticket is key to Maurice's search for a form of love between men. By meeting Risley and being introduced to Tchaikovsky's biography, he becomes acquainted with the options of remaining closeted (like Tchaikovsky) or leading a double life (like Wilde), but they remain only as options in a novel insistent on offering a happy ending. Violet Tonks's ticket thus contributes to navigating Maurice, though falsely and thus fruitlessly, through a mixture of despair, confusion, and defiance after he learns the news of Clive's engagement. The ticket allows Maurice to explore his queer genealogy, paving the ground for his reunion or acquaintance with Wilde and Tchaikovsky, from whom he ends up making a departure. Once again, Forster employs, however obliquely, women as facilitators to relations between men.

---

[92] *M*, p. 123.   [93] *M*, p. 137.   [94] *M*, pp. 221–22.

[95] For discussion of Kitty specifically, and of women characters in *Maurice* more generally, see Gemma Moss, 'Women In and Out: Forster, Social Purity and Florence Barger', and Anna Watson, '"Flat pieces of cardboard stamped with a conventional design": Women and Narrative Exclusion in E. M. Forster's *Maurice*', both in *Twenty-First-Century Readings of E. M. Forster's* Maurice, ed. Emma Sutton and Tsung-Han Tsai (Liverpool: Liverpool University Press, 2020), pp. 52–74 and 101–26.

[96] Keeling, 'No Trace of Presence', pp. 89–93.   [97] *M*, p. 137.

It is possible to discern a sustained reluctance to side with the professional women in the three texts we have discussed. Socially active and politically mindful, the three women characters are not matriarchs who are pivotal to a domestic scene or youths that question social norms, both of which frequent Forster's texts elsewhere. Instead, the roles they serve all involve a backward glance into disparate fragments of the past which the three texts urge readers to defy. In Vashti's antiquarian intellectualism, Dorothea's enthusiasm for 'the folk', and Violet Tonks's inadvertent contribution to Maurice's reappraisal of his queer antecedents, Forster constructs his visions by casting aside the values and concepts resurrected by or through these women characters, suggesting his perception of them as part of patriarchal culture. Vashti's musicological lectures help the Machine repress a body like Kuno's in an unspecified future; Dorothea's folksong collecting neglects individuals in an unfinished novel; and Violet Tonks's ticket almost deflects Maurice from his quest for a friend in an unpublishable work. All these demonstrate that Forster plots his more and more explicit representations of homosexual desire via the repeated device of belittling and rejecting professional women. Consequently, although Forster shows an awareness of the gendering of professionalism, his championing of musical amateurism seems to be underpinned not only by a contempt for professionals but also by an aversion to women.

Postlude

Forster's weekly contributions to the column, 'Notes on the Way', for the feminist journal *Time & Tide* in November 1935 addressed a variety of topical political events and social phenomena at the time, such as elections in Britain, the rise of fascist and anti-fascist movements in France, and the annihilation of human civilization that the development of science may facilitate. Yet it is his steadfast belief in the role of art in a time of crisis that ran through these pieces. In one of them, Forster's conclusion is a profoundly suggestive passage on music's power to mitigate individuals' experience of political turmoil:

> Trying to escape from [all the political affairs] and to unmuddle myself a little, I put one or two of Hugo Wolf's songs upon the gramophone before concluding these notes. There, sure enough, was our problem, transferred into terms of music, and solved. There was the contest – not indeed between outer and inner, public and private, but between two distinct sorts of sounds: piano-sounds and voice-sounds. Hugo Wolf is the only song-writer I know who allows each sort of sound to go its own way. In many musicians (Schubert for instance) the piano accompanies the voice, in others it echoes the voice (e.g. Schumann's 'Nussbaum'), in others it alternates. Wolf alone seems able to create two independent and continuous streams of music, whose true relation is not revealed until the close. The piano generally goes on longest. The final bars of the piano in 'Nun wandre Maria' or 'Anacreon's Grave' or 'Ganymede' have a retrospective value which bears no relation to the notes struck. They throw back to the beginning and make the two streams into one. And this, it seems to me, is what great art does in these worrying times. It solves none of our bothers, personal or political, but it reveals a world where they might have been solved. Nor is this the end of the mystery; instead of being tantalized and irritated by such elusiveness and unpracticability, we are actually comforted, and return to what we choose to call 'actual life' with a better heart.[1]

---

[1] 'Notes on the Way', in *PT*, pp. 286–90 (pp. 289–90).

160   *E. M. Forster and Music*

Arguing for the strength and relevance of Hugo Wolf's music, the central idea of the passage recalls Forster's words on art more generally in a previous contribution to the same column: despite not being 'drugs' and 'not guarantee[ing] to act [upon us] when taken', art 'mustn't be brushed aside like a butterfly. It is not all gossamer, what we have delighted in, it has become part of our armour, and we can gird it on'.[2] By perceiving Wolf's lieder as an example of artistic unity where an enlightening synthesis of human voice and piano takes place, Forster uses such formal wholeness as a metaphor for the resolution of ideological differences. Specifically, if read alongside *Aspects of the Novel*, his comment on how the piano postludes to the three songs 'throw back to the beginning and make the two streams into one' recalls his notion of 'difficult' rhythm as a narrative device that retrospectively brings everything together at the close of a book. This fascination with a musical narrative's ability to transcend the constraints of the linearity of time – with an artwork as a closed, self-sufficient organic entity – demonstrates an attention to form and produces a celebration of the songs' autonomy. Forster's strategy of highlighting the interdependence of the artistic and the political thus paradoxically emphasizes the separation of the two worlds: it is the internal logic of Wolf's songs that helps him 'unmuddle' himself; their formal integrity reminds him of the possibility of resolution and reconciliation and sustains him through the often puzzling and unpredictable political affairs of 'actual life'.

Thematically, Forster's decision to conclude this categorically political piece of writing with his personal reflection on Wolf's music expresses his primary intention to highlight the individual and the subjective against external event-fulness. He opens the 'Notes' with a disclaimer: 'Italy, Abyssinia, the League, the election. The notes for the month must begin with this sinister text, but I am too much muddled to elucidate it, muddled as well as worried, and hope to pass on next week to matters nearer my competence'.[3] After this, he turns to personal well-being. Wondering why, 'in spite of all the disorder, our private lives often remain happy and docile', Forster suggests that the priority of self and the longing for pleasure mean that, despite the awareness that 'it's ghastly' outside, 'when they get the chance they can't help having a pleasant time'.[4] Consequently, '[c]onstant happiness is only for the obtuse, but patchy happiness seems to be a possibility for all well-developed men and women'.[5] Referring to a concert experience where he was made uncomfortable and ashamed by a fellow concertgoer 'bleating out apologetically' about leaving political work behind to have a brief moment of relaxation, Forster complains

---

[2] *AH*, pp. 70–71.   [3] *PT*, p. 286.   [4] *PT*, p. 287.   [5] *PT*, p. 287.

Postlude

161

that 'his patches of happiness hadn't coincided with my own'.[6] Read in relation to this incident, his description of the impact of Wolf's music on him becomes an unapologetic demonstration of not solipsistic joy but individual independence. By underlining the contribution of Wolf's music to his personal equilibrium at the end of the 'Notes', Forster responds to public stigmas surrounding the enjoyment of arts in the midst of political crisis and defends his selfhood and subjectivity, thus refusing – as in his silence about Wagner in the coming years – to be subsumed by the collective thinking in many concurrent political causes. Also, in terms of form, if we attend to the essay's form and read the discursiveness of the 'Notes' as a patchwork of intersected subject matters, Forster's conclusion with Wolf's music concretizes a treasured patch of happiness and leverages against political and social turbulence.

The praise Forster gave to the Austrian composer of Slovene origin Hugo Wolf (1860–1903) is, however, surprising, given that he often derided composers who were heralded as Wagner's successors at the time.[7] We saw in Chapter 4, for example, the satire of Richard Strauss's use of chromaticism in *The Longest Journey*. In 1964, when Forster was 85 years old, he commented in his *Commonplace Book* on Gustav Mahler and Europe's post-Wagnerian musical landscape:

> *Mahler.* 3rd Symphony 4th Symphony Song of Earth per gramophone and in that order of approval. Find little originality in him and seriousness rather than profundity, but wish I had found him sooner. Certainly, like many others, he loves beauty and wishes it hadnt to be left, so his company is congenial and his tediousness easy to condone. What a curse orchestral prolixity was in the early half of this century! Composers were allowed too many instruments and too much time. Size not fully filled and too readily worshipped by Central Europe. Wagner, the leader here, but he *had* something thoughtful to say.[8]

On the one hand, claiming that Mahler's music lacked 'profundity', Forster challenges the widely circulated notion, as well as Mahler's self-characterization, of his music as philosophically significant in that it demands a listener's intellectual engagement.[9] On the other, Forster's

---

[6] *PT,* p. 287.

[7] Amanda Glauert, *Hugo Wolf and the Wagnerian Inheritance* (Cambridge, UK: Cambridge University Press, 1999).

[8] *CB,* pp. 253–54. The last sentence of the quotation recalls Margaret Schelgel's words: 'But, of course, the real villain is Wagner'. *HE,* p. 37.

[9] This notion continues nowadays. For example, in his essay, Morten Solvik comments that 'Any thorough understanding of Gustav Mahler and his music must probe the complexities of his thoughts about life and existence. Mahler's pursuit of these fundamental questions went far beyond idle speculation, haunting his personal reflections and informing his artistic project with a nearly obsessive quality. In significant ways, Mahler's works represent a response to this existential

162   *E. M. Forster and Music*

objection to Mahler's and other contemporary central European composers' preference for expanded instrumentation and orchestral force in their often lengthy compositions is not uncommon: Mahler was, and still is, criticized for creating sounds that are too loud, evoking emotions that are too raw, in a manner that is both violent and oversentimental.[10] Read alongside his critique of Mahler, Forster's admiration of Wolf's lieder suggests a wariness of what he perceived as unnecessary grandiosity and a preference for compression and crystallization. His choice of something small and quiet like the lieder in the 'Notes' can be read as suggestive, then, of Forster's resistance to the grandiloquence in contemporary political utterances.

Forster's comparison of Wolf with Schubert and Schumann reflects the way Wolf's music grew increasingly popular in Britain in the first decades of the twentieth century. Ernest Newman's endorsement of Wolf, including his 1907 biography of the composer and other short essays, often relies on a comparison between Wolf and Schubert (partially because both set some of the same poems by Goethe), characterizing the former as meticulously matching music's expressivity with its poetic source and the latter as spontaneously writing his melodious songs.[11] Although critics have disputed Newman's assessment,[12] this perception of Wolf's composition as an intellectual enterprise – his music as intimately interactive with its poetic language, his oeuvre as elevating the status of the German lieder – has continued in modern scholarship on Wolf.[13] Forster's praise of Wolf's complexity over Schubert's and Schumann's 'simplicity' paints a similar picture of the development of the genre of the lieder. Complimenting Wolf's ability to use the piano to construct a narrative parallel to that of the

---

inquiry, an extension of an overriding need to somehow fathom the universe'. Morten Solvik, 'The Literary and Philosophical Worlds of Gustav Mahler', in *The Cambridge Companion to Mahler*, ed. Jeremy Barham (Cambridge, UK: Cambridge University Press, 2007), pp. 21–34 (p. 21).

[10] For the reception of Mahler in the twentieth century, see Leon Botstein, 'Whose Gustav Mahler? Reception, Interpretation, and History', in *Mahler and His World*, ed. Karen Painter (Princeton: Princeton University Press, 2002), pp. 1–54.

[11] Ernest Newman, *Hugo Wolf* (London: Methuen, 1907). See also Ernest Newman, 'Hugo Wolf and the Lyric', *The Musical Times*, 1 November 1915, 649–51.

[12] Newman's comparison has been contested by his contemporaries: see e.g. A. H. Fox Strangways, 'Schubert and Wolf', *Music & Letters*, 23.2 (1942), 126–34. More recently, Lawrence Kramer's work on Wolf seeks to redefine the composer's relationship with Schubert: see e.g. 'Decadence and Desire: The *Wilhelm Meister* Songs of Wolf and Schubert', *19th-Century Music*, 10.3 (1987), 229–42. Kramer also examines the construction of 'the Wolf legend': 'Hugo Wolf: Subjectivity in the Fin-de-Siècle Lied', in *Song Acts: Writing on Words and Music* (Leiden: Brill, 2017), pp. 146–77.

[13] See e.g. Eric Sams, *The Songs of Hugo Wolf* (Bloomington: Indiana University Press, 1992), especially the introductory chapter 'Wolf as a Song-writer', pp. 1–42.

Postlude 163

poem – that is, to use the piano not as an accompaniment but as a companion, or even a commentator sometimes – Forster presents Wolf as a post-Wagnerian composer whose major work encapsulates the dramatic tension between word and music and augments the expressive power of the song form.

The fact that the musical expression Wolf inherited and matured is distinctly German indicates Forster's attempt to combat English insularity through an evocation of Europe as sharing the same cultural heritage. As Laura Tunbridge has noted, 'If a community were being imagined through lieder performance in London between the wars it was one ... less about nationalism than about cosmopolitanism'.[14] By discussing Wolf, Forster made more than just an anti-Nazi move to embrace German culture; more broadly, it echoed contemporary voices from the anti-fascist Left by declaring Europe's solidarity on the cultural front. This is particularly evident in his reference to 'Anacreon's Grave'. Comprising only twenty-one bars, Wolf's song is a setting of Goethe's poem *Anakreons Grab*, a 'moving hail and farewell to the ancient Greek poet whose verse had been a major inspiration in [Goethe's] youth'.[15] As Eric Sams comments,

> Goethe's beautiful lines, replete with reverence, are rounded by their elegiac metre into a classical object of shapely perfection. Wolf's music recreates their form and content, and further adds a new reverence and beauty of its own. His setting seems to express not only the poem but the actual experience he imagines as having inspired it, namely the unexpected chance discovery of a real tomb in a living landscape.[16]

The postlude, departing from the high arpeggios that answer the poet earlier in the song, revolves warmly around the tonic chord before fading away (*verklingend*) and finally resting on the dominant, expressing Anacreon's protected rest and the poet's quiet retreat. Paying homage to the two previous homages (Wolf's homage to Goethe and Goethe's homage to Anacreon), Forster's reference to the song acknowledges his artistic inheritance, containing the multilayered pasts in the present. That these pasts transcend national boundary is pertinent to the political commentary Forster is making in the 'Notes': he cautions readers not to take the fascist group *Croix de Feu* in France as simply 'Foreign News'.[17]

---

[14] Laura Tunbridge, 'Singing Translations: The Politics of Listening Between the Wars', *Representations*, 123.1 (2013), 53–86 (p. 76).

[15] Eric Sams and Susan Youens, 'Wolf, Hugo (Filipp Jakob)', *Grove Music Online*, www.oxfordmusiconline.com [accessed 10 May 2018].

[16] Sams, *Songs*, pp. 218–19.   [17] *PT*, p. 289.

E. M. Forster and Music

Forster therefore emphasizes connections, both cultural and political, across nations and through time.

Against external upheavals, Forster once again turns to the value of personal relationships. 'Nun wandre Maria', from Wolf's *Spanisches Liederbuch*, sets to music Joseph's solicitude for Mary on their long journey to Bethlehem. Throughout the song, the consistency of the parallel thirds in the piano's right hand is a motif associated with companionship.[18] Wolf's song presents Joseph's words as comforting and understanding, their journey as a concerted endeavour to reach the good rest promised at the destination, as evoked by the piano's postlude which 'finds and holds, for the first time in the song, the tonic-major key'.[19] The warmth of the company is maintained in the postlude and the distress on the journey is relieved by the tonal resolution. If uncharacteristic in drawing inspiration from Christianity, Forster's reference to the song is characteristic of his advocacy of personal relationships and suggests his continuing faith in the private bonding between individuals in the face of political crises and uncertainties.

As we saw in the last chapter, Forster's depictions of personal bonding are often charged with homoeroticism, here in particular exemplified by his listening to Wolf's 'Ganymede'. Listening on his gramophone in order to 'escape' certainly reveals Forster's social exclusivity, but what might also be encapsulated in his listening to the German lieder sung in their original language in a secluded environment is a heightened sense of intimacy between the listener, the singer, and the composer.[20] Known for its exploration of the erotic symbolism of Goethe's poem, Wolf's song captures Ganymede's desire to soar and intoxication with the loveliness of nature created by Zeus, which gradually transform into a fervent wish to join the god.[21] The postlude represents this as physical fervour: after the lyric ends with a prayer, 'Alliebender Vater' (all-loving father), the piano repeats the melody to 'In diesen Arm' (in your arm), which appeared earlier in the song, thus characterizing Ganymede's worship of Zeus as a bodily yearning. In complimenting Wolf on his sophisticated use of the piano postlude, Forster implicitly endorses Wolf's interpretation of the erotic dynamic of Goethe's *Ganymed*, thus unveiling his own reading of the poem as focused on its representation of the homoerotic desire for physical intimacy. That Forster says that 'we are actually comforted' by songs like Wolf's thus has an overtone of sexual consummation: what

---

[18] Sams, *Songs*, p. 26.   [19] Sams, *Songs*, p. 254.   [20] Tunbridge, 'Singing Translations', p. 76.
[21] Sams, *Songs*, pp. 243–44.

Postlude 165

perhaps could not be articulated in public is expressed unabashedly in his references to the music.

***

The scrutiny of textual details in the oeuvre of an author who, like Forster, seems to have become overly familiar among critics and readers might seem to some counterintuitive. Nearly every critical attempt in recent years to re-evaluate Forster's worth as a writer, especially a modernist one, has seemed more and more reluctant to focus solely on his texts and instead become eager to align Forster with other writers, usually those who came after him, to show the legacies of Forster's ideas. In the twenty-first century, the aim of these accounts has been to resurrect Forster's cultural status, literary credentials, and posthumous influence against the castigations of queer and postcolonial readings in the 1980s and 1990s. Arguing for Forster's relevance to our current world by unearthing and underlining postmodern complexities in his work, these accounts have recycled the image of Forster as a sage produced by liberal humanist criticism. The problem with these recent assessments of Forster, however, is that, for all their intention of returning the critical spotlight to Forster, one has to ask why Forster cannot be studied on his own terms. The very fact that these critics emphasize, but do not examine, Forster's merit is baffling: it presents Forster's ideas as an established system, a set of stable criteria even, and suggests, perhaps inadvertently, that close-reading textual evidence with its historical contexts in mind is unnecessary. To put the issue bluntly, can 'Forster's legacies' really bring new life to and drive fresh critical discussions within Forster scholarship?

As I have been at pains to demonstrate with an exclusive focus on Forster's representations of music, a return to the text and its contexts may be a better critical strategy to uncover unexpected nuances in and stimulate new understandings of Forster's work – especially when, as is widely agreed, the work is characterized by irony, irresolution, and ambivalence. As Santanu Das elegantly describes it, '[t]here is always something that eludes, unsettles, lingers' in Forster's fiction, an 'unresolved tension' which 'fills his protagonists with a strange restlessness and propels them from their solid, secure worlds into "adventures" in which we no longer know where the exhilaration ends and the anguish begins'.[22] While this

---

[22] Santanu Das, 'E. M. Forster', in *The Cambridge Companion to English Novelists*, ed. Adrian Poole (Cambridge, UK: Cambridge University Press, 2009), pp. 345–60 (p. 346).

166   *E. M. Forster and Music*

distinct feature of Forster's writing has often been interpreted by legacies studies as a kind of Forsterian ethics that informs subsequent generations of writers' efforts in negotiating the conflicts of an increasingly diversified society, some of Forster's works have been more amenable than others to this sort of treatment – hence the disproportionate amount of critical interest in *A Passage to India*. The previous chapters have demonstrated that these imbalances can be redressed by a renewed probing into the whole repertoire of Forster's writings. And this has allowed us to recognize contradictions such as those between his anti-imperialism and the limitations of his cross-cultural epistemology, his inheritance of literary heritage and his ahistorical conception of literary creativity, his attraction to masculine athleticism and his wariness of unbound heroism, his misogyny and his celebration of classless intermingling. More importantly, what emerges from the previous chapters' discussion of the political significance of Forster's musical emphases is the striking fact that, despite all our professed familiarity with Forster's output, hidden details in his oeuvre remain to be uncovered. As I have illustrated, renowned texts – such as *Aspects of the Novel*, *A Passage to India*, *Where Angels Fear to Tread*, *The Longest Journey*, 'What I Believe', and 'The Machine Stops' – gain added layers of meaning and become endowed with new implications for our understanding of Forster's ideology when we consider their musical representations and relate them to his lesser-known texts. The latter approach is itself an attempt to do justice to the breadth and scope of Forster's writing; my intention to highlight the versatility of Forster's musical enthusiasms has made visible a Forster who produced a wide range of writings apart from his novels and short stories, and whose concerns often went beyond his self-affiliation to 'the fag-end of Victorian liberalism'.[23] As we saw in his interest in Hugo Wolf's lieder in 'Notes on the Way', this is an individual, though quiet and unassuming, who is acutely aware of his own cultural baggage but at the same time disquietingly critical of political currents in 1930s Europe.

If we were confined to using one word to summarize Forster's attitude towards the contentious relationship between music and politics, his favourite term 'muddle' would be a good choice. As a writer for whom 'muddle' – confusion, falsity, misunderstanding, entanglement – blossoms into creativity and whose work cultivates and explores the 'muddle' in human society, Forster's statement that 'music is so very queer that an amateur is bound to get muddled when writing about it' accrues a fittingly

---

[23] 'The Challenge of our Time' (1946), in *TCD*, pp. 54–58 (p. 54).

Postlude

paradoxical overtone. It seems that Forster relished the condition of 'get [ting] muddled' when writing about music, as if it were a welcome outcome that his willingness to try out various routes but commit to none inevitably entails. From the politicized field of musical cultures, Forster's depictions of 'muddle' acquire their creative energy. By persistently situating music within its cultural milieu and highlighting it as an event that interacts with its surroundings – as we saw in the opening of 'Not Listening to Music' – Forster does more than write about music. That is, he experiments with the referential and associative capabilities of musical representations, thereby alluding to multifarious – and sometimes conflicting – ideological viewpoints. For Forster, the 'muddle' when writing about music is a forte, serving as a conduit for him to reflect on and respond to politics of various kinds and sustain their irreconciliation.

Frequently, it seems that it is our own preconceptions with what music is and should be that prevent us from accessing Forster's musical politics. The perception of music, especially Western classical music, as abstract and autonomous still underpins many discourses upon music today, be they concert programmes, reviews, criticisms, or studies of aesthetics. The publications of the conservative philosopher Roger Scruton perhaps best illustrate the continuance of such a perception. In 1997, Scruton wrote that 'In hearing', we undergo 'the pure event, in which no individual substances participate, and which therefore *becomes* the individual object of our thought and attention';[24] then, in 2009, 'sounds heard as music are heard in abstraction from their physical causes and effects';[25] and most recently, music is 'an abstract, non-representational art' that 'avails itself of temporal organization in a non-physical space'.[26] This abstraction of music, as I have argued at the beginning of my study, too willingly resorts to a universalizing understanding of music and has underlain and shaped previous readings of Forster's use of music. What I would like further to point out here is that often it has also directed readers' attention to details in Forster's work that eulogize music as essentially just a conveyer of inexplicable moments of artistic intimacy. Zadie Smith, for instance, makes a passing remark that Forster's 'idealisation of music' is one of the things at which he 'fails'.[27] Paradoxically, Smith's reworking of the

---

[24] Roger Scruton, *The Aesthetics of Music* (Oxford: Oxford University Press, 1997), p. 12.

[25] Roger Scruton, *Understanding Music: Philosophy and Interpretation* (London: Continuum, 2009), p. 7.

[26] Roger Scruton, *Music as an Art* (London: Bloomsbury, 2018), p. 124.

[27] Zadie Smith, 'Love, actually', *Guardian*, 1 November 2003, www.theguardian.com/books/2003/nov/01/classics.zadiesmith [accessed 10 May 2018].

168   *E. M. Forster and Music*

Beethoven concert in *Howards End* into an open-air performance of Mozart's *Requiem* where issues of race, class, and economics are intertwined in *On Beauty* (2005) suggests her awareness of the political charge of Forster's representations of music. Perhaps Smith's comment refers to Forster's frequently quoted opening remark in 'The *Raison d'Être* of Criticism' that music, he believed, 'is the deepest of the arts and deep beneath the arts'.[28] However, distilling this particular statement from the context where it was uttered would be, as I suggested in Chapter 5, to neglect Forster's eagerness to justify his speech as an amateur in front of trained musicologists. Also, it is worth recalling his long description about being distracted during a concert in 'Not Listening to Music'. Indeed, music may have provided Forster with an emotive, profoundly intimate space, but what has become evident in our discussion is that his engagement with musics also galvanized him to make sense of his surroundings and look into a wide range of topical subject matters of the time.

In discussing the sheer range of musical representations in his writing and their political ramifications, we have uncovered a Forster more eclectic and versatile than the 'gay' writer that recent criticism has highlighted, most clearly evidenced by the central tenet of Wendy Moffat's biography of Forster that everything 'start[s] with the fact that he was homosexual'.[29] As we have seen, while Forster's representations of music consistently produce queer resonances, there are many other political dimensions of his engagement with music being ignored by the critical tendency to focus simply on issues of sexuality in Forster's work. This can be exemplified by the approach critics have taken to Forster's collaboration with Eric Crozier on the libretto of Benjamin Britten's opera *Billy Budd* (1951). The history of their adaptation of Melville's novella into an all-male opera has been well documented. The project started in 1948 when Britten approached Forster; the work was originally commissioned for the Festival of Britain in 1951. Having finished the libretto with Crozier first, Forster's subsequent grumblings about Britten's slowness and comments on the music Britten had drafted (most memorably, his critique of Britten's draft of Claggart's monologue as 'soggy depression' without '*passion*') were received by the composer as unwelcome interventions, resulting in mild frictions between the two friends.[30] Though delayed, the production received a huge wave of advance publicity; the dismissive tone adopted by some of the previews and reviews was partially a reaction against the hype surrounding the

---

[28] *TCD*, p. 105.   [29] Moffat, *Forster*, pp. 3–21.   [30] *SL*, II, p. 242.

Postlude

169

opera's premiere in the Royal Opera House on 1 December 1951.[31] Afterwards, Forster was gracious, writing to Britten to say that the opera was his 'Nunc Dimittis, in that it dismisses me peacefully and convinces me I have achieved'.[32] Given the fact that it was Forster's major late creative project, plus the continuing rise in the opera's reputation and the frequency with which it is staged (most recently in the Royal Opera House in April 2019), it is not surprising that *Billy Budd* has received increasing critical attention in studies of Forster and music. What is surprising is that these critics seem to have been driven by the same concern with Forster's homosexuality. As I have pointed out in the Introduction, recent critics such as David Deutsch and Josh Epstein have examined the queer significance of Forster's work on the opera, thus following Clifford Hindley, Philip Brett, Mary C. Francis, and many others by reading the opera primarily as a crystallization of Forster's desire to 'write about profound relationships between men: symbolically to evoke the power of homosexual love without being in any way sexually explicit'.[33] While many other critics, whether in musicology or in literary studies, analyse Forster's part in the construction of the tensions between the opera's music and words,[34] their intermedial analyses also frequently allude to the sexual identity of the composer and the co-librettist as a formative factor to the style and aesthetics of *Billy Budd*.

This tendency to identify the creative process and 'message' of the opera as distinctly homosexual, however, has hindered us from accessing and assessing the political significance of *Billy Budd* in its specific historical moment. Whereas Melville's novella itself has been discussed in terms of a

---

[31] Paul Kildea, *Selling Britten: Music and the Market Place* (Oxford: Oxford University Press, 2002), p. 130.

[32] *SL*, II, p. 246. For Forster's work on the opera, see Furbank, *Forster*, II, pp. 283–86.

[33] The quotation is from Philip Brett, *Music and Sexuality in Britten: Selected Essays*, ed. George E. Haggerty (Berkeley: University of California Press, 2006), p. 72. Mary C. Francis also gives the same interpretation of Forster's intention of collaborating on *Billy Budd*: it was 'a late chance to achieve something he had not done in his published writing: publicly address the idea of homosexual love'. Mary C. Francis, '"A Kind of Voyage": E. M. Forster and Benjamin Britten's *Billy Budd*', in *Biographical Passages: Essays in Victorian and Modernist Biography*, ed. Joe Law and Linda K. Hughes (Columbia: University of Missouri Press, 2000), pp. 44–64 (p. 51). Clifford Hindley's gay reading of the opera, such as his article 'Love and Salvation in Britten's "Billy Budd"', *Music & Letters*, 70.3 (1989), 363–81, is illuminating but also contentious in Britten studies. One can also argue that Eve Kosofsky Sedgwick's reading of Melville's novella in *Epistemology of the Closet* (1990) participated in these assessments of the opera.

[34] Fillion, *Difficult Rhythm*, pp. 123–37; Alder and Hauck, *Music and Literature*, pp. 131–78. Claire Seymour's suggestion that the libretto seeks resolution whereas Melville's text is full of uncertainty is, however, unconvincing: Claire Seymour, *The Operas of Benjamin Britten: Expression and Evasion* (Woodbridge: Boydell, 2004), pp. 132–59.

E. M. Forster and Music

wide spectrum of subjects ranging from philosophy to law, it prompts one to contemplate why the opera has not been subjected to equally varied approaches. While Hanna Rochlitz, both in her book *Sea-Changes: Melville – Forster – Britten* and her chapter on *Billy Budd* for Kate Kennedy's edited collection *Literary Britten*, has produced exceptionally detailed accounts of the opera's composition and provided analyses of its echoes with Forster's other works,[35] it is in J. P. E. Harper-Scott's recent argument for a historicist confrontation with the 'ideological component' of Britten's operas that my discussion sees our understanding of *Billy Budd* being enriched and complicated.[36] In his theoretically dense but power- fully delivered analysis of the opera, Harper-Scott argues against 'privileg [ing] the gay interpretation', overthrowing previous criticism's universal- izing understanding of *Billy Budd* as a work about 'love' or 'salvation', and proposing that, instead of 'offer[ing] a vision of a better world', the opera 'merely outline[s]' a structure of ideological violence.[37] Although I have reservations about his insistence on the separation of identity politics from the need to restore the opera's historical specificity (more about this later), many of his observations are compelling, such as his comments on Vere – whose inaction during the trial and hanging of Billy feeds into 'the hegemonic power of rule' and its paranoia about the threat of mutiny – as 'liberal to a fault';[38] on the omnipresent B-flat/B-natural semitone as a 'false opposition' between sovereign power and its imagined resistance;[39] and on the chords during the Interview scene as 'ideological normalization' ('they do not *change* anything in the course of the opera or *invent* or *discover* anything new that might emerge ... as a redemptive possibil- ity').[40] Most importantly, drawing continuity between 'the state of excep- tion' of the post-revolutionary moment in 1797 (in the narrative time frame) and that in the 1950s which held postwar British citizens in its thrall when totalitarianism, capitalism, and democracy were vying for global ascendency,[41] Harper-Scott's study of *Billy Budd*'s presentation of systemic and symbolic violence represents a burgeoning line of inquiry

---

[35] Hanna Rochlitz, *Sea-Changes: Melville – Forster – Britten* (Göttingen: Universitätsverlag Gttingen, 2012). Hanna Rochlitz, "'I *have* read *Billy Budd*': The Forster–Britten Reading(s) of Melville', *in Literary Britten: Words and Music in Benjamin Britten's Vocal Works*, ed. Kate Kennedy (Woodbridge: Boydell & Brewer, 2018), pp. 296–317.

[36] J. P. E. Harper-Scott, *Ideology in Britten's Operas* (Cambridge, UK: Cambridge University Press, 2018), p. 3.

[37] Harper-Scott, *Ideology*, pp. 79 and 171.   [38] Harper-Scott, *Ideology*, pp. 152 and 150.

[39] Harper-Scott, *Ideology*, p. 156.   [40] Harper-Scott, *Ideology*, p. 164.

[41] Harper-Scott, *Ideology*, p. 144.

Postlude

into the political suggestiveness of Britten's operas in relation to the time and surroundings of their making.[42]

One element that has not yet been addressed is the opera's representation of race. Melville scholars have examined the narrator's fleeting glimpse at an old black sailor at the beginning of the story and commented on the ambiguity of the portrayal of Billy's and Claggart's racial identity, raising questions about Melville's attitudes towards race, slavery, national imagining, and colonialism.[43] The opera does not include the old black sailor, which in some way is understandable as the action between the Prologue and the Epilogue concentrates on the events onboard the *Indomitable*. However, although whiteness is never referred to as an element of the 'beauty' of Billy Budd, the majority of the singers who have sung the title role are white.[44] While the ways in which race is cast on stage and screen are subjected to increasing scrutiny and adjustments in recent years, it seems that the world envisioned and constructed by the opera at the very beginning was a predominantly white one. The 1966 BBC recording of the opera in its revised two-act form, for example, featured a thoroughly white main cast and choir. It is extremely telling, then, if we look back at Forster's excitement about the appearance of the American baritone Theodor Uppman, who sang the title role in the premiere: Forster found Uppman 'really splendid', admired his 'good physique' and 'fair curly hair', and said that he 'found nothing that contradicted the part', suggesting a homoerotic adoration of qualities conventionally associated with ideas about Caucasian male beauty.[45]

Intriguingly, there was a non-white singer in the original cast: the Māori bass-baritone Inia Te Wiata, who sang the role of Dansker, the veteran sailor who acts as a cautionary voice to Billy, although this seems – in

---

[42] These works include Heather Wiebe, *Britten's Unquiet Pasts: Sound and Memory in Postwar Reconstruction* (Cambridge, UK: Cambridge University Press, 2012), and Christopher Chowrimootoo, *Middlebrow Modernism: Britten's Operas and the Great Divide* (Oakland: University of California Press, 2018).

[43] See e.g. John Bryant, 'How Billy Budd Grew Black and Beautiful: Versions of Melville in the Digital Age', *Leviathan: A Journal of Melville Studies*, 16.1 (2014), 60–86; Brian R. Pellar, *Moby-Dick and Melville's Anti-Slavery Allegory* (New York: Palgrave Macmillan, 2017), p. 189; Cynthia J. Davis, 'Nation's Nature: "Billy Budd, Sailor," Anglo-Saxonism, and the Canon', in *Race and the Production of Modern American Nationalism*, ed. Reynolds J. Scott-Childress (New York: Garland, 1999), pp. 43–65; Klaus Benesch, 'The Language of Gesture: Melville's Imaging of Blackness and the Modernity of *Billy Budd*', *La Clé des Langues*, January 2010, http://cle.ens-lyon.fr/anglais/ litterature/litterature-americaine/the-language-of-gesture-melville-s-imaging-of-blackness-and-the-modernity-of-billy-budd [accessed 27 April 2019].

[44] One of the exceptions is the British baritone Roderick Williams, who recently appeared as the title role in Opera North's 2016 production of *Billy Budd*.

[45] *SL*, II, pp. 245 and 246.

modern terms – not a colour-conscious but a colour-blind casting decision. Born in 1915 in Otaki, New Zealand, Te Wiata's singing talent was noted and showcased early in his life when he toured as a soloist with a mission choir, but he only received formal musical training after he sailed to Britain in 1947.[46] After he started auditioning for the Royal Opera House in 1950, his breakout year came shortly: in 1951, he appeared in *The Magic Flute* (as the Speaker of the Temple) alongside Britten's partner Peter Pears (as Tamino), in Ralph Vaughan Williams's new work *The Pilgrim's Progress* (as Bunyan), in Purcell's *The Fairy-Queen* (as one of the Masquers), and in *Billy Budd*. With the rise of Te Wiata's career as an opera singer came the gradual blurring of his Māori identity. The more visibility he gained in the contemporary British press, the less he was presented as Māori, a scenario not dissimilar from other Māori people and indigenous Australians whose process of becoming famous often still entails the repression of their aboriginality, the recognition of their cultural root giving way to nationalization or internationalization.[47] In early April 1951, for example, Te Wiata's personal background was detailed in a full paragraph in *The Stage* for the upcoming premiere of *The Pilgrim's Progress*, while he was simply namechecked by the same newspaper in November for the publicity of *Billy Budd*.[48] If this reflected the different importance of the roles he played in the two operas, it could also suggest the British public's growing familiarity with his name. Contemporary reviews of him were mostly cursory, focusing on his performances without mentioning his race: he was described as 'dignified and adequate' as Bunyan by Hubert Foss, the musical editor for Oxford University Press;[49] his 'brusque, embittered taciturnity' as Dansker was preferred by the musicologist Patricia Howard to Owen Brannigan's interpretation of the role in the 1968 Decca recording of the opera.[50] Although Forster noted his Māori identity when becoming extremely moved by his duet with Billy at a rehearsal,[51] there is no evidence indicating that Te Wiata was cast in *Billy Budd* because of his

---

[46] These biographical details of Inia Te Wiata's life can be found in Beryl Te Wiata, 'Story: Te Wiata, Inia Morehu Tauhia Watene Iarahi Waihurihia', *Te Ara: The Encyclopedia of New Zealand*, https://teara.govt.nz/en/biographies/5t12/te-wiata-inia-morehu-tauhia-watene-iarahi-waihurihia [accessed 30 June 2019].

[47] Karen Fox, *Māori and Aboriginal Women in the Public Eye: Representing Difference, 1950–2000* (Canberra: ANU E Press, 2011), p. 63.

[48] Anon., 'New Opera', *The Stage*, 12 April 1951, 7. Anon., 'Covent Garden: "Billy Budd" Premiere"', *The Stage*, 1 November 1951, 8.

[49] Hubert Foss, '"The Pilgrim's Progress"', *The Musical Times*, 92.1300 (Jun 1951), 275.

[50] Patricia Howard, 'Review of Britten, *Billy Budd*. Soloists/Ambrosian Opera Chorus/LSO/Britten', *The Musical Times*, 109.1510 (1968), 1125.

[51] *SL*, II, p. 245.

Postlude 173

non-whiteness, nor was it quoted as a reason for his second appearance in Britten's work – as the blind ballad singer in another Covent Garden production, *Gloriana* (1953), a role specifically written for him by Britten. Even though he was listed as one of the 'dominion['s] representatives' at Queen Elizabeth II's coronation, this reveals the way in which his racial and national background was used to underline not the nation's ambition for diversification but the absorption of others at the centre of the Commonwealth.[52] Te Wiata's appearance in *Billy Budd*, then, seemed an inadvertent spark of cultural diversity rather than a conscious attempt to engage with some of the racial issues raised in Melville's text.

Yet *Billy Budd* did not premiere in a vacuum: Britain in the early 1950s witnessed the heightened social prejudices against non-white settlers from the Empire's previous colonies (the 'Windrush generation' included). If one resists such contextualization and prefers to think about the artistic realm of Covent Garden as insulated from the outside world of social changes, the truth was that the subject of race and colonialism created a West End bestseller just next door. In the aforementioned issue of *The Stage* where the publicity of *Billy Budd* appeared, the article beneath it was an interview of Oscar Hammerstein and Richard Rodgers, the writer and the musician behind the immensely successful musical, *South Pacific*.[53] An import from Broadway, *South Pacific* defied British critics' derision, both before and after its opening night on 1 November 1951, and went on a long run of more than 800 performances at the Theatre Royal, Drury Lane.[54] Set in a South Pacific island during the Second World War, the musical's plot revolves around two intercultural romances: an American nurse with a French plantation owner who has two mix-raced children and an American lieutenant with a Tonkinese girl. One of its famous – and controversial – numbers is a song sung by the young lieutenant, 'You've Got to Be Carefully Taught', which challenged explicitly the inculcation of racism in contemporary American society. Although the representations of race and intercultural relations in the musical are obviously not without

---

[52] Anon., 'Music for the Coronation', *The Musical Times*, 94.1325 (Jul 1953), 307.

[53] Anon., '"South Pacific" Team: Rodgers and Hammerstein in London', *The Stage*, 1 November 1951, 8.

[54] Writing in *Observer* from New York in April 1951, Kenneth Harris asked: 'Why are the musicals [*South Pacific* and *Guys and Dolls*] so popular, even with sophisticated playgoers?'. Kenneth Harris, 'It's That Broadway Melody', *The Observer*, 15 April 1951, 5. *The Guardian*'s review of the opening night of *South Pacific* was wry: 'Had it been a new play by Shakespeare and a new opera by Mozart rolled into one, expectation could hardly have run higher.' [Philip Hope-Wallace], 'Review of "South Pacific"', *Guardian*, 2 November 1951, 5.

problems and have since then been examined and critiqued,[55] the musical was an evident attempt at interrogating these issues and provoking its audiences to reflect on them, a bold departure from the widely circulated perception of Broadway musicals as light and entertaining. In contrast, the concurrent *Billy Budd* seemed whitewashed. With terms such as 'Beauty', 'Handsome', 'good', and 'evil' scattered in their unqualified form in the libretto, the story onboard the *Indomitable* asks metaphysical questions and explores the entanglement of human relationships. The story is elevated to the universal when Vere says, 'Plutarch – the Greeks and the Romans – their troubles and ours are the same', but such an elevation hides a Eurocentric outlook, perhaps on both the librettists' and the production's sides. By cutting out Melville's allusions to racial inequality and slavery and by selecting an original cast that was predominantly white, *Billy Budd*, in its attempt to complicate the power dynamics between individuals and their community, too readily accepted race as irrelevance and allowed non-whiteness to remain invisible – not just from a twenty-first-century point of view but in comparison to *South Pacific*. It is in the accentuation of the differences between the two works – in terms of genre, style, theme, and reception – that we also underline the fact that they were staged at the same time and nearby, and consider, however uncomfortably, how Forster, alongside his collaborators, envisioned – or failed to envision – racial relations in the opera, thus questioning to what extent *Billy Budd* reflected (or shunned) a national and racial imagining of Britishness in the early 1950s.

Ultimately, then, *Billy Budd* is not just a 'gay' opera, or – to put it in another way – critics should not merely view the opera with the prior knowledge of Forster's and Britten's homosexuality. Instead, as Harper-Scott has persuasively argued, it is necessary to pay attention to the 'material' and the 'historical'.[56] However, when he resists not only the symbolic or abstract readings of *Billy Budd* but also what he calls 'the (neo) liberal doctrine of capitalist-realist identity politicking', Harper-Scott limits his historicist discussion to a no less abstract forum of Western ideological conflicts, thus falling short of truly restoring the historical elements and the material experiences surrounding the creation of the opera from ideas to stage.[57] What we have seen from this case of *Billy Budd* reminds us of the fertile ground for discussion when we conceptualize 'politics' in its most protean form and remember that Forster was

---

[55] Jim Lovensheimer, *South Pacific: Paradise Rewritten* (Oxford: Oxford University Press, 2010).
[56] Harper-Scott, *Ideology*, p. 171.   [57] Harper-Scott, *Ideology*, p. 114.

writing at a time of changes and in a space by no means homogenized. On the one hand, *Billy Budd*, like *A Diary for Timothy*, was a collaborative project to which Forster devoted himself in the second half of his career. It is not coincident that both the documentary and the opera, only a few years apart, delivered an examination of war's impact on personal relations and exposed the disquieting uncertainty and alienation of human community. The fact that Forster found creative energy in these collaborative, intermedial projects – into which he never ventured in the Edwardian years – says as much about his cultural status at the time (that he was being sought after) as about his sense of the value of artistic collaboration as a restorative force for postwar British society. On the other, in light of the opera's problematic engagement with issues of racial identity, all these concerns of *Billy Budd* – the 'war's impact on personal relations', the 'alienation of human community', and even 'postwar British society' – need to be qualified and de-universalized. Registering the various forms of social stratification, we are enabled to make a more nuanced reflection on political divisions and issues of intersectionality and discover music – as an artwork as well as a cultural event – at its most multivalent.

And it is here we return our focus to the political significance of Forster's engagement with and representations of music. Instead of regarding his fascination with music purely as an indebtedness to music as a concept, a metaphor, or an aesthetic form, we have listened to the political resonances of his reflection on music. In his employment of rhythm as a racialized term, his portraits of Western musical instruments as enmeshed in the operation of Empire, his inheritance of literary and musical heritage as nationally specific, his wariness of the appropriations of Wagner's and Beethoven's music for purposes of war, and his critique of musical scholarship as a gendered arena, we have retrieved a Forster no longer just merely enchanted with the formalist or expressive qualities of Western art music, but acutely attuned to musics in their plurality, actuality, and political suggestiveness. By redressing previous criticism's tendency to draw the affinity between Forster's conception of 'rhythm' and the style of his prose, we have discovered his, and other contemporary writers', conscious engagement with racial and evolutionary discourses about rhythm. Moreover, as we have seen, beyond this emblematic example, there is a wide variety of musical and political intersections in Forster's oeuvre that are cultural-historically specific and complex, but they cannot be simply subsumed under the master narrative of modernist intermediality. What is particularly revealing is the fact that Forster consistently formulated some of his most abiding ideological concerns – including but not limited to issues of sexuality – through drawing music into his writing. If the political energy of Forster's brief discussion of Hugo Wolf's music in 1935 reminds us of the overtones his references to music – however passing – can generate, the revelation of the whiteness of *Billy Budd* is a timely signal for readers in the twenty-first century to reach beyond existing critical parameters and stay alert to the conditioning forces of our own perspectives. In his representations of music, we have seen Forster test the boundary of epistemology, gauge the pressure of colonial conventions on personal relations, expose the performativity of national characteristics, redefine heroism and hero-worship, and search for ways to bring homosexual desires into his writing, whether publishable or not. At the heart of Forster's engagement with music is his protean interest in a broad range of topical subjects and political issues. This correlation between music and politics, then, has taken us back to acknowledging and interpreting the multiple frontiers of Forster's ideological exploration and the many concerns he registers and raises in his work. His six novels may be widely known and extensively studied, but unexplored corners – many and meaningful – remain in his oeuvre. Here, the textual nuances of Forster's musical representations offer good evidence of how 'our most musical novelist' bore witness to and commented, if sometimes contradictorily, on various political factors and cultural matrices of his time. In retrieving a sense of Forster's musical representations as a conflicted space where politics and aesthetics intersect, we have brought to the fore the ideological contention in Forster's writing, recuperating the value of close-reading the relation and tension between text and context as a critical approach that may yield further interpretative possibilities for future critical analyses. It is from this recuperation that we might start to reread – and perhaps also listen to – Forster intently.

Bibliography

Achebe, Chinua, 'An Image of Africa: Racism in Conrad's *Heart of Darkness*', in *Hopes and Impediments: Selected Essays* (New York: Doubleday, 1989), pp. 1–20.

Adorno, Theodor, *In Search of Wagner*, trans. Rodney Livingstone, with foreword by Slavoj Žižek (London: Verso, 2009).

Albright, Daniel, ed., *Modernism and Music: An Anthology of Sources* (Chicago: University of Chicago Press, 2004).

Alder, Erik, and Dietmar Hauck, *Music and Literature: Music in the Works of Anthony Burgess and E. M. Forster, An Interdisciplinary Study* (Tübingen: Francke, 2005).

Anderson, Perry, 'Nation-States and National Identity', *London Review of Books*, 9 May 1991, 3–8.

Anon., 'Covent Garden: "Billy Budd" Premiere', *The Stage*, 1 November 1951, 8.

'Music for the Coronation', *The Musical Times*, 94.1325 (Jul 1953), 307.

'New Opera', *The Stage*, 12 April 1951, 7.

'"South Pacific" Team: Rodgers and Hammerstein in London', *The Stage*, 1 November 1951, 8.

Ardis, Ann L., *Modernism and Cultural Conflict, 1880–1922* (Cambridge, UK: Cambridge University Press, 2002).

Armstrong, Paul B., *Play and the Politics of Reading: The Social Uses of Modernist Form* (Ithaca: Cornell University Press, 2005).

'Two Cheers for Tolerance: E. M. Forster's Ironic Liberalism and the Indirections of Style', *Modernism/modernity*, 16.2 (2009), 281–99.

Ashbrook, William, *Donizetti and His Operas* (Cambridge, UK: Cambridge University Press, 1982).

'Lucia di Lammermoor ("Lucy of Lammermoor")', *Grove Music Online*, www.oxfordmusiconline.com [accessed 10 May 2018].

Baedeker, Karl, *Italy: Handbook for Travellers: Second Part: Central Italy and Rome*, 13th ed. (Leipsic: Baedeker, 1900).

Barthes, Roland, *Beethoven the Creator*, trans. Ernest Newman (New York: Harper & Brothers, 1929).

Bates, Eliot, 'The Social Life of Musical Instruments', *Ethnomusicology*, 56.3 (2012), 363–95.

Bibliography

Baucom, Ian, *Out of Place: Englishness, Empire, and the Locations of Identity* (Princeton: Princeton University Press, 1999).

Beauman, Nicola, *Morgan: A Biography of E. M. Forster* (London: Hodder & Stoughton, 1993).

Benesch, Klaus, 'The Language of Gesture: Melville's Imaging of Blackness and the Modernity of *Billy Budd*', *La Clé des Langues*, January 2010, http://cle.ens-lyon.fr/anglais/litterature/litterature-americaine/the-language-of-gesture-melville-s-imaging-of-blackness-and-the-modernity-of-billy-budd [accessed 27 April 2019].

Benson, Stephen, *Literary Music: Writing Music in Contemporary Fiction* (Aldershot: Ashgate, 2006).

Bentley, Eric, *The Cult of the Superman: A Study of the Idea of Heroism in Carlyle and Nietzsche, with Notes on Other Hero-Worshippers of Modern Times* (London: Hale, 1947).

Berlioz, Hector, *The Memoirs of Hector Berlioz*, ed. and trans. David Cairns (London: Victor Gollancz, 1969).

Bhabha, Homi K., 'Of Mimicry and Man: The Ambivalence of Colonial Discourse', in *The Location of Culture* (London: Routledge, 1994), pp. 121–31.

Biddle, Ian, *Music, Masculinity and the Claims of History: The Austro-German Tradition from Hegel to Freud* (Farnham: Ashgate, 2011).

Binckes, Faith, *Modernism, Magazines, and the British Avant-Garde* (Oxford: Oxford University Press, 2010).

Björkén-Nyberg, Cecilia, '"Listening, Listening": Music and Gender in *Howards End, Sinister Street* and *Pilgrimage*', in *Literature and Music*, ed. Michael J. Meyer (Amsterdam: Rodopi, 2002), pp. 89–115.

The Player Piano and the Edwardian Novel (Edinburgh: Edinburgh University Press, 2015).

Black, Jeremy, *Italy and the Grand Tour* (New Haven: Yale University Press, 2003).

Bolton, Thaddeus L., 'Rhythm', *The American Journal of Psychology*, 6.2 (1894), 145–238.

Botstein, Leon, 'Whose Gustav Mahler? Reception, Interpretation, and History', in *Mahler and His World*, ed. Karen Painter (Princeton: Princeton University Press, 2002), pp. 1–54.

Bowen, Elizabeth, 'A Passage to E. M. Forster', in *Aspects of E. M. Forster*, ed. Oliver Stallybrass (London: Edward Arnold, 1969), pp. 1–12.

Bowlby, Rachel, 'Jacob's Type', in *Feminist Destinations and Further Essays on Virginia Woolf* (Edinburgh: Edinburgh University Press, 1997), pp. 85–99.

Boyden, David D., and Ann M. Woodward, 'Viola', *Grove Music Online*, www.oxfordmusiconline.com [accessed 10 May 2018].

Boyes, Georgina, *The Imagined Village: Culture, Ideology and the English Folk Revival* (Manchester: Manchester University Press, 1993).

Brett, Philip, *Music and Sexuality in Britten: Selected Essays*, ed. George E. Haggerty (Berkeley: University of California Press, 2006).

Bibliography

'Musicality, Essentialism, and the Closet', in *Queering the Pitch: The New Gay and Lesbian Musicology*, ed. Philip Brett, Elizabeth Wood, and Gary C. Thomas (New York: Routledge, 1994), pp. 9–26.

'Musicology and Sexuality: The Example of Edward J. Dent', in *Queer Episodes in Music and Modern Identity*, ed. Sophie Fuller and Lloyd Whitesell (Urbana: University of Illinois Press, 2002), pp. 177–88.

Brett, Philip, Elizabeth Wood, and Gary C. Thomas, ed., *Queering the Pitch: The New Gay and Lesbian Musicology* (New York: Routledge, 1994).

Bristow, Joseph, *Effeminate England: Homoerotic Writing after 1885* (New York: Columbia University Press, 1995).

'*Fratrum Societati*: Forster's Apostolic Dedications', in *Queer Forster*, ed. Robert K. Martin and George Piggford (Chicago: University of Chicago Press, 1997), pp. 113–36.

Britain, Ian, *Fabianism and Culture: A Study in British Socialism and the Arts, c. 1884–1918* (Cambridge, UK: Cambridge University Press, 1982).

Britten, Benjamin, 'Some Notes on Forster and Music', in *Aspects of E. M. Forster*, ed. Oliver Stallybrass (London: Edward Arnold, 1969), pp. 81–86.

Brooke, Rupert, *Democracy and the Arts* (London: Rupert Hart-Davis, 1946).

Brown, Bill, 'The Secret Life of Things (Virginia Woolf and the Matter of Modernism)', *Modernism/modernity*, 6.2 (1999), 1–28.

Brown, E. K., 'Rhythm in E. M. Forster's *A Passage to India*', in *E. M. Forster: A Passage to India, A Casebook*, ed. Malcolm Bradbury (London: Macmillan, 1970), pp. 93–113.

Brown, Malcolm Hamrick, 'Tchaikovsky and His Music in Anglo-American Criticism, 1890s–1950s', in *Queer Episodes in Music and Modern Identity*, ed. Sophie Fuller and Lloyd Whitesell (Urbana: University of Illinois Press, 2002), pp. 134–49.

Brown, Tony, 'E. M. Forster's *Parsifal*: A Reading of *The Longest Journey*', *Journal of European Studies*, 12.1 (1982), 30–54.

Bryant, John, 'How Billy Budd Grew Black and Beautiful: Versions of Melville in the Digital Age', *Leviathan: A Journal of Melville Studies*, 16.1 (2014), 60–86.

Buck, Claire, *Conceiving Strangeness in British First World War Writing* (Basingstoke: Palgrave Macmillan, 2015).

Bucknell, Brad, *Literary Modernism and Musical Aesthetics: Pater, Pound, Joyce, and Stein* (Cambridge, UK: Cambridge University Press, 2001).

Burnham, Scott, *Beethoven Hero* (Princeton: Princeton University Press, 1995).

Burra, Peter, 'Introduction to the Everyman Edition', in E. M. Forster, *A Passage to India*, ed. Oliver Stallybrass (London: Edward Arnold, 1978), pp. 315–27.

Buzard, James, *The Beaten Track: European Tourism, Literature, and the Ways to Culture, 1800–1918* (Oxford: Oxford University Press, 1993).

Cammarota, Richard S., 'Musical Analogy and Internal Design in *A Passage to India*', *English Literature in Transition*, 18.1 (1975), 38–46.

Bibliography

Campbell, Murray, 'Overtone', *Grove Music Online*, www.oxfordmusiconline.com [accessed 10 May 2018].

Caporaletti, Silvana, 'Science as Nightmare: "The Machine Stops" by E. M. Forster', *Utopian Studies*, 8.2 (1997), 32–47.

Carbajal, Alberto Fernández, *Compromise and Resistance in Postcolonial Writing: E. M. Forster's Legacy* (Basingstoke: Palgrave Macmillan, 2014).

Cavalié, Elsa, and Laurent Mellet, ed., *Only Connect: E. M. Forster's Legacies in British Fiction* (Bern: Peter Lang, 2017).

Cheyette, Bryan, *Constructions of 'The Jew' in English Literature and Society: Racial Representations, 1875–1945* (Cambridge, UK: Cambridge University Press, 1993).

Cheyette, Bryan, and Laura Marcus, ed., *Modernity, Culture, and 'the Jew'* (Cambridge, UK: Polity, 1998).

Chowrimootoo, Christopher, *Middlebrow Modernism: Britten's Operas and the Great Divide* (Oakland: University of California Press, 2018).

Clayton, Martin, and Bennett Zon, ed., *Music and Orientalism in the British Empire, 1780s–1940s: Portrayal of the East* (Aldershot: Ashgate, 2007).

Cole, Sarah, *Modernism, Male Friendship, and the First World War* (Cambridge, UK: Cambridge University Press, 2003).

Collini, Stefan, *Public Moralists: Political Thought and Intellectual Life in Britain 1850–1930* (Oxford: Clarendon, 1991).

Connor, Steven, 'The Modern Auditory I', in *Rewriting the Self: Histories from the Renaissance to the Present*, ed. Roy Porter (London: Routledge, 1997), pp. 203–23.

Cooper, John Xiros, ed., *T. S. Eliot's Orchestra: Critical Essays on Poetry and Music* (New York: Garland, 2000).

Cregan-Reid, Vybarr, 'Modes of Silence in E. M. Forster's "Inferior" Fiction', *English Literature in Transition*, 56.4 (2013), 445–61.

da Sousa Correa, Delia, 'Katherine Mansfield and Music: Nineteenth-Century Echoes', in *Celebrating Katherine Mansfield*, ed. Gerri Kimber and Janet Wilson (Basingstoke: Palgrave Macmillan, 2011), pp. 84–98.

Das, Santanu, 'E. M. Forster', in *The Cambridge Companion to English Novelists*, ed. Adrian Poole (Cambridge, UK: Cambridge University Press, 2009), pp. 345–60.

Davis, Cynthia J., 'Nation's Nature: "Billy Budd, Sailor," Anglo-Saxonism, and the Canon', in *Race and the Production of Modern American Nationalism*, ed. Reynolds J. Scott-Childress (New York: Garland, 1999), pp. 43–65.

Dawson, Graham, *Soldier Heroes: British Adventure, Empire and the Imagining of Masculinities* (London: Routledge, 1994).

Dean, Winton, *Essays on Opera* (Oxford: Clarendon, 1990).

Delany, Paul, '"Islands of Money": Rentier Culture in E. M. Forster's *Howards End*', *English Literature in Transition*, 31.3 (1988), 285–96.

Deutsch, David, *British Literature and Classical Music: Cultural Contexts 1870–1945* (London: Bloomsbury, 2015).

Bibliography

'The Pianola in Early Twentieth-Century British Literature: "Really it is a wonderful machine"', *English Literature in Transition*, 58.1 (2015), 73–90.

'Reconnecting Music to *Howards End*: Forster's Aesthetics of Inclusion', *LIT*, 21.3 (2010), 163–86.

Dickinson, Goldsworthy Lowes, 'Anglo-India', in *Appearances* (Garden City: Doubleday, Page & Company, 1914), pp. 15–17.

DiGaetani, John Louis, *Richard Wagner and the Modern British Novel* (Cranbury: Associated University Presses, 1978).

Dormon, James H., 'Shaping the Popular Image of Post-Reconstruction American Blacks: The "Coon Song" Phenomenon of the Gilded Age', *American Quarterly*, 40.4 (1988), 450–71.

duPlessis, Nicole, 'Transcendence, Transformation, and the Cultural Economy of Literacy in E. M. Forster's "The Celestial Omnibus" and "Other Kingdom"', *LIT*, 21.2 (2010), 81–100.

Dyson, George, and William Drabkin, 'Chromatic', *Grove Music Online*, www .oxfordmusiconline.com [accessed 10 May 2018].

Elgar, Edward, *A Future for English Music and Other Lectures*, ed. Percy M. Young (London: Dobson, 1968).

Ellis, Steve, *British Writers and the Approach of World War II* (Cambridge, UK: Cambridge University Press, 2014).

Epstein, Josh, *Sublime Noise: Musical Culture and the Modernist Writer* (Baltimore: John Hopkins University Press, 2014).

Farrell, Gerry, *Indian Music and the West* (Oxford: Oxford University Press, 2004).

Fifield, Peter, "'I often wish you could answer me back: and so perhaps do you!": E. M. Forster and BBC Radio Broadcasting', in *Broadcasting in the Modernist Era*, ed. Matthew Feldman, Erik Tonning, and Henry Mead (London: Bloomsbury, 2014), pp. 57–77.

Fillion, Michelle, *Difficult Rhythm: Music and the Word in E. M. Forster* (Urbana: University of Illinois Press, 2010).

'Edwardian Perspectives on Nineteenth-Century Music in E. M. Forster's *A Room with a View*', *19th-Century Music*, 25.2–3 (2001–2), 266–95.

Firchow, Peter E., 'Germany and Germanic Mythology in *Howards End*', *Comparative Literature*, 33.1 (1981), 50–68.

Fiske, Roger, *Scotland in Music: A European Enthusiasm* (Cambridge, UK: Cambridge University Press, 1983).

Flaubert, Gustave, *The Letters of Gustave Flaubert: 1830–1857*, ed. and trans. Francis Steegmuller (Cambridge, MA: Harvard University Press, 1980).

Madame Bovary, ed. Margaret Cohen, trans. Eleanor Marx Aveling and Paul de Man (New York: Norton, 2005).

Foata, Anne, 'The Knocking at the Door: A Fantasy on Fate, Forster and Beethoven's Fifth', *Cahiers Victoriens et Édouardiens*, 44 (1996), 135–45.

Fordham, Finn, *I Do I Undo I Redo: The Textual Genesis of Modernist Selves in Hopkins, Yeats, Conrad, Forster, Joyce, and Woolf* (Oxford: Oxford University Press, 2010).

Forster, E. M., *Abinger Harvest and England's Pleasant Land*, ed. Elizabeth Heine (London: Andre Deutsch, 1996).

Albergo Empedocle and Other Writings, ed. and intro. George H. Thomson (New York: Liveright, 1971).

Alexandria: A History and a Guide and Pharos and Pharillon, ed. Miriam Allott (London: Andre Deutsch, 2004).

Arctic Summer and Other Fiction, ed. Elizabeth Heine and Oliver Stallybrass (London: Edward Arnold, 1980).

Aspects of the Novel and Related Writings, ed. Oliver Stallybrass (London: Edward Arnold, 1974).

Commonplace Book, ed. Philip Gardner (Stanford: Stanford University Press, 1985).

Goldsworthy Lowes Dickinson and Related Writings, ed. Oliver Stallybrass (London: Edward Arnold, 1973).

The Hill of Devi and Other Indian Writings, ed. Elizabeth Heine (London: Edward Arnold, 1983).

Howards End, ed. Oliver Stallybrass (London: Edward Arnold, 1973).

The Journals and Diaries of E. M. Forster, ed. Philip Gardner, 3 vols (London: Pickering & Chatto, 2011).

The Longest Journey, ed. Elizabeth Heine (London: Edward Arnold, 1984).

The Machine Stops and Other Stories, ed. Rod Mengham (London: Andre Deutsch, 1997).

The Manuscripts of A Passage to India, ed. Oliver Stallybrass (London: Edward Arnold, 1978).

Maurice, ed. Philip Gardner (London: Andre Deutsch, 1999).

Nordic Twilight (London: Macmillan, 1940).

A Passage to India, ed. Oliver Stallybrass (London: Edward Arnold, 1978).

The Prince's Tale and Other Uncollected Writings, ed. P. N. Furbank (London: Andre Deutsch, 1998).

A Room with a View, ed. Oliver Stallybrass (London: Edward Arnold, 1977).

Selected Letters of E. M. Forster, ed. Mary Lago and P. N. Furbank, 2 vols (London: Collins, 1983–85).

Two Cheers for Democracy, ed. Oliver Stallybrass (London: Edward Arnold, 1972).

The Uncollected Egyptian Essays of E. M. Forster, ed. Hilda D. Spear and Abdel-Moneim Aly (Dundee: Blackness Press, 1988).

Where Angels Fear to Tread, ed. Oliver Stallybrass (London: Edward Arnold, 1975).

Forsyth, Cecil, *Music and Nationalism: A Study of English Opera* (London: Macmillan, 1911).

Foss, Hubert, '"The Pilgrim's Progress"', *The Musical Times*, 92.1300 (Jun 1951), 275.

Fox, Karen, *Māori and Aboriginal Women in the Public Eye: Representing Difference, 1950–2000* (Canberra: ANU E Press, 2011).

Fox Strangways, A. H., 'Schubert and Wolf', *Music & Letters*, 23.2 (1942), 126–34.

Bibliography

Francis, Mary C., '"A Kind of Voyage": E. M. Forster and Benjamin Britten's *Billy Budd*', in *Biographical Passages: Essays in Victorian and Modernist Biography*, ed. Joe Law and Linda K. Hughes (Columbia: University of Missouri Press, 2000), pp. 44–64.

Freedgood, Elaine, *The Ideas in Things: Fugitive Meaning in the Victorian Novel* (Chicago: University of Chicago Press, 2006).

Freedman, Jonathan, *The Temple of Culture: Assimilation and Anti-Semitism in Literary Anglo-America* (Oxford: Oxford University Press, 2000).

Fuller, Sophie, and Nicky Losseff, ed., *The Idea of Music in Victorian Fiction* (Aldershot: Ashgate, 2004).

Furbank, P. N., *E. M. Forster: A Life*, 2 vols (London: Secker & Warburg, 1977–78)

Furbank, P. N., and F. J. H. Haskell, 'E. M. Forster: The Art of Fiction No. 1', *The Paris Review*, 1 (1953), 28–41.

Gardner, Philip, ed., *E. M. Forster: The Critical Heritage* (London: Routledge & Kegan Paul, 1973).

George Gordon Byron, *Childe Harold's Pilgrimage* in *Byron: Poetical Works*, ed. Frederick Page (Oxford: Oxford University Press, 1970).

Gillett, Paula, 'Ambivalent Friendships: Music-Lovers, Amateurs, and Professional Musicians in the Late Nineteenth Century', in *Music and British Culture, 1785–1914: Essays in Honour of Cyril Ehrlich*, ed. Christina Bashford and Leanne Langley (Oxford: Oxford University Press, 2000), pp. 321–40.

Musical Women in England, 1870–1914: "Encroaching on All Man's Privileges" (New York: St Martin's Press, 2000).

Gilliam, Bryan, and Charles Youmans, 'Strauss, Richard', *Grove Music Online*, www.oxfordmusiconline.com [accessed 10 May 2018].

Glauert, Amanda, *Hugo Wolf and the Wagnerian Inheritance* (Cambridge, UK: Cambridge University Press, 1999).

Goldman, Jane, 'Forster and Women', in *The Cambridge Companion to E. M. Forster*, ed. David Bradshaw (Cambridge, UK: Cambridge University Press, 2007), pp. 120–37.

Golston, Michael, *Rhythm and Race in Modernist Poetry and Science* (New York: Columbia University Press, 2008).

Goodlad, Lauren M. E., 'Where Liberals Fear to Tread: E. M. Forster's Queer Internationalism and the Ethics of Care', *Novel*, 39.3 (2006), 307–36.

Goscilo, Margaret, 'Forster's Italian Comedies: Que[e]rying Heterosexuality Abroad', in *Seeing Double: Revisioning Edwardian and Modernist Literature*, ed. Carola M. Kaplan and Anne B. Simpson (Basingstoke: Macmillan, 1996), pp. 193–214.

Green, Lucy, *Music, Gender, Education* (Cambridge, UK: Cambridge University Press, 1997).

Grey, Thomas S., 'Wagner's *Die Meistersinger* as National Opera (1868–1945)', in *Music and German National Identity*, ed. Celia Applegate and Pamela M. Potter (Chicago: University of Chicago Press, 2002), pp. 78–104.

Bibliography

Hai, Ambreen, *Making Words Matter: The Agency of Colonial and Postcolonial Literature* (Athens: Ohio University Press, 2009).

Halliday, Sam, *Sonic Modernity: Representing Sound in Literature, Culture and the Arts* (Edinburgh: Edinburgh University Press, 2013).

Hankins, Sarah, 'Queer Relationships with Music and an Experiential Hermeneutics for Musical Meaning', *Women & Music: A Journal of Gender and Culture*, 18 (2014), 83–104.

Harker, Dave, *Fakesong: The Manufacture of British 'Folksong', 1700 to the Present Day* (Milton Keynes: Open University Press, 1985).

Harper-Scott, J. P. E., *Ideology in Britten's Operas* (Cambridge, UK: Cambridge University Press, 2018).

Harris, Kenneth, 'It's That Broadway Melody', *Observer*, 15 April 1951, 5

Hawkins, Hunt, 'Forster's Critique of Imperialism in *A Passage to India*', *South Atlantic Review*, 48.1 (1983), 54–65.

Hayes, Nick, 'More Than "Music-While-You-Eat"? Factory and Hostel Concerts, "Good Culture" and the Workers', in *'Millions Like Us'?: British Culture in the Second World War*, ed. Nick Hayes and Jeff Hill (Liverpool: Liverpool University Press, 1999), pp. 209–35.

Herring, Scott, 'Material Deviance: Theorizing Queer Objecthood', *Postmodern Culture*, 21.2 (2011), www.pomoculture.org/2013/09/03/material-deviance-theorizing-queer-objecthood/ [accessed 30 May 2018].

Herz, Judith Scherer, 'Forster's Sentences', *English Literature in Transition*, 55.1 (2012), 4–18.

   'Listening to Language', in *A Passage to India: Essays in Interpretation*, ed. John Beer (Basingstoke: Macmillan, 1985), pp. 59–70.

   '"This Is the End of Parsival": The Orphic and the Operatic in *The Longest Journey*', in *Queer Forster*, ed. Robert K. Martin and George Piggford (Chicago: University of Chicago Press, 1997), pp. 137–50.

Hindley, Clifford, 'Love and Salvation in Britten's "Billy Budd"', *Music & Letters*, 70.3 (1989), 363–81.

Ho, Janice, *Nation and Citizenship in the Twentieth-Century British Novel* (Cambridge, UK: Cambridge University Press, 2015).

[Hope-Wallace, Philip], 'Review of "South Pacific"', *Guardian*, 2 November 1951, 5.

Howard, Patricia, 'Review of Britten, *Billy Budd*. Soloists/Ambrosian Opera Chorus/LSO/Britten', *The Musical Times*, 109.1510 (1968), 1125.

Huebner, Steven, 'Faust (ii)', *Grove Music Online*, www.oxfordmusiconline.com [accessed 10 May 2018].

Hughes, Meirion, and Robert Stradling, *The English Musical Renaissance 1840–1940: Constructing a National Music*, 2nd ed. (Manchester: Manchester University Press, 2001).

Hutcheon, Linda, '"Sublime Noise" for Three Friends: Music in the Critical Writings of E. M. Forster, Roger Fry and Charles Mauron', in *E. M. Forster: Centenary Revaluations*, ed. Judith Scherer Herz and Robert K. Martin (London: Macmillan, 1982), pp. 84–98.

Bibliography 185

Irving, David R. M., 'Comparative Organography in Early Modern Empires', *Music & Letters*, 90.3 (2009), 372–98.

'The Dissemination and Use of European Music Books in Early Modern Asia', *Early Music History*, 28 (2009), 39–59.

Isherwood, Christopher, *Down There on a Visit* (New York: Farrar, Straus and Giroux, 2013).

Jackson, Kevin, *Humphrey Jennings* (London: Picador, 2004).

James, Henry, 'Charles de Bernard and Gustave Flaubert: The Minor French Novelists' (1876), in *Henry James: Literary Criticism*, ed. Leon Edel, 2 vols (Cambridge, UK: Cambridge University Press, 1984), II, pp. 159–83.

Jander, Owen, and Ellen T. Harris, 'Coloratura', *Grove Music Online*, www .oxfordmusiconline.com [accessed 10 May 2018].

Jennings, Humphrey, dir., *A Diary for Timothy*, in *Humphrey Jennings Collection* (UK: Crown Film Unit, 1945; DVD, Film First, 2005).

Johannmeyer, Anke, '"For Music Has Wings": E. M. Forster's "Orchestration" of a Homophile Space in *The Longest Journey*' (unpublished MA thesis, Uppsala University, 2009).

Johnson, Henry M., 'An Ethnomusicology of Musical Instruments: Form, Function, and Meaning', *JASO*, 26.3 (1995), 257–69.

Joyce, James, *Dubliners*, ed. Jeri Johnson (Oxford: Oxford University Press, 2000).

Keeling, Bret L., '"No Trace of Presence": Tchaikovsky and the Sixth in Forster's *Maurice*', *Mosaic: A Journal for the Interdisciplinary Study of Literature*, 36.1 (2003), 85–101.

Kerman, Joseph, *Musicology* (London: Fontana, 1985).

Kermode, Frank, *Concerning E. M. Forster* (London: Weidenfeld & Nicolson, 2009).

Kershaw, Ian, *1889–1936: Hubris* (Harmondsworth: Penguin, 1999).

Kildea, Paul, *Selling Britten: Music and the Market Place* (Oxford: Oxford University Press, 2002).

Koestenbaum, Wayne, *The Queen's Throat: Opera, Homosexuality, and the Mystery of Desire* (New York: Poseidon, 1993).

Kramer, Lawrence, *Classical Music and Postmodern Knowledge* (Berkeley: University of California Press, 1995).

'Culture and Musical Hermeneutics: The Salome Complex', *Cambridge Opera Journal*, 2.3 (1990), 269–94.

'Decadence and Desire: The *Wilhelm Meister* Songs of Wolf and Schubert', *19th-Century Music*, 10.3 (1987), 229–42.

'Hugo Wolf: Subjectivity in the Fin-de-Siècle Lied', in *Song Acts: Writing on Words and Music* (Leiden: Brill, 2017), pp. 146–77.

Music as Cultural Practice, 1800–1900 (Berkeley: University of California Press, 1990).

Lago, Mary, *E. M. Forster: A Literary Life* (Basingstoke: Macmillan, 1995).

Landon, Brooks, *Science Fiction after 1900: From the Steam Man to the Stars* (New York: Routledge, 2002).

Bibliography

Lansbury, Coral, *Arcady in Australia: The Evocation of Australia in Nineteenth-Century English Literature* (Carlton: Melbourne University Press, 1970).

Large, David C., 'Wagner's Bayreuth Disciples', in *Wagnerism in European Culture and Politics*, ed. David C. Large and William Weber (Ithaca: Cornell University Press, 1984), pp. 72–133.

Large, David C., and William Weber, ed., *Wagnerism in European Culture and Politics* (Ithaca: Cornell University Press, 1984).

Law, Joe, 'The "perniciously homosexual art": Music and Homoerotic Desire in *The Picture of Dorian Gray* and Other *Fin-de-Siècle* Fiction', in *The Idea of Music in Victorian Fiction*, ed. Sophie Fuller and Nicky Losseff (Aldershot: Ashgate, 2004), pp. 173–96.

Lehmann, John, *Rupert Brooke: His Life and His Legend* (London: Weidenfeld & Nicolson, 1980).

Leppert, Richard, *The Sight of Sound: Music, Representation, and the History of the Body* (Berkeley: University of California Press, 1993).

Lewis, Rachel, 'What's Queer about Musicology Now?', *Women & Music: A Journal of Gender and Culture*, 13 (2009), 43–53.

Lindenberger, Herbert, *Opera: The Extravagant Art* (Ithaca: Cornell University Press, 1984).

Lovensheimer, Jim, *South Pacific: Paradise Rewritten* (Oxford: Oxford University Press, 2010).

Lucas, John, 'E. M. Forster: An Enabling Modesty', *EREA*, 4.2 (2006), 34–44.

Lucas, W. J., 'Wagner and Forster: *Parsifal* and *A Room with a View*', in *Romantic Mythologies*, ed. Ian Fletcher (London: Routledge & Kegan Paul, 1967), pp. 271–97.

McClary, Susan, *Feminine Endings: Music, Gender, and Sexuality* (Minneapolis: University of Minnesota Press, 2002).

McWilliams-Tullberg, Rita, *Women at Cambridge: A Men's University – Though of a Mixed Type* (London: Victor Gollancz, 1975).

Mackay, Robert, 'Safe and Sound: New Music in Wartime Britain', in *'Millions Like Us'? British Culture in the Second World War*, ed. Nick Hayes and Jeff Hill (Liverpool: Liverpool University Press, 1999), pp. 179–208.

Malik, Charu, 'To Express the Subject of Friendship: Masculine Desire and Colonialism in *A Passage to India*', in *Queer Forster*, ed. Robert K. Martin and George Piggford (Chicago: University of Chicago Press, 1997), pp. 221–35.

Mandler, Peter, *The English National Character: The History of an Idea from Edmund Burke to Tony Blair* (New Haven: Yale University Press, 2006).

Mann, Thomas, *Pro and Contra Wagner*, trans. Allan Blunden (London: Faber and Faber, 1985).

Mao, Douglas, 'The Point of It', in *Utopianism, Modernism, and Literature in the Twentieth Century*, ed. Alice Reeve-Tucker and Nathan Waddell (Basingstoke: Palgrave Macmillan, 2013), pp. 19–38.

Solid Objects: Modernism and the Test of Production (Princeton: Princeton University Press, 1998).

Bibliography

Marcus, Laura, 'The Rhythm of the Rails: Sound and Locomotion', in *Sounding Modernism: Rhythm and Sonic Mediation in Modern Literature and Film*, ed. Julian Murphet, Helen Groth, and Penelope Hone (Edinburgh: Edinburgh University Press, 2017), pp. 193–210.

Markley, A. A., 'E. M. Forster's Reconfigured Gaze and the Creation of a Homoerotic Subjectivity', *Twentieth-Century Literature*, 47.2 (2001), 268–92.

Marsh, Richard O., *White Indians of Darien* (New York: G. P. Putnam's Sons, 1934).

Martin, Jane, *Women and the Politics of Schooling in Victorian and Edwardian England* (London: Leicester University Press, 1999).

Martin, William, *Joyce and the Science of Rhythm* (New York: Palgrave Macmillan, 2012).

Mathew, Nicholas, *Political Beethoven* (Cambridge, UK: Cambridge University Press, 2013).

May, William, 'Modernism's Handmaid: Dexterity and the Female Pianist', *Modernist Cultures*, 8.1 (2013), 42–60.

Mayhew, Henry, *London Labour and the London Poor*, 4 vols (London: Frank Cass, 1967).

Medalie, David, *E. M. Forster's Modernism* (Basingstoke: Palgrave, 2002).

Mellor, Leo, *Reading the Ruins: Modernism, Bombsites and British Culture* (Cambridge, UK: Cambridge University Press, 2011).

Mendenhall, Allen, 'Mass of Madness: Jurisprudence in E. M. Forster's *A Passage to India*', *Modernist Cultures*, 6.2 (2011), 315–37.

Meredith, Christabel M., *The Educational Bearings of Modern Psychology* (Boston: Houghton Mifflin, 1916).

Moe, Nelson, *The View from Vesuvius: Italian Culture and the Southern Question* (Berkeley: University of California Press, 2002).

Moffat, Wendy, *E. M. Forster: A New Life* (London: Bloomsbury, 2010).

'E. M. Forster and the Unpublished "Scrapbook" of Gay History: "Lest We Forget Him!"', *English Literature in Transition*, 55.1 (2012), 19–31.

'The Narrative Case for Queer Biography', in *Narrative Theory Unbound: Queer and Feminist Interventions*, ed. Robyn Warhol and Susan S. Lanser (Columbus: The Ohio State University Press, 2015), pp. 210–26.

Moss, Gemma, 'Music, Noise, and the First World War in Ford Madox Ford's *Parade's End*', *Modernist Cultures*, 12.1 (2017), 59–77.

'Music in E. M. Forster's *A Room with a View* and *Howards End*: The Conflicting Presentation of Nineteenth-Century Aesthetics', *English Literature in Transition*, 59.4 (2016), 493–509.

'Women In and Out: Forster, Social Purity and Florence Barger', in *Twenty-First-Century Readings of E. M. Forster's* Maurice, ed. Emma Sutton and Tsung-Han Tsai (Liverpool: Liverpool University Press, 2020), pp. 52–74.

Moylan, Tom, *Scraps of the Untainted Sky: Science Fiction, Utopia, Dystopia* (Boulder: Westview, 2000).

Bibliography

Myers, C. S., 'A Study of Rhythm in Primitive Music', *The British Journal of Psychology*, 1.4 (1905), 397–406.

Neal, Brandi A., 'Coon Song', *Grove Music Online*, www.oxfordmusiconline.com [accessed 10 May 2018].

Newman, Ernest, *Hugo Wolf* (London: Methuen, 1907).

'Hugo Wolf and the Lyric', *The Musical Times*, 1 November 1915, 649–51.

Newark, Cormac, '*Faust*, Nested Reception and La Castafiore', *Cambridge Opera Journal*, 25.2 (2013), 165–84.

Opera in the Novel from Balzac to Proust (Cambridge, UK: Cambridge University Press, 2011).

Nordau, Max, *Degeneration*, trans. anon. (Lincoln: University of Nebraska Press, 1993).

Zionism: Its History and Its Aims, trans. Israel Cohen (London: English Zionist Federation, 1905).

O'Callaghan, Katherine, ed., *Essays on Music and Language in Modernist Literature: Musical Modernism* (New York: Routledge, 2018).

O'Grady, Deirdre, *The Last Troubadours: Poetic Drama in Italian Opera, 1597–1887* (London: Routledge, 1991).

Outka, Elizabeth, *Consuming Traditions: Modernity, Modernism, and the Commodified Authentic* (Oxford: Oxford University Press, 2008).

Owen, Barbara, and Alastair Dick, 'Harmonium', *Grove Music Online*, www.oxfordmusiconline.com [accessed 10 May 2018].

Parker, Lisa, 'The Expansion and Development of the Music Degree Syllabus at Trinity College Dublin during the Nineteenth Century', in *Music and Institutions in Nineteenth-Century Britain*, ed. Paul Rodmell (Farnham: Ashgate, 2012), pp. 143–60.

Parrinder, Patrick, *Nation and Novel: The English Novel from its Origins to the Present Day* (Oxford: Oxford University Press, 2006).

Parry, Benita, '*A Passage to India*: Epitaph or Manifesto?', in *E. M. Forster: A Human Exploration: Centenary Essays*, ed. G. K. Das and John Beer (London: Macmillan, 1979), pp. 129–41.

'The Politics of Representation in *A Passage to India*', in *A Passage to India: Essays in Interpretation*, ed. John Beer (Basingstoke: Macmillan, 1985), pp. 27–43.

Postcolonial Studies: A Materialist Critique (London: Routledge, 2004).

Pasler, Jann, 'The Utility of Musical Instruments in the Racial and Colonial Agendas of Late Nineteenth-Century France', *Journal of the Royal Musical Association*, 129.1 (2004), 24–76.

Peat, Alexandra, *Travel and Modernist Literature: Sacred and Ethical Journeys* (New York: Routledge, 2011).

Pellar, Brian R., *Moby-Dick and Melville's Anti-Slavery Allegory* (New York: Palgrave Macmillan, 2017).

Peraino, Judith A., *Listening to the Sirens: Musical Technologies of Queer Identity from Homer to Hedwig* (Berkeley: University of California Press, 2006).

Picker, John M., *Victorian Soundscapes* (Oxford: Oxford University Press, 2003).

Bibliography

Plain, Gill, *Literature of the 1940s: War, Postwar and 'Peace'* (Edinburgh: Edinburgh University Press, 2013).

Pordzik, Ralph, 'Closet Fantasies and the Future of Desire in E. M. Forster's "The Machine Stops"', *English Literature in Transition*, 53.1 (2010), 54–74.

Potter, Pamela M., *Most German of the Arts: Musicology and Society from the Weimar Republic to the End of Hitler's Reich* (New Haven: Yale University Press, 1998).

'Music in the Third Reich: The Complex Task of "Germanization"', in *The Arts in Nazi Germany: Continuity, Conformity, Change*, ed. Jonathan Huener and Francis R. Nicosia (New York: Berghahn, 2006), pp. 85–110.

Presner, Todd Samuel, *Muscular Judaism: The Jewish Body and the Politics of Regeneration* (London: Routledge, 2007).

Prieto, Eric, *Listening In: Music, Mind, and the Modernist Narrative* (Lincoln: University of Nebraska Press, 2002).

Quinn, Martin, and Safaa Hejazi, 'E. M. Forster and *The Egyptian Mail*: Wartime Journalism and a Subtext for *A Passage to India*', *English Literature in Transition*, 25.3 (1982), 131–45.

Rau, Petra, *English Modernism, National Identity and the Germans, 1890–1950* (Farnham: Ashgate, 2009).

Reid, Susan, 'In Parts: Bodies, Feelings, Music in Long Modernist Novels by D. H. Lawrence and Dorothy Richardson', *Pilgrimage: A Journal of Dorothy Richardson Studies*, 7 (2015), 7–29.

Richardson, Dorothy, *Pilgrimage*, 4 vols (London: Virago, 1979).

Rochlitz, Hanna, '"I *have* read *Billy Budd*": The Forster–Britten Reading(s) of Melville', in *Literary Britten: Words and Music in Benjamin Britten's Vocal Works*, ed. Kate Kennedy (Woodbridge: Boydell & Brewer, 2018), pp. 296–317.

Sea-Changes: Melville – Forster – Britten (Göttingen: Universitätsverlag Göttingen, 2012).

Rodmell, Paul, ed., *Music and Institutions in Nineteenth-Century Britain* (Farnham: Ashgate, 2012).

Roerick, William, 'Forster and America', in *Aspects of E. M. Forster*, ed. Oliver Stallybrass (London: Edward Arnold, 1969), pp. 61–72.

Rosenbaum, S. P., 'Towards a Literary History of *Monteriano*', *Twentieth-Century Literature*, 31.2–3 (1985), 180–98.

Ross, Alex, *The Rest Is Noise: Listening to the Twentieth Century* (New York: Picador, 2007).

Roszak, Suzanne, 'Social Non-Conformists in Forster's Italy: Otherness and the Enlightened English Tourist', *Ariel: A Review of International English Literature*, 45.1–2 (2014), 167–94.

Rushton, Julian, 'Quarter-tone', *Grove Music Online*, www.oxfordmusiconline .com [accessed 10 May 2018].

Rutherford, Jonathan, *Forever England: Reflections on Race, Masculinity and Empire* (London: Lawrence & Wishart, 1997).

Said, Edward W., *Musical Elaborations: The Wellek Library Lectures at the University of California, Irvine* (New York: Columbia University Press, 1991).

Bibliography

Sams, Eric, *The Songs of Hugo Wolf* (Bloomington: Indiana University Press, 1992).

Sams, Eric, and Susan Youens, 'Wolf, Hugo (Flipp Jakob)', *Grove Music Online*, www.oxfordmusiconline.com [accessed 10 May 2018].

Scarry, John, 'William Parkinson in Joyce's "The Dead"', *Journal of Modern Literature*, 3.1 (1973), 105–7.

Schaff, Barbara, 'Italianised Byron – Byronised Italy', in *Performing National Identity: Anglo-Italian Cultural Transactions*, ed. Manfred Pfister and Ralf Hertel (Amsterdam: Rodopi, 2008), pp. 103–21.

'John Murray's *Handbooks to Italy*: Making Tourism Literary', in *Literary Tourism and Nineteenth-Century Culture*, ed. Nicola J. Watson (Basingstoke: Palgrave Macmillan, 2009), pp. 106–18.

Scher, Steven Paul, ed., *Music and Text: Critical Inquiries* (Cambridge, UK: Cambridge University Press, 1992).

Scruton, Roger, *The Aesthetics of Music* (Oxford: Oxford University Press, 1997). *Music as an Art* (London: Bloomsbury, 2018).

Understanding Music: Philosophy and Interpretation (London: Continuum, 2009).

Sedgwick, Eve Kosofsky, *Epistemology of the Closet* (Berkeley: University of California Press, 1990).

Sessions, Roger, 'The Scope of Music Criticism', in *Music and Criticism: A Symposium*, ed. Richard F. French (Cambridge, MA: Harvard University Press, 1948), pp. 35–51.

Seymour, Claire, *The Operas of Benjamin Britten: Expression and Evasion* (Woodbridge: Boydell, 2004).

Shaheen, Mohammad, *E. M. Forster and the Politics of Imperialism* (Basingstoke: Palgrave Macmillan, 2004).

Shapiro, Alexander H., 'McEwan and Forster, the Perfect Wagnerites', *The Wagner Journal*, 5.2 (2011), 20–45.

Sharpe, Jenny, *Allegories of Empire: The Figure of Woman in the Colonial Text* (Minneapolis: University of Minnesota Press, 1993).

Shaw, George Bernard, *The Perfect Wagnerite*, 2nd ed. (London: Constable, 1908).

Showalter, Elaine, '*A Passage to India* as "Marriage Fiction": Forster's Sexual Politics', *Women & Literature*, 5.2 (1977), 3–16.

Simon, Richard Keller, 'E. M. Forster's Critique of Laughter and the Comic: The First Three Novels as Dialectic', *Twentieth-Century Literature*, 31.2–3 (1985), 199–220.

Slade, Carole, 'E. M. Forster's Piano Players', *University of Windsor Review*, 14.2 (1979), 5–11.

Smart, Mary Ann, 'Donizetti, (Domenico) Gaetano (Maria): Biography', *Grove Music Online*, www.oxfordmusiconline.com [accessed 10 May 2018].

'The Silencing of Lucia', *Cambridge Opera Journal*, 4.2 (1992), 119–41.

Smith, Zadie, 'Love, actually', *Guardian*, 1 November 2003, www.theguardian .com/books/2003/nov/01/classics.zadiesmith [accessed 10 May 2018].

Bibliography

Smither, Howard E., 'Oratorio', *Grove Music Online*, www.oxfordmusiconline.com [accessed 10 May 2018].

Snyder, Carey J., *British Fiction and Cross-Cultural Encounters: Ethnographic Modernism from Wells to Woolf* (New York: Palgrave Macmillan, 2008).

Solie, Ruth A., *Music in Other Words: Victorian Conversations* (Berkeley: University of California Press, 2004).

Solvik, Morten, 'The Literary and Philosophical Worlds of Gustav Mahler', in *The Cambridge Companion to Mahler*, ed. Jeremy Barham (Cambridge, UK: Cambridge University Press, 2007), pp. 21–34.

Spotts, Frederic, *Bayreuth: A History of the Wagner Festival* (New Haven: Yale University Press, 1994).

Stape, J. H., ed., *E. M. Forster: Interviews and Recollections* (Basingstoke: Macmillan, 1993).

Steinweis, Alan E., *Art, Ideology, and Economics in Nazi Germany: The Reich Chambers of Music, Theater, and the Visual Arts* (Chapel Hill: University of North Carolina Press, 1993).

Stevenson, Randall, 'Forster and Modernism', in *The Cambridge Companion to E. M. Forster*, ed. David Bradshaw (Cambridge, UK: Cambridge University Press, 2007), pp. 209–22.

Stone, Wilfred, *The Cave and the Mountain: A Study of E. M. Forster* (Stanford: Stanford University Press, 1966).

'Forster on Love and Money', in *Aspects of E. M. Forster*, ed. Oliver Stallybrass (London: Edward Arnold, 1969), pp. 107–21.

Suleri, Sara, *The Rhetoric of English India* (Chicago: University of Chicago Press, 1992).

Sutton, Emma, *Aubrey Beardsley and British Wagnerism in the 1890s* (Oxford: Oxford University Press, 2002).

'"English Enthusiasts": Vernon Lee and Italian Opera', in *Exiles, Emigrés and Intermediaries: Anglo-Italian Cultural Transactions*, ed. Barbara Schaff (Amsterdam: Rodopi, 2010), pp. 375–402.

'Foreign Bodies: Mark Twain, Music and Anglo-American Identity', *Symbiosis*, 8.1 (2004), 109–19.

'"Putting Words on the Backs of Rhythm": Woolf, "Street Music", and *The Voyage Out*', in *Rhythm in Literature after the Crisis in Verse*, Special Issue of *Paragraph*, ed. Peter Dayan and David Evans, 33.2 (2010), 176–96.

'"The Music Spoke For Us": Music and Sexuality in *Fin-de-siècle* Poetry', in *The Figure of Music in Nineteenth-Century British Poetry*, ed. Phyllis Weliver (Aldershot: Ashgate, 2005), pp. 213–29.

Virginia Woolf and Classical Music: Politics, Aesthetics, Form (Edinburgh: Edinburgh University Press, 2013).

Tambling, Jeremy, 'Scott's "Heyday" in Opera', in *The Reception of Sir Walter Scott in Europe*, ed. Murray Pittock (London: Continuum, 2006), pp. 285–92.

Te Wiata, Beryl, 'Story: Te Wiata, Inia Morehu Tauhia Watene Iarahi Waihurihia', *Te Ara: The Encyclopedia of New Zealand*, https://teara.govt.nz/en/biographies/5t12/te-wiata-inia-morehu-tauhia-watene-iarahi-waihurihia [accessed 30 June 2019].

Bibliography

Tresch, John, and Emily I. Dolan, 'Toward a New Organology: Instruments of Music and Science', *Osiris*, 28.1 (2013), 278–98.

Trilling, Lionel, *E. M. Forster: A Study*, 2nd ed. (London: New Directions, 1964).

Trillini, Regula Hohl, *The Gaze of the Listener: English Representations of Domestic Music-Making* (Amsterdam: Rodopi, 2008).

Trotter, David, *Paranoid Modernism: Literary Experiment, Psychosis, and the Professionalization of English Society* (Oxford: Oxford University Press, 2001).

Tsai, Tsung-Han, 'Music as Queering in E. M. Forster's *Goldsworthy Lowes Dickinson*', *Music & Letters*, 99.1 (2018), 1–15.

'"Worse than irritated – namely insecure": Forster at Bayreuth', in *Wagner and Literature*, Special Issue of *Forum for Modern Language Studies*, ed. Michael Allis, 50.4 (2014), 466–81.

Tunbridge, Laura, 'Singing Translations: The Politics of Listening Between the Wars', *Representations*, 123.1 (2013), 53–86.

Turner, Henry S., 'Empire of Objects: Accumulation and Entropy in E. M. Forster's *Howards End*', *Twentieth-Century Literature*, 46.3 (2000), 328–45.

Twain, Mark, *A Tramp Abroad* (New York: Penguin, 1997).

Vaget, Hans Rudolf, 'Hitler's Wagner: Musical Discourse as Cultural Space', in *Music and Nazism: Art under Tyranny, 1933–1945*, ed. Michael H. Kater and Albrecht Riethmüller (Laaber: Laaber, 2003), pp. 15–31.

Vaughan Williams, Ralph, *English Folk-Songs* (London: English Folk Dance and Song Society, 1966).

Von Glahn, Denise, and Michael Broyles, 'Art Music', *Grove Music Online*, www.oxfordmusiconline.com [accessed 30 December 2018].

Waddell, Nathan, 'Modernism and Music: A Review of Recent Scholarship', *Modernist Cultures*, 12.2 (2017), 316–30.

Moonlighting: Beethoven and Literary Modernism (Oxford: Oxford University Press, 2019).

Walsh, Stephen, 'Stravinsky, Igor', *Grove Music Online*, www.oxfordmusiconline .com [accessed 10 May 2018].

Warner, Michael, ed., *Fear of a Queer Planet: Queer Politics and Social Theory* (Minneapolis: University of Minnesota Press, 1993).

Watson, Anna, '"Flat pieces of cardboard stamped with a conventional design": Women and Narrative Exclusion in E. M. Forster's *Maurice*', in *Twenty-First-Century Readings of E. M. Forster's* Maurice, ed. Emma Sutton and Tsung-Han Tsai (Liverpool: Liverpool University Press, 2020), pp. 101–26.

Weatherhead, Andrea K., '*Howards End*: Beethoven's *Fifth*', *Twentieth-Century Literature*, 31.2–3 (1985), 247–64.

Weiner, Marc A., *Richard Wagner and the Anti-Semitic Imagination* (Lincoln: University of Nebraska Press, 1995).

Weliver, Phyllis, *The Musical Crowd in English Fiction, 1840–1910: Class, Culture and Nation* (Basingstoke: Palgrave Macmillan, 2006).

'A Score of Change: Twenty Years of Critical Musicology and Victorian Literature', *Literature Compass*, 8.10 (2011), 776–94.

Bibliography

Women Musicians in Victorian Fiction, 1860–1900: Representations of Music, Science and Gender in the Leisured Home (Aldershot: Ashgate, 2000).

Westburg, Barry R., 'Forster's Fifth Symphony: Another Aspect of *Howards End*', *Modern Fiction Studies*, 10.4 (1964), 359–65.

Whelan, Kevin, 'The Memories of "The Dead"', *The Yale Journal of Criticism*, 15.1 (2002), 59–97.

Wiebe, Heather, *Britten's Unquiet Pasts: Sound and Memory in Postwar Reconstruction* (Cambridge, UK: Cambridge University Press, 2012).

Wild, Jonathan, *The Rise of the Office Clerk in Literary Culture, 1880–1939* (Houndmills: Palgrave Macmillan, 2006).

Wilde, Alan, *Art and Order: A Study of E. M. Forster* (London: Peter Owen, 1965).

Wilenski, R. H., 'How I Listen to Music', *Listener*, 2 February 1939, 281.

Williams, Simon, *Wagner and the Romantic Hero* (Cambridge, UK: Cambridge University Press, 2004).

Wolf, Werner, *The Musicalization of Fiction: A Study in the Theory and History of Intermediality* (Amsterdam: Rodopi, 1999).

Woolf, Virginia, *The Essays of Virginia Woolf*, ed. Andrew McNeillie (vols I–IV) and Stuart N. Clarke (vols V–VI), 6 vols (London: Hogarth Press, 1986–2011).

Three Guineas (Harmondsworth: Penguin, 1977).

The Waves, ed. Michael Herbert and Susan Sellers, with research by Ian Blyth (Cambridge, UK: Cambridge University Press, 2011).

Zeikowitz, Richard E., ed., *Letters between Forster and Isherwood on Homosexuality and Literature* (Basingstoke: Palgrave Macmillan, 2008).

Zhou, Mi, 'Sublime Noise: Reading E. M. Forster Musically' (unpublished doctoral thesis, University of Cambridge, 2009).

Zon, Bennett, 'The "Non-Darwinian" Revolution and the Great Chain of Musical Being', in *Evolution and Victorian Culture*, ed. Bernard Lightman and Bennett Zon (Cambridge, UK: Cambridge University Press, 2014), pp. 196–226.

Representing Non-Western Music in Nineteenth-Century Britain (Rochester: University of Rochester Press, 2007).

Archival Sources

The Papers of E. M. Forster, King's College Library, Cambridge.

Index

Achebe, Chinua, 38
Addinsell, Richard, 4
Adorno, Theodor, 26, 107
Albright, Daniel, 9
Aldeburgh Festival, 84, 146–47
amateurism, 5–6, 13, 15, 19–20, *See also* music
and professionalism
Anderson, Perry, 99
anti-Semitism, 16, 19, 107, 110, 116–18, 120
Armstrong, Paul B., 27, 41, 43

Baedeker Guides, 80, 89, 94–96
Barger, Florence, 155
Bayreuth, 105, 111, 124, 129–31, 140
BBC, 3, 106, 127, 129, 140, 171
'Beachcomber', 129
Beale, Dorothea, 153
Beckett, Samuel, 8
Beethoven, Ludwig van, 1–4, 7, 14–15, 101,
105, 107–9, 127–28, 134, 137–38, 168,
175
Coriolan Overture, Op. 62, 134
Piano Sonata No. 23, Op. 57, 1–4, 21,
134
Piano Sonata No. 28, Op. 101, 107
Piano Sonata No. 32, Op. 111, 137
Symphony No. 5, Op. 7, 7, 15, 127–28,
137–38
Bentley, Eric, 129–30
Cult of the Superman, The, 129–30
Bergson, Henri, 40
Berlioz, Hector, 76, 89, 97, 100
Bhabha, Homi K., 73
Biddle, Ian, 136
Bismarck, Otto von, 129
Bolton, Thaddeus L., 24, 25
Bowen, Elizabeth, 6
Bowlby, Rachel, 108
Brahms, Johannes, 14–15
Vier ernste Gesänge, Op. 121, 15
Vier Gesänge, Op. 17, 15

Brannigan, Owen, 172
Brett, Philip, 54, 71, 136, 169
Britain, Ian, 152
Britten, Benjamin, 6–7, 168–75
Billy Budd, 20, 168–76
Gloriana, 173
Broadwood, Lucy, 148
Brooke, Rupert, 152–53
Democracy and the Arts, 152
Brown, E. K., 7, 23
Browne, Thomas, 132
Bucknell, Brad, 9
Burra, Peter, 6, 8
Buzard, James, 92, 95
Byron, George Gordon, Lord, 92–93, 99, 100
Childe Harold's Pilgrimage, 92–93

Cammarano, Salvadore, 77
Carlyle, Thomas, 129
Cheltenham Ladies' College, 153
Chopin, Frédéric, 68
chromaticism, 68, 71, 121, 161
Cole, Arthur, 110
Conrad, Joseph, 38
Heart of Darkness, 38
coon song, 94–98
Croix de Feu, 163
Crozier, Eric, 168

Darling, Josie, 53
Darling, Malcolm, 53, 122, 153
Das, Santanu, 165
Day-Lewis, Cecil, 122
decadence, 118–19
Defoe, Daniel, 87
degeneration, 118–21
Deutsch, David, 11, 169
Dickinson, Goldsworthy Lowes, 17, 22, 27–31,
35, 40, 45, 47, 54
'Anglo-India', 28–33, 35, 38, 40, 45, 47, 49, 53
Appearances, 27

194

Index

Donizetti, Gaetano, 76–85, 90, 95–98, 100
  Lucia di Lammermoor, 76–85, 90, 96–98
Dostoevsky, Fyodor, 82, 87

Egyptian Mail, The, 31
Elgar, Edward, 36, 75–76, 143
  Dream of Gerontius, The, 36
Eliot, George, 87
empire, 28, 32, 47, 49, 54, 56, 59, 61, 70, 72, 76, 121, 173, *See also* music and colonialism
Epstein, Josh, 11, 169
eugenics, 118–19

Fabianism, 151–53
fascism, 108, 126, 159, 163, *See also* Nazism
Fay, Eliza, 32
Festival of Britain, The, 168
Fillion, Michelle, 11–12, 18, 77, 80, 108, 119, 156
First World War, 22, 31, 85, 101, 122
Flaubert, Gustave, 77, 79–85, 87, 99, 100
  Madame Bovary, 77, 79–82
folk music, 142–43, 147–53
Fordham, Finn, 8, 10
Forster, E. M.
  'A Musician in Egypt', 32–35, 41–44, 53
  'A Note on the Way', 20
  'A View without a Room', 122
  'Advance, India!', 63–64
  'Anonymity: An Enquiry', 86
  'Beethoven's Piano Sonatas', 107–9, 127
  'Eliza in Egypt', 32
  'George Crabbe and Peter Grimes', 84
  'Handel in Egypt', 35–40, 42, 49
  'Jew-Consciousness', 116
  'Not Listening to Music', 12–13, 106, 167–68
  'Notes on the English Character', 98
  'Notes on the Way', 159–66
  'Our Second Greatest Novel?', 82
  'Pessimism in Literature', 87, 110–12
  'Post-Munich', 123–26, 128
  'Racial Exercise', 116
  'Revolution at Bayreuth', 19, 105, 129–31
  'Sunday Music', 100–1
  'The C Minor of that Life', 105, 133
  'The Celestial Omnibus', 132–33
  'The Duty of Society to the Artist', 152
  'The English Character', 98–99
  'The Eternal Moment', 95
  'The Functions of Literature in War-time', 101
  'The Machine Stops', 19–20, 137–46, 155–56, 158, 166
  'The Nazis and Culture', 104

'The *Raison d'Être* of Criticism', 129, 133–35, 138, 144, 168
'Three Countries', 17
'Webb and Webb', 151
'What I Believe', 108, 123–25, 166
Abinger Harvest, 31, 63
Alexandria: A History and a Guide, 37
Arctic Summer, 19–20, 137–38, 143, 146–56, 158
Aspects of the Novel, 4, 7, 16–17, 22–24, 39–47, 56, 83, 85–87, 160, 166
Commonplace Book, 129, 161–62
Hill of Devi, The, 42, 44–45, 48–49, 54–55, 67
Howards End, 4, 14–15, 29, 49, 72–73, 75–76, 137–38, 168
Longest Journey, The, 19, 112–22, 127, 132, 161, 166
Maurice, 154, 156–58
Nordic Twilight, 19, 103–6, 108–9, 111, 122, 125, 131
Passage to India, A, 8, 16–17, 23–24, 30–31, 34–35, 38–45, 49–74, 78, 95, 166
Pharos and Pharillon, 31
Room with a View, A, 122, 137
Two Cheers for Democracy, 106
Where Angels Fear to Tread, 18, 76–100, 112, 166
Forsyth, Cecil, 76
Foss, Hubert, 172
Francis, Mary C., 169
Franck, César, 32
Frederick the Great, 129
Freedman, Jonathan, 118
Fry, Roger, 9

George, Stefan, 129
Gerhardt, Elena, 1, 2
Goethe, Johann Wolfgang von, 162–64
Golston, Michael, 26–27
Goodlad, Lauren M. E., 78
Göring, Hermann, 104, 122
Gounod, Charles, 29–30
  Faust, 29
gramophone, 64–65, 159, 161, 164
Green, Lucy, 144

Hai, Ambreen, 43
Hammerstein, Oscar, 173
Handel, George Frideric, 35–38, 47, 53
  Israel in Egypt, 37
  Messiah, 35–38, 47, 53
Hankins, Sarah, 71
Hardy, Thomas, 87

Index

harmonium, 61–67, 95, 121
Harper-Scott, J. P. E., 170–71, 174
Hegel, Georg Wilhelm Friedrich, 118
Heine, Elizabeth, 112, 119, 146
Hejazi, Safaa, 38, 40
heroism, 103–31
Herring, Scott, 51
Herz, Judith Scherer, 7
Hess, Myra, 1–4, 107
Hindley, Clifford, 169
Hitler, Adolf, 103, 105–6, 127
Howard, Patricia, 172
Hutcheon, Linda, 9
Hutt, Jenny, 4
Huxley, Aldous, 8

Isherwood, Christopher, 4, 110

James, Henry, 77, 81, 87
   Ambassadors, The, 77
Jennings, Humphrey, 1, 4
   Diary for Timothy, A, 1–4, 21, 175
   Pandæmonium 1660–1886, 4
Joyce, James, 8, 75
   'The Dead', 75

Karpeles, Maud, 148
Keeling, Bret L., 11
Keilberth, Joseph, 131
Kennedy, Kate, 170
Kerman, Joseph, 10
Kermode, Frank, 6, 7
Koestenbaum, Wayne, 71
Kramer, Lawrence, 5, 10, 13

Lucas, John, 109
Ludolf, G. H., 48

Mahler, Gustav, 161–62
   Das Lied von der Erde, 161
   symphonies, 161
Malik, Charu, 72
Manchester Guardian, The, 27
Mandler, Peter, 99
Mann, Maud, 52
Mann, Thomas, 107
Marcus, Laura, 24
Marsh, Richard O., 48, 51
Masood, Syed Ross, 27
Mauron, Charles, 9
Mayhew, Henry, 37–38
McClary, Susan, 10, 54, 71
Medalie, David, 7, 23–24
Melville, Herman, 168–69, 171, 173–74
   Billy Budd, Sailor, 168–69, 171, 173–74

Mendelssohn, Felix, 36
   Elijah, 36
Meredith, Christabel, 154–55
   *Educational Bearings of Modern Psychology,
      The*, 154
Meredith, Hugh O., 154
Meyerstein, E. H. W., 134
Moffat, Wendy, 168
Moss, Gemma, 138
Mozart, Wolfgang Amadeus, 168
   Magic Flute, The, 172
   Requiem, 168
Munich Agreement, 124
Murray, John, 93
music
   and antiquarianism, 20, 142, 146, *See also* folk
      music
   and colonialism, 16–17, 33–34, 41, 48–74,
      95, 142
   and epistemology. *See* rhythm and race
   and evolution, 25–26, 30, 36–37, 46, 116
   and gender, 3, 14–15, 19–20, 57–58, 132–58
   and homosexuality, 11, 54–55, 60, 70–72, 80,
      156, 164–65, 168–69
   and Jewishness, 2, 115–21
   and literary heritage. *See* Byron, George
      Gordon, Lord; Flaubert, Gustave; Scott,
      Walter; Twain, Mark
   and material culture, 48–74, 78
   and national character, 76–77, 87–100
   and nationalism, 2–3, 75–76
   and professionalism, 19–20, 135–36, 145–46,
      155–56
   and race, 171–75, *See also* coon song; music
      and Jewishness; rhythm and race
   and war, 1–4, 103–10, 122–28
   as a discipline, 132–58
   prose's 'musicality', 4, 7–8, 16, 22
musicology. *See* music, as a discipline
Mussolini, Benito, 127
Myers, C. S., 22, 25
   'A Study of Rhythm in Primitive Music', 22, 25

National Gallery concerts, 1, 107
Nautch, 69
Nazism, 19, 26, 101, 103–10, 122–29, 163
Newark, Cormac, 87
Newman, Ernest, 162
Nietzsche, Friedrich, 110, 123, 129
Nordau, Max, 118–21
   Die Entartung, 118

oratorio, 36–37
organology, 50
overtone, 69

Index

197

Parry, Benita, 44, 47, 56
Pears, Peter, 172
Pergolesi, Giovanni Battista, 150–51
phonograph, 48, 51
piano, 63, 67–72, 91, 132, 133, 159–60, 162, 164
pianola, 50
Plain, Gill, 3
Pound, Ezra, 26
Prieto, Eric, 8
Proust, Marcel, 7, 82, 87
  À la recherche du temps perdu, 7
Purcell, Henry, 172
  Fairy-Queen, The, 172

quarter-tone, 69
Quinn, Martin, 38, 40

Rama Rau, Santha, 39
Rau, Petra, 91
Redgrave, Michael, 4
rhythm, 7–8, 16–17, 22–47, 52, 78, 87, 141, 160
  and race, 16–17, 22–47
Richardson, Dorothy, 132
  Pointed Roofs, 132
'Roast Beef of Old England', 54
Rochlitz, Hanna, 170
Rodgers, Richard, 173
Rodmell, Paul, 135
Roland, Romain, 3
Rosenbaum, S. P., 77
Roszak, Suzanne, 88
Royal Albert Hall, 35
Royal Opera House, 169, 172
Rutherford, Jonathan, 58

Said, Edward W., 26
Sams, Eric, 163
Schaff, Barbara, 92
Scher, Steven Paul, 10
Schopenhauer, Arthur, 118
Schubert, Franz, 68, 159, 162
Schumann, Robert, 159, 162
  Der Nussbaum, 159
Scott, Walter, 77, 82–85, 97, 99, 100
  Bride of Lammermoor, The, 77, 83
Scruton, Roger, 167
Searight, Kenneth, 54
Second World War, 1–4, 101–2, 103–7, 122–28, 131, 140, 173
Sedgwick, Eve Kosofsky, 70
Sessions, Roger, 128
Shaheen, Mohammad, 56
Sharp, Cecil, 147
Sharpe, Jenny, 58

Shaw, George Bernard, 110
  Perfect Wagnerite, The, 110
Smith, Zadie, 167
  On Beauty, 168
Snyder, Carey J., 42
South Pacific, 173–74
Spencer, Herbert, 25, 36
  'The Origin and Function of Music', 25
Stage, The, 172–73
Stanford, Charles Villiers, 143
Stevenson, Randall, 9
Stone, Wilfred, 6, 115
Strauss, Richard, 76, 121, 161
Stravinsky, Igor, 150
  Pulcinella, 150
Sutton, Emma, 89, 93

Tchaikovsky, Pyotr Ilyich, 156–58
  Symphony *Pathétique*, 156–58
Te Wiata, Inia, 171–73
Terni, Enrico, 32–35
Tetrazzini, Luisa, 77
Time & Tide, 159
Tolstoy, Leo, 7, 82, 87
  War and Peace, 7
Tonic Sol-fa, 142
Trevelyan, R. C., 27, 54
Trotter, David, 135
Tukojirao III, the Maharajah of the state of Dewas Senior, 67
Tunbridge, Laura, 163
Turgenev, Ivan, 82
Turner, Henry S., 72–73
Twain, Mark, 93–94, 99, 100
  Tramp Abroad, A, 93–94

Uppman, Theodor, 171

Vaughan Williams, Ralph, 149, 172
  Pilgrim's Progress, The, 172
viola, 57–61

Wigmore Hall, 20
Wagner, Richard, 18–19, 26, 32, 93, 101–2, 103–34, 139, 161, 175
  Das Judenthum in der Musik, 116
  Das Rheingold, 119, 132–33
  Die Walküre, 101, 111
  Götterdämmerung, 104, 112
  Lohengrin, 93
  Parsifal, 104
  Ring, The, 18, 103–4, 107, 109–16, 122–26, 130–32
  Siegfried, 111–12, 114, 130
  Tristan und Isolde, 18, 68

Index

Warner, Michael, 80
Webb, Beatrice, 151, 153
Weliver, Phyllis, 10
Wells, H. G., 139
Wharton, Edith, 29
  Age of Innocence, 29
Wild, Jonathan, 137
Wilde, Alan, 88
Wilde, Oscar, 156–57
  Picture of Dorian Gray, The, 70
Wilenski, R. H., 106
Windgassen, Wolfgang, 131
Wolf, Hugo, 20, 159–66, 176
  'Anacreon's Grave', 159, 163–64
  'Ganymede', 159, 164–65
  'Nun wandre Maria', 159, 164
Wolf, Werner, 13–14

Woolf, Virginia, 38, 82, 103, 107, 152,
  155–56
  'On Re-reading Novels', 82–83
  Three Guineas, 155–56
  'Scott's Character', 82
  'Street Music', 38
  Room of One's Own, A, 152
  Waves, The, 103
  Years, The, 38, 107
Working Men's College, 110
Wright, Basil, 4

Yeats, W. B., 26

Zhou, Mi, 11–12, 52
Zionism, 118, 120
Zon, Bennett, 25

CPSIA information can be obtained
at www.ICGtesting.com
Printed in the USA
LVHW111224030821
694401LV00002B/100